American Signatures

Oklahoma Project for Discourse and Theory

Oklahoma Project for Discourse and Theory

Series Editors

Robert Con Davis, University of Oklahoma
Ronald Schleifer, University of Oklahoma

Advisory Board

Maya Angelou, Wake Forest University
Jonathan Culler, Cornell University
Jacques Derrida, University of California, Irvine
Shoshana Felman, Yale University
Henry Louis Gates, Jr., Cornell University
Sandra M. Gilbert, Princeton University
Edmund Leach, Oxford University
Richard Macksey, Johns Hopkins University
J. Hillis Miller, University of California, Irvine
Marjorie Perloff, Stanford University
Edward W. Said, Columbia University
Thomas A. Sebeok, Indiana University at Bloomington
Gayatri Chakravorty Spivak, University of Pittsburgh

American Signatures

Semiotic Inquiry and Method

by Thomas A. Sebeok

edited by Iris Smith

University of Oklahoma Press : Norman and London

Library of Congress Cataloging-in-Publication Data

Sebeok, Thomas Albert, 1920–
    American signatures : semiotic inquiry and method / by Thomas
A. Sebeok ; edited by Iris Smith.
        p. cm. — (Oklahoma project for discourse and theory ; v. 6)
    Includes bibliographical references and index.
    ISBN 0-8061-2310-9 (alk. paper)
    1. Semiotics. 2. Semiotics—United States. I. Smith, Iris (Iris
L.) II. Title. III. Series.
P99.S3 1990
302.2—dc20
                                       90–50239

The paper in this book meets the guidelines for permanence and durability of the Committee on Production Guidelines for Book Longevity of the Council on Library Resources, Inc. ∞

American Signatures: Semiotic Inquiry and Method is volume 6 in the Oklahoma Project for Discourse and Theory.

For JAS

. . . signify, I pray you . . .
Here will we sit, and let the sounds of music
Creep into our ears; soft stillness and the night
Become the touches of sweet harmony.
Sit, Jessica . . .
But, whilst this muddy vesture of decay
Doth grossly close it in, we cannot hear it.

The Merchant of Venice 5.1. 51–65

Solitary, singing in the West, I strike up for a New World.

—Walt Whitman, "Starting from Paumanok"

Contents

Series Editors' Foreword

When we began the Oklahoma Project for Discourse and Theory several years ago, one of our goals was to publish at some point a book devoted to contemporary semiotics. We wanted such a book because cultural studies, the primary commitment of the Oklahoma Project, began in the 1950s as an attempt to apply semiotic analysis to the study of culture. Stuart Hall, Richard Johnson, and others have written about the origins of cultural studies in the work of F. R. Leavis, Raymond Williams, and at the Birmingham center in England in conjunction with the semiotic enterprise of Ferdinand de Saussure and Claude Lévi-Strauss. Semiotics is thus a key component of the Oklahoma Project for Discourse and Theory—hence *American Signatures: Semiotic Inquiry and Method*, by Thomas A. Sebeok, one of the most respected and well known semioticians in the world.

Sebeok shows in this book, however, that semiotics—which indeed inaugurated cultural theory—also has a complex history as a body of specifically "semiotic" inquiry and methodology. That history, at least as expansive as that of cultural studies proper, is necessarily international in scope and ranges from Sebeok's own origins in Eastern Europe (Hungary) through the academic centers of Western Europe, North America, and beyond. But while the history and development of semiotics is global, one can gain a significant understanding of the field by looking intently at the American staging of semiotics. Issues relating to great American figures in the field, such as Charles A. Peirce, Roman Jakobson, and Thomas A. Sebeok himself, illuminate the advent of semiotics in American academic and intellectual life, that is, they show how semiotics developed as an "American" practice with ties to other areas of social, scientific, and humanistic inquiry as practiced in America. Sebeok's *American Signatures* is dedicated precisely to understanding the strand of American intellectual life that goes under the name *semiotics.*

The task at hand, however, is an ambitious one. American semiotics consists of a large assortment of specialties, and as Bruno Latour has shown recently from a theoretical perspective, and as other philosophers of science have argued as well, a semiotic analysis may be a privileged instrument of inquiry—perhaps unique in contemporary discourse—in its ability to move with great descriptive and analytic power through scientific, social science, and humanistic texts. Those within the field of semiotic study know that Sebeok has been demonstrating such power through his voluminous store of semiotic analysis for over forty years. He has done groundbreaking interdisciplinary research on analyses of social discourse, language, medicine, veterinary medicine, and zoosemiotics, and these categories only begin to suggest the almost boundless appetite of semiotics as Sebeok conceives and practices it, and as he has inspired many other prominent semioticians to practice it.

Thus, in its understanding of the history of American semiotics, in its critical inventory of semiotic methodology, and in its assessments of work still to be done, *American Signatures* is an authoritative engagement with the past, present, and future of semiotics in America, a critical engagement by the person most qualified to write the account.

American Signatures—in its transdisciplinary expanse and critical formulations—is evidence of the ongoing commitment to cultural criticism that underlies the Oklahoma Project for Discourse and Theory.

Robert Con Davis
Ronald Schleifer

Norman, Oklahoma

Acknowledgments

We offer our thanks to the following individuals and organizations for their assistance: to Susan Petrilli, of the Istituto di Filosofia del Linguaggio at the University of Bari, Italy, for providing the transcript of her interview; to Joyce Dewsbury of the University Archives, University of Florida; Christian Kloesel, Director of the Peirce Edition Project, Indiana University; and Evan P. Young of the Research Center for Language and Semiotic Studies, Indiana University, for their help in acquiring photographs; and to Patricia L. Dornbusch of the University of Oklahoma Press for her invaluable editorial assistance.

T. A. S.
I. S.

I also extend my thanks to Michael L. Johnson, Mary Lamb, Richard Lanigan, and Simone Zelitch, valued readers and listeners, and to Hans J. Fischer, my keenest reader, for his indispensable support.

I. S.

American Signatures

Introduction
Thomas A. Sebeok: "The Semiotic Self" in America

by Iris Smith

"There is no 'American school' of semiotics." No one who knows Thomas A. Sebeok or his work would be surprised to hear him say this. The geographical boundaries of the United States—or those of Canada, Brazil, France, or Sebeok's own Hungarian homeland—certainly have not contained, and do not appear to have significantly shaped, the development of semiotics in the last hundred years. Sebeok's life is a case in point. Born in Budapest and raised in that region of Europe between the world wars, Sebeok followed his father to the United States in 1937, attending the University of Chicago shortly thereafter. His father, an economist, had arrived in 1936. In 1941, after beginning graduate work at Princeton, Sebeok visited New York City periodically to study with another international, the newly arrived Roman Jakobson. As Sebeok himself has commented, how could such a thing as an "American school" (or a Prague school, for that matter) account for the varied expanse of Jakobson's work? Indeed, where could Sebeok himself, who travels and corresponds incessantly, and whose writings are translated into many languages, be classified?

Besides the inadequacy of the notion of national schools, there is also the difficulty of the term *American*. In the title of this book Sebeok uses the term to mean "pertaining to the United States," as a convenience for drawing the limits of his study. It cannot be denied, though, that this word slops over rather messily (and usefully) into other realms. At roughly the same time that Sebeok came to the United States, the original edition of the *Oxford English Dictionary* (*OED*) defined *American* as "an aborigine of the American conti-

3

nent; now, called an 'American Indian.'...A native of America of
European descent; *esp.* a citizen of the United States" (1933: vol. 1,
p..279). The 1972 supplement to the *OED* updates its earlier definition to read, "Now simply, a native or inhabitant of North or South
America," adding (with the confusion that earlier appeared) "a citizen of the United States" (p. 75). (We should note the implicit class
and race assumptions of the earlier definition: only European Americans need apply. Perhaps, on the other hand, in limiting our definition
to the latter phrase, "a citizen of the United States," we shall be
accused of "Americanitis," which the original edition offers as "some
characteristically American penchant [esp. *fig.*, overweening or
blatant national conceit in American achievements]." It cannot be
denied that the narrow use of the term *American* excludes semioticians working throughout the two American continents. Their signatures remain to be traced.)

Setting aside the ambiguities of *American* as an indication of
nationality, we shall find that the word carries connotations central
to the study of signs as we know it today. Perhaps in exploring these
connotations we shall come to a better understanding of what Sebeok
means by "American Signatures." He has long maintained that
semiotics is best undertaken as a doctrine or teaching maneuver. In
the *Encyclopedic Dictionary of Semiotics* (*EDS*) John Deely reminds us that

> "doctrine," in Latin or English, refers first of all to a "teaching" in the
> most general sense, i.e., to *what* some person or persons, even un-
> known, assert to be the case about something. Thus, *doctrina* may
> concern natural reality or social reality, or any web and admixture of
> the two. In the systematic context of Latin scholasticism, with a
> remarkable constancy spanning the later centuries of that epoch—as
> illustrated, for example, early in Aquinas (c. 1266 [1952]:Iq.1) or late
> in Poinsot (1637 [1931]: disp. 2)—*doctrina* referred to a body of
> thought sensitive to its own implications and *striving* for consistency
> throughout, while achieving explanations (however provisional) at a
> level beyond what can be empirically circumscribed in unambiguous
> ways. Thus, the notion of *doctrina* is one of the avenues expressing
> the differing ways in which the sensory core of cognition is relied
> upon in dominant moods of thought which are typically "scientific"
> as contrasted with those that tend more to typically "philosophic"
> analysis. [Sebeok 1986c: vol. 1, p. 214]

For Sebeok as well, semiotics is best thought of as a teaching maneuver or as this "body of thought sensitive to its own implication...striving for consistency throughout." Sebeok's publications, plentiful and multifaceted, have attempted such a doctrine, but have never pretended to be directed at a rigidly defined group of readers. In fact, Sebeok's "congeners"—individuals of like mind—are located in many parts of the world, individuals who often first encounter semiotics in their reading. More than once a researcher has thought himself or herself alone in ranging beyond his or her own academic discipline, whether it be literary criticism, the history of philosophy, genetics, or marketing, into questions of meaning as sign production, only to discover that this "solitary" activity is common ground for numerous intellectual communities. As an Australian visitor attending the 1984 meeting of the Semiotic Society of America remarked, "I had assumed that I would be the only self-taught semiotician at this meeting. In fact, I find we are all self-taught!" This gentleman and I were both discovering that semiotics usually is—and by Sebeok's lights should be—a doctrine engaged and furthered by inquisitive (although not isolated) individuals.

Perhaps for this reason more than any other, Sebeok has never claimed a "Bloomington school," although he has taught at Indiana University since 1943. He prefers instead to speak and write (as he does in this volume) of individuals of like mind free to disagree. Certainly Sebeok has put much time and effort throughout his career into drawing congeners together, making many dialogues possible. Thus, while it is misleading to talk of schools, it is appropriate to speak of a community or communities in the doctrine of semiotics, and to seek out the relation of an individual scholar-scientist such as Sebeok to that community. (Nor is it irrelevant that Sebeok himself has long been a "congenial" force in the expansion of semiotics as a subject for academic study in the United States, and indeed in many other countries as well.)

In an article on "Semiosis and Semiotics: What Lies in Their Future?" (1988c), Sebeok maintains that semiotics is "the universal propensity of the human mind for reverie focused specularly inwards upon its own long-term cognitive strategy and daily maneuverings." In this statement Sebeok seems to isolate the individual, but he certainly would not take as his model the situation of Charles Sanders Peirce, who spent many of his later years in the relative isolation of his home at Milford, Pennsylvania, and the more complete isolation created by his inability to find a permanent university position. As Sebeok's own activities in the intellectual community of semiotics demonstrate, individual reflection must be measured against the reflections of others. Peirce himself, who with Charles Morris has been a key figure in Sebeok's efforts to redirect semiotic study toward John Locke's *doctrina signorum* (as Deely points out in Sebeok 1989b:x), often wrote of such a "community of inquirers." What is this community for Sebeok? As his readers already know, he divides semiotic inquiry into two traditions, the "minor" or language-based tradition inspired largely by the work of Ferdinand de Saussure, and the "major," or non linguistic-based, tradition of Locke, Peirce, and Morris. Sebeok has long disparaged the former as a community (my term) that has insisted on putting the linguistic cart before the semiotic horse. Still, the two have much in common. In Sebeok's work on the nature of semiosis (particularly on the semiotic self), both communities will find useful ideas.

In my own area, literary and performance theory, semiotics is largely an enterprise with a Sausurrean genealogy whose primary figures include Claude Lévi-Strauss, Roland Barthes, Jacques Lacan, A. J. Greimas, Roman Jakobson, Julia Kristeva, Umberto Eco, Paul de Man, and Jacques Derrida. The pantheon of what has come to be called "post-structuralism" is constantly in flux. While post-structuralism has dealt very little with the work of Morris or Sebeok, it has discovered the work of Peirce. Most interesting for the post-structuralists is the nature of the interpretant, a concept they have added to a glossary that draws more often on the phenomenology of Georg W. F. Hegel (Derrida, de Man) or psychoanalytic sign systems (Lacan, the French feminists, much film study of the 1970s and 80s). As Teresa de Lauretis says of the work of Eco in *Alice Doesn't* (a book that stands at the juncture of semiotics, feminism, and film study):

> Eco's debt to Peirce is extensive. The latter's concepts of interpretant and unlimited semiosis are pivotal to *A Theory of Semiotics*, which turns on the notion of a dialectic interaction between codes and modes of sign production. They serve to bridge the gap between discourse and reality, between the sign and its referent (the empirical object to which the sign refers); and so they usher in a theory of meaning as a continual cultural production that is not only suscep-

tible of ideological transformation, but materially based in historical change. [de Lauretis 1984:172]

Critics of film, mass culture, and, to a lesser extent, literature and theatre have come to the work of Peirce through Eco (and others) and have found useful the pragmatism of Peirce's semiotics (I am not speaking here of Peirce's own "pragmaticism"), in countering, for example, the idealist strictures of Freudian and Lacanian "subjects." At the same time, Peirce's schema of interpretants allows us to discuss material sign production in the realm of culture without forgetting the subject. As de Lauretis says, "The individual's habit as a semiotic production is both the result and the condition of the social production of meaning" (1984:179). Both subject and social reality are signs.

Peirce remarked long ago that by testing and retesting the individual's abductions, those abductions may approach the 'real': "The real, then, is that which, sooner or later, information and reasoning would finally result in, and which is therefore independent of the vagaries of me and you. Thus, the very origin of the conception of reality involves the notion of a COMMUNITY without definite limits, and capable of a definite increase of knowledge" (5.311).* Only the community can hope to approach the final interpretants of the "real"; the individual is limited by "ignorance and error" (5.317). In much the same manner, Sebeok sees the field or discipline of semiotics as one of scholar-scientists reaching for "a general unified perspective within...'ecumenical semiotics'" (Anderson et al. 1984:35). Like the expanding intellectual universe in which Sebeok sees himself, semiotics is "maturing" or "evolving," growing more complex (just as Peirce maintained the universe is moving from simplicity to complexity). Semiotics "provides the human sciences with a context for reconceptualizing foundations" (Anderson et al. 1984:35). As a doctrine it will edge toward (while not, in all probability, reaching) a "higher synthesis" that will illuminate numerous branches of the human sciences. (One such doctrine is the notion of Gaia.)

Drawing on Peirce's view of the community reaching for the

---

* References to the *Collected Papers of Charles Sanders Peirce* (1931–1966) are to volume and paragraph numbers according to the textual divisions established by the editors Charles Hartshorne and Paul Weiss.

"real," as well as on the work of Jakob von Uexküll and René Thom, Sebeok acknowledges that the members of the community participate variously in the creation of the "real." Here the "major" and "minor" traditions in semiotics find the most common ground. Saussurean "theorists" work from the premise that the arbitrary nature of language renders meaning something less than eternal truth. In literary theory, post-structuralists have expanded on this premise to the point that certain individuals have questioned our ability to determine meaning, or to distinguish fiction from nonfiction. The most significant contributions of the "major" tradition in semiotics are often defined in similar terms. As Roberta Kevelson notes, in both cases semiotics builds on paradigms, or referent beliefs, which are then put to the test in the context of free inquiry (Kevelson 1986:540).

In fact, this question of free inquiry brings together, in more definite terms, the relation of the individual semiotician to a community of inquirers. Sebeok has not written directly on the American contexts for such inquiry, but he has been remarkably consistent in treating the question of individuality, or, more broadly, "the semiotic self." In chapter 1 of this book, Sebeok explains that his friendship with the physician and writer Harley C. Shands sparked his interest in the semiotics of medicine. In recent years Sebeok has written extensively on the dual, immunologic and semiotic (or social), determinations of self. Drawing on Jakob von Uexküll's view of the overlapping *Umwelten* that constitute the self's interaction with another, he remarks:

> The notion "semiotic self" registers and emphasizes the fact that an animate is capable of absorbing information from its environment if and only if it possesses the corresponding key, or code. There must exist an internalized system of signposts to provide a map to the actual configuration of events. Therefore, "self" can be adequately grasped only with the concepts and terminology of the doctrine of signs. Another way of formulating this fact is that while living entities are, in one commonly recognized sense, open systems, their permeable boundaries permitting certain sorts of energy-matter flow or information transmissions to penetrate them, they are at the same time closed systems, in the sense that they make choices and evaluate inputs, that is to say, in their semantic aspect. [Sebeok 1989b:viii]

Moreover, "the closest link of the self in nature as well as in culture is with memory, both as a feature of a physical repository and as a social construct....It is the *articulatio secunda*, or the syntactic aspect of language, which provides the machinery whereby memory organizes...and finally imposes a coherent and personal narrative schema upon each of us" (vi). We become the *dramatis personae* of our own theatres of consciousness (a term Sebeok borrows from Peirce). Thus, for Sebeok the self is not identical to consciousness; instead, by means of "specular semiotics," "man converts his Umwelt into a unitary system of signs, a configuration"—and, no less, into the impression that in fact we are today the same engaging person we were yesterday.

There are a number of points to be made about the "semiotic self" in an "American" context. In the United States, popular sentiment has treated the individual as a measure of absolute value, and an absolute in itself. Because Peirce, Morris, Jakobson, Sebeok, and so many other semioticians have lived amidst this sentiment, we must wonder about the influence of these popular notions on their semiotics. Although the best known American Pragmatist, John Dewey, was more concerned with philosophy's place in community ethics than was Peirce, the latter addressed at least once the place for the individual in the political institutions of the United States. In 1871 he wrote:

> The question whether the *genus homo* has any existence except as individuals, is the question whether there is anything of any more dignity, worth, and importance than individual happiness, individual aspirations, and individual life. Whether men really have anything in common, so that the *community* is to be considered as an end in itself, and if so, what the relative value of the two factors is, is the most fundamental practical question in regard to every public institution the constitution of which we have it in our power to influence. [8.38]

Peirce's final remark here—"which we have it in our power to influence"—rests on an assumption fundamental to the conduct of semiotic inquiry: that the individual has the political right to influence the community. Of course the role of the citizen in regard to his or her country differs from the role of the inquirer within the semiotic community. We have seen that for Sebeok the semiotic self must be understood in semiotic terms; it now remains to explore how the activities of the semiotician—Peirce's inquirer—interact with those public institutions that are in themselves both open and closed systems, semiotic selves with shifting bureaucratic and democratic natures. In a position paper, Sebeok says with Myrdene Anderson, John Deely, Martin Krampen, Joseph Ransdell, and Thure von Uexküll: "In the humanities, social sciences, life sciences, and conceptual sciences...significant work tends to be accomplished by individual scholar-scientists in touch with themselves and their sibling disciplines, and hence aware of the value in exchange" (Anderson et al. 1984:8).

The influence of American political ideals on such ideas will not seem so far-fetched if we remember Charles Morris's assessment of the four "occasions" of American pragmatism, so closely related to the development of semiotics in the United States. Morris pointed out that the pragmatists—whom he identified as Charles S. Peirce, John Dewey, William James, and George Mead—had developed their ideas at the "occasion" of four historical influences: "1) the prestige which science and the scientific method enjoyed in the mid-nineteenth century; 2) the corresponding strength of empiricism in the then current philosophy; 3) the acceptance of biological evolution; 4) the acceptance of the ideals of American democracy" (1970:5). Morris points to the first, the scientific method, as the chief influence on Peirce's work. Still, the fourth is apparent in Peirce's 1871 remark quoted above. As has been pointed out, Peirce saw *semeiotic*, or logic, as encompassing all other realms of thought, including the political and ethical. I do not propose that Peirce's citizenship was important to his *semeiotic*, but rather that the democratic ideals he seems to have valued bore an optimism that touched his metaphysics, a universe evolving into greater complexity; contributed to his belief in scientific method and progress; and had a hand with these others in shaping his semiotic.

We might make use of American history, specifically the encounter of European individuals with the New World, as an event that has had tremendous effects on our "semiotic self." In *The Conquest of America*, Tzvetan Todorov (1984) draws a fascinating picture of the first encounters between European and American "selves" in the late fifteenth and the sixteenth centuries. Even more influential than the discovery of this other world is, as Todorov points out, the perspective of the European chronicler. Often the explorers recorded their own experiences in letters, diaries, and reports that have been largely responsible for our understanding (as well as our misunderstanding) of these events. The records of Christopher Columbus, for example, include unlikely conversations with Indians with whom he shared no common language. Noting at one point the great volume of fresh water discharged into the ocean near the Florida coast, Columbus concluded that the land ahead could not be an island. No, the Indians confirmed, it is in fact part of a larger continent (Todorov 1984:15). As well as Columbus has reasoned on the evidence of his senses, what can we make of the Indians' "confirmation"? Columbus's accounts, like most personal narratives, throw a web of expectations before him, making encounters with strange phenomena—Indians, stifling heat, flocks of parrots—into the signs of a foretold land whose outlines he already, in some sense, knows.

Todorov demonstrates quite convincingly that the conquerors' accounts of these events reflect two things: how disparate were the Europeans' and Americans' senses of self and how loud the clash of these self-images still sounds today. After giving an "exemplary history" of the recorded interactions between Europeans (Columbus and Hernando Cortes figure prominently) and Americans (primarily the Aztecs and Mayas), Todorov draws a number of conclusions. The Europeans' experience of language—that is, as a tool for integrating the community and identifying and manipulating the Other—met with incomprehension, the Americans having no sense of language as a concrete instrument of action on an Other. Thus, the Europeans failed to perceive the Americans as members of the human community. What should have enabled the Europeans to engage the Indians in dialogue—that is, a European sense of the human Other—actually inhibited a real dialogue and helped to set Europe on the road to the domination of these and many other peoples.

Further, Todorov characterizes the discovery of perspective in European art and the discovery of the New World as two contemporaneous historical moves "to validate a single and individual viewpoint" (1984:121). This startling relation exists "by reason of the transformation that both facts simultaneously reveal and produce in

human consciousness" (1984:121). Todorov sets out to "read" the
modern individualist ideology that guided these explorers and art-
ists, an ideology he sees as dying out today. "A man's life belongs
to himself and has nothing to do with anyone else's" (1984:254),
says this ideology. Nonsense, replies Todorov; history permits us to
reflect upon ourselves and to know ourselves through the Other. In
the cases of Cortes and Columbus that Other is the Indian; Cortes
and Columbus themselves are Others for us. Knowledge must be
acquired, claims Todorov, not to gain power as Cortes did, but to
resist it. This view in certain respects is consonant with Sebeok's
view of the semiotic self, and before it, with Jakob von Uexküll's
work on *Umwelten*, as well as with Peirce's ideas on the community
of inquirers. Roberta Kevelson connects Peirce's belief in freedom
of inquiry to a taste in later American work for paradigm, or provisional belief: "Characteristic of semiotics in the United States is
the belief that freedom of inquiry is truncated and restrained whenever
extra-scientific dogma is permitted to govern the methodological
processes as well as the conclusions of scientific inquiry. Such
dogma is not always explicit. It may be implied in the style of
inquiry" (1986:522–523). Is this concern for the influence of dogma
on scientific inquiry not implied as well in Sebeok's notion of the
semiotic self?

Sebeok could be considered one instance of that "international"
(Todorov 1984:250) who is replacing the earlier, colonizing self:
that is, one who affirms the Other's exteriority while recognizing
the Other as subject. Unlike Sebeok's semiotic self, this international self is offered as a "new exotopy" or as a characteristic feature of
our time. Quoting Hugh of St. Victor, Todorov proposes: "The man
who finds his country sweet is only a raw beginner; the man for
whom each country is as his own is already strong; but only the man
for whom the whole world is as a foreign country is perfect (I
myself, a Bulgarian living in France, borrow this quotation from
Edward Said, a Palestinian living in the United States, who himself
found it in Erich Auerbach, a German exiled in Turkey)" (1984:250).

It is entirely appropriate that Sebeok's accounts in this book of
figures in American semiotics are personal accounts: the accounts
of a chronicler, of one who was there, who *witnessed*. Moreover, in
the metaphor of the signature, we find yet another indexical link to

the semiotic self. Signatures certainly may be seen as traces of their authors' uniqueness; but in this volume the traces are further removed, viewed through the speculum of Sebeok's memory. In his recent essay "The Semiotic Self Revisited" (1989a), Sebeok once again chronicles a personal experience, this time to illustrate the "iconic spatial expressions" of social position that help to determine the semiotic self:

> In my father's household, in interwar Hungary, he, the "head" of the family, was seated during meals, as you would expect, at the "head" of the table. On Sundays and most other holidays, the midday (main, often extended) family meal of the day began almost invariably with chicken soup. Cooked in the broth, there floated the severed head of a rooster, cockscomb prominently displayed. The maid always served my father first, ladling out of the tureen the rooster's head into his bowl, beak facing my father. After he had finished his soup, he would pick up the head, munch on the comb, then, with a special instrument, trephine the skull and suck the brain out. When my father was absent, protocol demanded that the elder son, myself, be served the head, with the same tasty rite ensuing. [p. xi]

Sebeok ruminates on these iconic signs as the representation of the self within a family community that clearly delineated who "had maximum access to amenities and information" (p. xi). One could also see these signs as indexical: instructions that guide and reinforce the behavior of servants, wife, and children, as well as head of household.

The vividness of Sebeok's description of the scene recalls the fascination of a young boy who not only witnesses such a rite but invests himself in the position of the father, whom he is expected to replace and imitate. (One wonders how he might have described the scene had he been the second son? or perhaps the daughter?) As Sebeok himself says, "The mechanisms at work here were incorporated, indeed, drummed into my *self*, which, as Peirce however wisely observed (5.642), 'is only inferred,' for 'your neighbors are, in a measure, yourself, and in far greater measure than...you would believe' (7.571)." Interestingly, in retelling this tale, Sebeok as author takes a more estranged position; while he retains the position of subject, he looks upon the scene with an ethnographer's eye. Nor can we overlook that Sebeok did not, in fact, go on to take his father's place in this aristocratic European milieu. Instead, he (and his father) came to America.

Now, I do not mean to suggest that by leaving Europe Sebeok left behind all of the European notions of self and other implied by this anecdote. Indeed, if any one individual has had a prime influence on Sebeok's notion of the semiotic self, it is the European Jakob von Uexküll. Semiotics as a discipline (and Sebeok with it) has flourished as a result of a robust and complicated dialogue between Europe and the United States (and Canada, let us not forget), and more recently between these intellectual communities and those elsewhere that have since begun to interact with ours.

We are not unaware that, in calling this collection *American Signatures: Semiotic Inquiry and Method*, we have broached difficult, unresolved issues. Nor will these issues become less complicated. For example, Sebeok speculates (after Margulis and Sagan 1986b) that *Homo sapiens* may one day find itself to be a "rudimentary organ, a delicately dissected nervous system attached to electronically driven plastic arms." This project of "cybersemiosis" may test what Peirce has called the "evolution of mind," and may run counter to other, humanistic conceptions of the individual found in the community of inquirers and drawn from cultural presuppositions, originally fostered in the Renaissance and later given expression in the political institutions of the United States. In such a context, how will current semiotic views of self and other work together with a democratic notion of "value in exchange" to sculpt a rich and useful role for semiotics? Moreover, what happens to the idea of the individual, indeed the semiotic self, when we begin to speak of cybersemiosis? Where does "individual happiness," as Peirce put it, fit in a cybersemiotic world?

With these thoughts in mind, a few words need to be said about the organization of this collection of essays. In writing his history of semiotics in the United States (published here for the first time, as chapter 1), Sebeok has proceeded, as one might expect, from self to other selves. Formally, chapter 1 is divided into three parts: a chronicle of significant individuals in U.S. semiotics, a report on "organizational aspects" of semiotics in this country; and projections for future teaching and research. Looked at informally, however, Sebeok uses his own history to trace ideas from one individual to the next, tying together personalities, events, and speculation. He unearths and explores the work of selected figures who remain little known (such as the banker, lawyer, and language theorist Alexander Bryan Johnson or the university teacher Ethel Albert), and puts them in perspective with figures we know well: Peirce, Morris, Jakobson, Margaret Mead, Kenneth Pike, and others. In chapter 2, "Vital Signs," Sebeok approaches a similar task, that of chronicling the state of semiotics in the 1980s. Here he does not confine himself to the United States. As in chapter 1, he looks ahead to developments in the sciences that hold challenges for semioticians.

Published here for the first time in English, as an addendum to chapter 1, Susan Petrilli's interview with Sebeok adds further reflections on his own development as a semiotician and on his ties to Jakobson and Morris. Sebeok has called Peirce, Jakobson, and Morris the three most important U.S. figures in the history of semiotics. While he discusses all three throughout this book, it would not be complete without Sebeok's essay "Roman Jakobson's Teaching in America" (chapter 3), which deals with the reception of Jakobson's work in the United States. In fact, given Jakobson's impact on semiotics in the Western hemisphere, this essay could have been titled, after Todorov, "Jakobson's Conquest of America."

This autobiographically oriented section of the book is followed by a selection of essays that demonstrates the development of a number of ideas in Sebeok's work. As John Deely has noted, since the 1950s Sebeok's work has shifted from specific area studies to broader-ranging ruminations on the nature of language, the human being ("man") as a sign, and the place of semiotics within the human sciences. The broader view is already present in chapter 4, "Is a Comparative Semiotics Possible?" There Sebeok speculates on a general theory of semiotics, using the genetic code as prototype, but he is already skeptical of the term "theory":

> It remains to be seen whether a general theory of semiotics can be constructed such that the problems and solutions relating to the natural languages can themselves be reformulated in an interesting way. At present, the trend continues in the opposite direction, that is, the descriptions of other sign systems tend to more or less slavishly imitate—despite occasional warnings, e.g., by Lévi-Strauss (1945)—and more often than not quite erroneously, the narrow internal mod-

els successfully employed by linguists. The literature of semiotics is thus replete with mere restatements rather than solutions of problems, and the need for different kinds of theory at different levels of "coding" appears pressing.

Sebeok ends chapter 4 by calling for a "well-developed theory of signs" that would seek out a "single template" that could account for the many varieties of zoosemiotics. Could, he asks, the sciences of linguistics and genetics converge? (In later essays he will answer, "yes.")

Elsewhere, Sebeok has proposed "communication" as one of two facets of semiosis (the other being signification), and as the feature that allows us to distinguish the vital from the inanimate. Communication is not synonymous with "language," although many may think it to be so; nor can the "origins of language" be sought in the communication systems of our ancestor species. (What has been called language in this context must be termed speech, while language itself, for Sebeok, becomes a "primary modeling system," an idea he explicates in chapter 6.)

On a related issue, John Deely, in his introduction to the second edition of *The Sign and Its Masters* (Sebeok 1989b), sees Sebeok holding firmly to the "broader view" despite others' objections that semiotics cannot "subtend the work of speculative and practical understanding alike." Deely maintains, after Sebeok, that "it will be semiotics that must assimilate our understanding of nature along with our understanding of discourse in its contrastive order as 'culture'" (Sebeok 1989b:xi). Our selection here of recent essays should make clear Sebeok's views on the relations between semiotics in the natural and human realms. Chapter 5, for example, concludes that the many methods of classifying "animal" may not be incompatible, but complementary. In that chapter Sebeok draws on the *Umweltforschung*, or "study of phenomenal worlds, self worlds or the subjective universe" of Jakob von Uexküll. Among these worlds are the indexical movements by which plants respond to the rays of the sun, and the sign action by which a cow recognizes such plants as food and consumes them. In each organism's *Umwelt* the same signs may play entirely different roles.

Uexküll's *Umwelten* are discussed as "models" in chapter 6, where Sebeok argues that whereas "language evolved as an adaptation,...speech developed out of language as a derivative 'exaptation' over a succeeding period of approximately two million years." Thus, "natural languages" came about primarily for modeling purposes, rather than for communication, which then—as now—is in many instances accomplished by nonverbal means. Language becomes a secondary modeling system, that is, a representation of current, and possible, worlds.

We follow this essay with one that tackles, head-on, the conflict between the major and minor traditions in semiotics. Chapter 7, "Linguistics and Semiotics," concludes, of course, that of the two designations "semiotics" has the only truly catholic compass.

While in chapter 5, Sebeok juxtaposed ideas from Uexküll with the work of the Moscow-Tartu school of semioticians, in chapter 8 he places Uexküll in the context of Peirce, in order to discuss the relative constancy of subjects and objects. Peirce and Uexküll seem to agree that, as the universe is "perfused with signs," the "subject" and "object" are perfused as well. The subject (Uexküll's "meaning-receiver")—in this case President Ulysses S. Grant, near death from cancer of the throat—equates life with his access to speech. Grant perceived himself deprived of "life," that is, of verbal semiosis, before his actual death; yet his predicament demonstrates the two functions of language: that of modeling the self (in this case, as "verb") and that of communicating with the Other.

As a final note, it is important to ask how semiotics as an activity of individual scholar-scientists is making its way in a world divided into nation-states. In his essay "Pandora's Box in Aftertimes" (in Sebeok 1986d), Sebeok takes us on an excursion into "applied" semiotics, with its combination of "policy and action with information" (p. 51). As a consultant to a government-funded study on nuclear waste disposal, Sebeok seems to have found himself viewed, not as a policymaker, nor as one who implements that policy, but as a resource of "information," as Sebeok sees it in its popular guise. An unusual role for a semiotician to play, it opens interesting questions about governments' understanding of the nature of semiotics as an activity. Government agencies seldom grasp semiotics as a doctrine, even in its institutionalized forms on American college campuses; yet, it often exists there by virtue of partial funding with federal grant monies. Indeed, where semiotics does take a formal existence in academia, how many of these universities consider it to be a marginal program, one of the first to go in times of budget difficulties? How many institutions claim a program in semiotics "on paper" but have little funding to back it up? How does semiotics sustain itself in the academic community? Sebeok has claimed that, despite these very real difficulties, "ecumenical" semiotics has benefited from its rather unorthodox and perhaps more flexible position in the academic bureaucracy, while established departments in other fields must struggle to effect even minor change.

These are important questions if we are to assert that semiotics is the activity of individual scholar-scientists. (Both Charles Morris and John Dewey pointed out some time ago that American pragmatism would never have had the impact it has delivered without its criticism of American society, a just corollary to its praise of American democratic ideals.) While the lone intellectual Peirce may currently be considered the preeminent intellectual forebear of the "major" tradition in the United States, it was the congenial, well-established academic Morris—as Sebeok points out—who first taught a course in semiotics, at the University of Chicago. We often walk a fine line between a traditional notion of American individualism, visible in Sebeok's talk of "masters," and a persistent urge, created in part by the configurations of our academic *Umwelten*, to rethink the Cartesian foundations of that individualism by means of Peirce's semiotic, Thom's catastrophe theory, and Uexküll's theory of meaning. Where does the individual scholar-scientist situate himself or herself in a nation-state that is more accurately termed the post-modern, post-industrial complex? Does such a setting promise the continuation of intellectual genealogies, a family of masters passing the doctrine from one generation to the next? Within the academic community, perhaps. Outside it, government may cast the semiotician in a different role: as a consultant to the technologies of cybernetics, nuclear waste disposal, and any number of other, government-regulated "evolutions." But we are, as semioticians (in the plural), also a group of constituencies often uncomfortable with such prospects. These trends, these contradictions, and the richness of the dialogue, can be seen in the work of Thomas A. Sebeok.

PART ONE

Semiotic Bearings

CHAPTER ONE

Semiotics in the United States
The View from the Center

I.

Il n'y a ni beaux ni vilains sujets...on pourrait presque établir comme axiome, en se posant au point de vue de l'Art pur, qu'il n'y en a aucun, le style étant a lui tout seul une manière absolue de voir les choses.—Flaubert to Louise Colet, January 16, 1852

Semioticians are, at least as regards one point, in full agreement: that no comprehensive (let alone "complete") treatise—or even a handy compendium—dealing with the history of semiotics as yet exists. Moreover, as Umberto Eco has emphasized (Forthcoming), no such monumental achievement can nowadays be even contemplated by any single would-be author.

At best, some of us are ready to contribute bits and pieces in the expectation that such scraps of *bricolage*, or recoding, may eventually be gathered up into a reasonably integrated collective mythic record (cf. Bouissac 1976). It is well to remember that Claude Lévi-Strauss's *bricoleur* practices applied semiotics, for, as his originator said, the *bricoleur* works with signs, hallowed in tradition. These signs "resemble images in being concrete entities but they resemble concepts in their powers of reference," and these "images and con-

---

This chapter was written expressly for this book. Two other versions are also in preparation: another article version, which will differ in several substantive particulars from this one, and a book-length version that will appear first in Italian, in a series titled *Strumenti*, edited by Umberto Eco for Bompiani (Milan), and afterward in English and other languages.

cepts play the part," in the Saussurean mode, "of the signifying and signified respectively" (Lévi-Strauss 1962b:18).

There is as yet, too, a far from universal consensus among semioticians as to *what* mosaic fragments will be pertinent to such an envisaged synthesis, or precisely how the parts, once identified, ought to be combined, for "the decision as to what to put in each place also depends on the possibility of a different element there instead, so that each choice which is made will involve a complete reorganization of the structure, which will never be the same as one vaguely imagined, nor as some other which might have been preferred to it" (Lévi-Strauss 1962b:19).

As Alain Rey pointed out in his rich and fruitful consideration of this issue, "Criteria for relevance are...linked to the perspective, or 'theoretical style' of each text; then to its objects; and finally to its method" (1984:92). In my view, the midmost target of semiotics is, indeed, as Rey so persuasively argued, *epistemology*, understood in the broad sense of the cognitive constitution of living entities, comprehending the physiological and psychological makeup of each in their interaction. In semiotics, we must in any case think of ourselves both as working within a tradition that changes over time and as trying to grasp things as they "really are."

The currently fashionable tag "cognitive science" seems to me, at best, a stylistic and methodological variant, commonly involving computers, for semiotics; at worst it seems a historically untutored, pretentious relabeling of an ancient multidisciplinary endeavor concerned with mediating structures, viz., signs, intervening between stimuli and responses, i.e., between objects and interpretants (see particularly Richard Parmentier's treatment of this issue in Mertz and Parmentier 1985: chap. 2 in particular). The goal of both semioticians and cognitive scientists, especially those experimenting with artificial neural networks, is to reach an understanding of the basic mechanisms of thought, especially human reasoning, image schemata, learning, perception and "preconceptual" structures, motor control, development, emotion, and, of course, language. This commonality becomes quite clear from reading such recent books as, among others, the ones by George Grace (1987), Mark Johnson (1987), George Lakoff (1987), Lakoff and Johnson (1980), and Ronald Langacker (1987). A unified theory of human cognition, and of cognition throughout the animal world generally, is our ultimate shared ambition, in order to bridge the yawning gulf between our understanding of the chemistry of neurons and of their biology, and to synthesize a wealth of particulars being daily uncovered by neuroscience. The details of the biology of the artificial must be mapped onto the biology of the "real" cells that compose the brain. As a shorter-range goal—to be achieved in the next decade perhaps—it should be possible to build a computer to simulate by means of electronic "neurons" events in the brain of a honeybee, a social creature with a remarkably sophisticated semiosic endowment.

The burden of this particular account is to depict in rough-hewn fashion the story of semiotics in this country, past and present, and perhaps to extrapolate cautiously from the known to the unknown. I intend to stay clear of a rigid chronology here, relying instead on the quasicinematic principle of flashbacks and flashforwards, transporting my reader as and where appropriate within the confines of my own tenaciously associative memory. So the following narrative will on occasion proceed by rapid projection of discrete snapshots of persons, ideas, incidents, and maybe of dreams as well—onto the reader's mental screen. Excessive engagement with history can be stultifying, but some measure of it is imperative.

The boundaries of the United States are of course far more permeable than most. Roman Jakobson and a throng of other academics, myself included, were trained, more or less, in other conventions, and worked for a varying number of years in foreign parts. The sources of U.S. semiotics are thus many, and its potency radiates all over the world. The ongoing dialectic between the local and the global must be borne constantly in mind lest this story turn into distasteful fiction. The expression "Anglo-Saxon semioticians," on occasion set off against "structuralist semioticians" (Harland 1987:4), and at other times against "Continental semioticians," is a bogus opposition, bordering on racism, to which Jakobson's cosmopolitan career stands not alone in giving the lie.

My inclination is to assign to the "great elders," as Roland Barthes (1988:6) referred to them—such canonical protagonists as Charles Sanders Peirce, Charles Morris, and Roman Jakobson (the first and third of whom have inspired reams of nervous exegetic literature)—walk-on parts when called upon, and to place center stage instead their precursors, contemporaries, epigones, acolytes, and scores of other competent artisans. In short, instead of starring Hamlet, I want, like Tom Stoppard, to feature Rosencrantz and Guildenstern.

Of course the temporal dimensions of my harlequin braid enfold but a moment in history. Of forty thousand antecedent generations of humans, less than one-thousandth—about a century and a half— produced the actors in this domestic saga. The first one hundred years or so of this period are already a matter of more or less detailed, if nonetheless controversial, record, on which this essay may throw a different light. As to the most recent third, I remain, if not an altogether innocent bystander, at least one living witness.

Any inquiry of this sort must of course yield a highly eccentric, not to say idiosyncratic, narrative—or even a quirky one. Quirkiness and prejudice are valuable, I think, if only because they counteract cliché. Each of the two previous attempts to limn semiotics in the United States—Wendy Steiner's (1978) and Roberta Kevelson's (1986)—bears its peculiar subjective mark. The two differ in conception and perspective, as well as in style and execution, but more important, the latter chooses to ignore entirely the earlier. The two pieces might be regarded as balancing each other to a degree; when combined, they complement this third, perhaps more irreverent, report. Of course the views put forth here inevitably relate to the context from which they issue.[1]

Although Peirce served as Steiner's pillar of departure and, not surprisingly, continued as Kevelson's uncontested hero, my own biases as to the genesis of semiotics in this country lead back unswervingly to Alexander Bryan Johnson (1786–1867), that "homespun genius on the American frontier," in Allen Read's apt phrase (1973:192) characterizing this wealthy Utica, New York (though English-born), banker and lawyer. Johnson also became, many years *avant la lettre Peircienne*, America's first near-great semiotician. The inscription on his gravestone neatly sums up how Johnson perceived himself: "The author of many books: / A lawyer by education: / A banker during active life: / A student of philosophy always." His philosophical intention and manner seem uncannily and particularly reminiscent of Wittgenstein's in the *Tractatus* (1921–22) (cf. Drake, in Todd and Blackwood 1969:8).

Fig. 1-1
Alexander Bryan Johnson.

When I coined the expression "neglected figures in the history of semiotic inquiry" (Sebeok 1989b:187, in reference to Jakob von Uexküll), I had not anticipated that I would be starting a mini-trend pursued in repeated section headings at annual meetings of the Semiotic Society of America, aimed variously at relocating those figures already housed elsewhere or relabeling others identified as "cryptosemioticians" (Sebeok 1989:9, 259; Rey 1984:92). But if anyone qualifies under this rubric, it is surely Johnson, ignored in his lifetime but since "rediscovered" at least twice: first in 1947 (A. Johnson 1947; see also Rynin 1967 and Drake, in Todd and Blackwood 1969) and next at a conference held in 1967 that was aimed (with little success) at durably rehabilitating him (see Todd and Blackwood 1969). That conference was attended by, among others,

Max Black, who offered a critical assessment of Johnson's language theories in modern perspective (Todd and Blackwood 1969:49–66), and by K. T. Fann, himself the author of the first serviceable monograph on Peirce's theory of abduction (1970).

There is no question that Johnson was well aware of, indeed was indebted to, the passage at the end of John Locke's 1690 *Essay Concerning Human Understanding*, later adopted by Peirce as well, about the Doctrine of Signs (A. Johnson 1947:15). Johnson, in fact, deemed his own work exactly that new and other "sort of logic and critic" that John Locke only dreamed of, adding however, in his typically wry fashion: "What a painful but too late a dawning of light, must this have been!" (1947:15).

This is not the place to reappraise Johnson's always subtle, always fascinating, if sometimes flawed, reflections upon "the relation [as he phrased the topic in the subtitle of his *Treatise on Language*] which words bear to things," on the philosophy of language, especially semantics, and on a host of other perennial semiotic conundrums. These cogitations are well and critically appraised by David Rynin, who believed Johnson to have been a thinker of the highest rank (exalted at length in Johnson 1947:30, 430; concisely in Rynin 1967; see also Todd and Blackwood 1969).

Here, I would point to one of Johnson's extraordinarily prophetic, fecund, far-reaching, and to me most congenially linking insights: "My lectures," he proclaimed before the Utica Lyceum in 1825, "will endeavour to subordinate language to nature—to make nature the expositor of words, instead of making words the expositors of nature. If I succeed, the success will ultimately accomplish a great revolution in every branch of learning" (Johnson 1947:40).

His pivotal apprehension was, in brief, that language cannot explain the world, but that the world explains language. The opening sentence of his first numbered paragraph reads: "Man exists in a world of his own creation" (1947:29). This statement can perhaps best be compared with Wittgenstein's first unforgettable numbered sentence: "The world is everything that is the case" (quoted in Johnson 1947:29). (This view was remolded a century or so later by Niels Bohr in his famous maxim, "We are suspended in language in such a way that we cannot say what is up and what is down. The word 'reality' is also a word, a word which we must learn to use correctly"; quoted, *inter alia*, in French and Kennedy 1985:302.)

It should be noted that by "nature" Johnson plainly meant— precisely as Uexküll did by the German word *Natur* (cf. Sebeok 1986d:73)—"reality as it appears to us in objects apprehended" (Rynin 1967:287). He saw that this reality, which he divided into three irreducible categories, was composed of signs and sign-processes (see also Cassirer 1944:23). These categories, roughly speaking, are the external universe or creation, the subjective universe of internal consciousness, and intellectual, unverbal things. It should be noted, though, that Johnson used different terms at different times. By grouping existences into verbal vs. "unverbal" (his coinage?) and further dividing the latter into three fundamental types— sensations, emotions, and intellections—Johnson illuminated several seemingly obscure predicaments of the modern doctrine of signs. While he seems to attach little value to "verbal" thinking, his divagations about the "unverbal"—the basis for which he locates in what he calls the human "organism"—have a Kantian ring to them, but he does not make this debt explicit.

His deliberations about the meaning of "natural signs," which are not a part of language, and his assault on the human tendency to interpret linguistically the information of our senses, are in some ways deficient. (For instance, his distinction between words and sentences was, in retrospect, grossly inadequate.) However, these ideas have riveting implications. As Johnson himself notes: "That the significance of a man's language is limited to his sensible experience would be readily admitted, were we not embarrassed with one difficulty. Bonfire names a sight, and melody a sound. If these words possessed no other signification, we should immediately understand that the import of bonfire must ever be unknown to the blind, and the import of melody to the deaf. But these words, and nearly all others, possess a further signification: they name words also. This is an important distinction, and till you understand it, you will be liable to delusion" (Johnson 1947:149–150).

The first American grand master of the realm of the "unverbal," Garrick Mallery (1831–1894), happened likewise to be a jurist (admitted to the bar in Philadelphia in 1853), who thereafter made an illustrious career as a gallant soldier until disability from wounds received in the Civil War caused his retirement from the army in

1879. In 1876, during his six years of service in the Signal Service
Bureau (created in 1870), while on duty at Fort Rice, Dakota Territory, he became engrossed in the pictography and sign language of
the (Siouan) Dakota Indians. As a result of this work, he was
ordered the next year to report to Maj. John Wesley Powell, the
influential American geologist and ethnologist, in whose company
he conducted field work in the Rocky Mountains. Upon retiring
from the army, he joined the Bureau of Ethnology, then under
Powell's directorship, and produced a sequence of substantial and
still peerless works based on assiduous collection of original data on
sign language among North American Indians, supported by impressive comparative and philosophical ruminations (see, e.g., Mallery 1972 [1881] and Umiker-Sebeok and Sebeok 1978:1–437).

Fig. 1-2
Garrick Mallery. (Photo courtesy Smithsonian Institute)

While Johnson's work was semiotic in every respect except its terminology, Mallery, whom Georges Mounin dubbed "a born semiologist" (1985:73), was a semiotician *au pied de la lettre*. He employed both the technical noun—note its spelling (Sebeok 1985b:51–52)—and the adjective freely and with astonishing accuracy and versatility. (Incidentally, Mallery also cites and discusses George Dalgarno's *sematology* [1972:25–26].)

In 1880, for example, Mallery characterized his own writings as native semiotics (reprinted in Umiker-Sebeok and Sebeok 1978:8). In the same monograph (see Umiker-Sebeok and Sebeok 1978:43), and again in 1881 (Mallery 1972:74), he told of the white deafmutes' semiotic code and pointed out that signs in succession exhibit a semiotic syntax (Mallery 1972:150). Then we find this sentence: "Men, in groping for a mode of communication with each other, and using the same general methods, have been under many varying conditions and circumstances which have determined differently many conceptions and their semiotic execution, but there have also been many of both which were similar" (1972:74). And he spoke of the precise mode of semiotic expression of the several tribes (1972:88).

Mounin wondered "if Mallery had read Peirce...or if Peirce had read Mallery" (1985:74)—and so must we all. Charles Morris's oft-cited 1946 dictum, according to which "Peirce was the heir of the whole historical philosophical analysis of signs" (C. Morris 1971:337), turns out to have been exaggerated, for we have no reason to suspect that Peirce was acquainted with, among others, the writings of John Poinsot (cf. Deely, in Poinsot 1985:492 n. 132) or with those of Johnson, who died when Peirce was twenty-eight. By then, Peirce had already published more than what is now encompassed in the initial tome of his chronological writings (1982, covering 1857–1866). Mallery, furthermore, is never mentioned by Peirce, or vice versa, although I am convinced, with Max H. Fisch and Jean Umiker-Sebeok, that the two must at least have known of each other, and may well have intermingled socially (for grounds, see Umiker-Sebeok and Sebeok 1978:xxxii n. 6).

Mallery's thinking, like his nomenclature, is permeated with a fine semiotic sensibility, but the sources of both are still shrouded in mystery. Since the twenty-four parts of William Dwight Whitney's

The Century Dictionary and Cyclopedia (*CD*), for which we know Peirce wrote numerous entries, and where the very form *semiotics* is well attested, began appearing only in 1889 (see Whitney 1891, pt. 19, p. 5,486), I can but hazard the following guess—subject to refutation if eventual research in military history fails to bear it out—as to Mallery's use of *semiotics*: that, in the course of his protracted service in the Signal Service Bureau, he might have become inured to the military use of this term. The French word *sémiotique* comparably denoted in the nineteenth century the "art de faire manoeuvrer les troupes en leur indiquant les mouvement par signes" (Sebeok 1985b:54 n. 2).

The recorded usages of *semiotics* in America make for a far more complicated story than has hitherto been traced, but this history can only be hinted at here. This very form is listed in the U.S. printing of *The Imperial Dictionary of the English Language*, with definition one reading: "The doctrine or science of signs; the language of signs," followed by definition two: "In *pathol.* that branch which teaches how to judge of all the symptoms in the human body, whether healthy or diseased; symptomatology; semeiology" (Ogilvie 1883:vol. 4, p. 27). The listing then recurs, almost verbatim, under the lemma "semiotics, semeiotics" in the *CD* (Whitney 1891: pt. 19, p. 5,486). In Peirce's marked copy of the 1889 edition of the *CD* (duplicated afterward by several Peirce scholars), the item is marked in green, which may have meant (according to a personal communication I received from Christian J. W. Kloesel, director of the Peirce Edition Project) "that Peirce simply recommended that the *Imperial* definitions be included in the *CD*." At the least, it is clear that the *-ics* form was already in use when Peirce worked on his contributions for the *CD*, but we do not know how widely, and we still do not know where Mallery picked up the term or why Peirce apparently never employed it himself (at least in his identified writings).

Of course, Mallery's knowledge of the history of "the systematic use of gesture speech" (1972:23–35) from antiquity to his own times, including its uses by orators and actors, was also enviable. He could easily have absorbed ideas and vocabulary through his extensive readings, which ran from quotations of the Stoic Chrysippus to Canon De Jorio's encyclopedic 1832 treatise about inferences based on Neapolitan gestures to reconstruct those of the ancients (Magli 1986).

Mention of De Jorio brings us forward directly to David Efron, who, like Mallery, has been influenced by De Jorio's work. Paul Ekman characterizes Efron as another pioneer "contributor to the now rapidly growing field of research into facial expressions and body movement in social interaction" (Preface to Efron 1972:7). Born in Argentina (1904–), Efron wrote his exemplary book, *Gesture, Race, and Culture* [1972 (1941)], while at Columbia University, where he conducted his fieldwork under the direction of Franz Boas. Martha Davis rightly pointed out that "the wealth of information [comparing groups of Italian and Jewish immigrants] presented in text, drawings, and notation has yet to be developed with the vision and breadth that [he] displays here" (1972:59). Efron focused upon nonverbal behavior in conversational settings. The question to which he sought the answer, empirically, by a judicious mixture of qualitative and quantitative methods, was: Are gestures culturally determined? His provisional conclusion was affirmative, or at any rate, it ratified that this form of human behavior is not determined by biological descent.

Efron later gave evidence of his allegiance, if intermittent, to semiotic methods and goals, for he actively participated in the 1974 Congress of the International Association for Semiotic Studies, where he vigorously and profitability debated my own plenary lecture and gave a clever (but to me wholly unconvincing) paper of his own, making the strong-sounding though vacuous claim that telepathy not merely exists but is "of a semiotic character" (Efron 1979:221n., 1,102–1,108). Efron drew on Old World sources with erudition, especially on De Jorio's book, *La mimica degli antichi investigata nel gestire Napoletano* (1832). If he knew the works of Mallery (easily familiar to other students of Boas, such as A. L. Kroeber), he never cited them. On the other hand, his own subsequent influence was (if not always explicitly recognized) pervasive in specialized corners of semiotic endeavor, rechristened subsequently by such names as "nonverbal communication" (Ruesch and Kees 1956), "proxemics" (E. Hall 1968), "nonverbal behavior" (Ekman and Friesen 1969:63), and "kinesics" (Birdwhistell 1970).

Of the just aforementioned, Edward T. Hall, Paul Ekman, and

Ray Birdwhistell were among those who took part in the 1962 conference on paralinguistics and kinesics, sponsored by the Indiana University Research Center in Anthropology, Folklore, and Linguistics, and reported in *Approaches to Semiotics* (Sebeok et al. 1972). In the course of the conference, American semiotics was—at least, according to the informed judgment of one observer (Rey 1984:92)—"organized," in the sense that it acquired its "institutional existence." And Jurgen Ruesch, ten years after that conference, published his own massive book, with the reverberatory title *Semiotic Approaches to Human Relations* (1972). (Ten years earlier, Ruesch had already discussed, if succinctly, "the field of semiosis" [1961:453].) But what were the true attainments and consequences of that 1962 conference?

One unanticipated outcome was the distinctive, perhaps singularly blended, *contour* acquired by semiotics in this country over the two ensuing decades. I chose to shape the conference around five thematic areas: cultural anthropology, education, linguistics, psychiatry, and psychology. Many prominent individuals were, naturally, invited to represent each of these disciplines. Other participants, in my view, never (or only half-heartedly) chose to proclaim themselves "semioticians."

An arresting case in point was that of Erving Goffman (1922–1982), who at times liked to designate himself a "sociologist," but who often relished his preferred role as an "outsider" (e.g., Sebeok et al. 1972:139, 232). In 1970, Goffman and I amicably coorganized and ran an international conference (sponsored by the Wenner-Gren Foundation for Anthropological Research). We were in total concord on the venue (Amsterdam), the participants, and topics to be discussed (Sherzer 1971). Yet we could not agree on the title. I wanted it to contain the identifying trademark *Semiotics*. After all, it was aspects of that which we were to discuss. Goffman, who had, years before, published what I considered his most insightful contribution to semiotics, *Stigma* (1963; but see MacCannell 1983:23–29), and who later (1979) cheerfully offered his "Footing" to be first published in *Semiotica*, insisted that he did not wish his work pinned down by that term, indeed by any one term. Hence we compromised on the *ad hoc* weasel phrase "Interaction Ethology," which nobody has used before or since.

Goffman's objections are particularly ironic in view of the earlier circumstance that resuscitated semiotics in the context of the 1962 conference and brought about the term's all but universal use. Everyone now remembers Margaret Mead's (1901–1978) declaration at that conference that *semiotics* is "the one word, in one form or other, that has been used by people who are arguing from quite different positions." But few recall the context of the remark. In fact, the paragraph in question started out: "We have been challenged by Dr. Goffman to say what we are doing and we are, I think, conceivably working in a field which in time will include the study of all patterned communication in all modalities..." (Sebeok et al. 1972:275). No wonder then that Dean MacCannell could claim, in his loving and pensive necrology of Goffman: "Those of us in the areas of semiotics...can regard him as a forerunner" (1983:1).

By *contour*, I meant above to suggest the peculiar, if constantly shifting, interlacement—in part intellectual, in part intimate—of the contemporary American semiotics community, which I have elsewhere positioned within a global "semiotic web" (Sebeok 1985b, chap. 10; note that this metaphor is now also used as the title of a continuing series of yearbooks, the second of which appeared in 1988, and which I continue to coedit with Jean Umiker-Sebeok, who was also the rapporteuse of our Amsterdam forum [see Sebeok and Umiker-Sebeok 1987–89]).

A case in point: I had coedited the transactions of the 1962 conference with Margaret Mead's daughter, Mary Catherine Bateson (1939–), whose father, Gregory Bateson (1904–1980), in collaboration with Jurgen Ruesch (1909–), had written the best general book, to this day, on communication (Ruesch and Bateson 1951). David Lipset (1980: chap. 12) presents Bateson as a "communication theorist." He was a notably acute thinker about some of the deepest semiotic problems, including zoosemiotic. He took a leading part in our Amsterdam conference, as well as in an earlier symposium on animal communication (sponsored by the Wenner-Gren Foundation and held at Burg Wartenstein, Austria, in 1965), which I had organized around the subject of zoosemiotics (Sebeok and Ramsay 1969:30). Moreover, he also contributed a marvellous, oft-cited chapter to my first handbook on *Animal Communication* (1968:614–626).[2]

A surprising number of American scholars situated in a multiplicity of academic fields, and some fiction writers as well, clearly practice semiotics but are not routinely so reckoned when formal tallies are drawn up. Let me single out a few such prominent figures, placing each in his appropriate setting.[3]

Among linguists, I consider Kenneth L. Pike (1912–) an unusually splendid exemplar, not only because he was the author of "a neglected contemporary American classic of 'cryptosemiotics'" (Sebeok 1989b:259)—his monumental semiotic treatise on *Language in Relation to a Unified Theory of the Structure of Human Behavior* (Pike 1967)—but also because his name provides an opportunity for some further reflections about the relationship of autochthonous linguistics with its enveloping semiotic matrix.

Let us consider some of the strictly American reverberations of the mutually coordinate or, as the case may be, hierarchical relationship between these two. (Ramifications of a broader nature, both historically and geographically, are reviewed in Sebeok 1987b.) All linguists resident in America—including Edward Sapir, Leonard Bloomfield, Yuen Ren Chao, Roman Jakobson, Uriel Weinreich, J. H. Greenberg, Noam Chomsky, Sebastian Shaumyan, and Sydney Lamb, four of whom were immigrants—have paid heed to the matter either explicitly or at least implicitly. Whether using this or a cognate term or none, they take it for granted as most Europeans, notably Ferdinand de Saussure, did or do, that linguistics is indeed subsumed under semiotics. Bloomfield remarked that "linguistics is the chief contributor to semiotic" (Sebeok 1987b:7); Chao distinguished languages from "quasi languages," citing zoosemiotics as one category, gestures as another, and in general following the semiotic terminology of Charles Morris (Chao 1968:116, 195); Chomsky alluded to a "science of semiology," in the framework of which it is tempting to draw an analogy to rules of grammar (1980:253); Greenberg asserted that "the special position of linguistics arises" from the fact that it is "a part of the nascent subject of semiotics, the science of sign behavior in general" (Sebeok 1989b: chap. 16); Jakobson accused of "egocentrism" linguists "who insist on excluding from the sphere of semiotics signs which are organized in a different manner than those of language" (1980:19; cf. Eco 1987); Lamb not only claimed that "pure linguistics, properly conceived, leaned quite naturally to semiotics" (1984:9; cf. Sebeok, Lamb, and Regan 1988) but also named the instructional unit he founded in 1982 at Rice University the "Department of Linguistics and Semiotics"; Sapir viewed language as but one of the "specialized forms of symbolic behavior" (Sebeok 1987b:7); Shaumyan defined "linguistics as a part of semiotics that deals with natural sign systems, that is, with natural languages"(1987:18); and Weinreich spoke of semiotics as the study of signs and sign systems "of which language is but one variety" (1980:390).

Such views were also consonant with those of many U.S.-based philosophers, as wildly dissimilar in outlook as Rudolf Carnap, who classified linguistics as "the descriptive, empirical part of semiotic" (1942:13); Ernst Cassirer, who dogmatically asserted that "linguistics is a part of semiotics" (1945:119); Susanne Langer, who, in her "general theory of symbolism" (1942:116) distinguishes between "verbal and non-verbal formulation"; Jacques Maritain (see especially 1957, and cf. Deely 1986); Wilbur Urban (1939:229—"Communication by language is...but one phase of a more general phenomenon"); or even Alfred North Whitehead, who delivered a series of lectures at the University of Virginia on *Symbolism* (1927: chap. 7 is on "Language"), and who discoursed at length on the question, What is "significance"? (1919: vol. 12, chap. 1).

Charles Morris, who rightly considered "the term 'language'...vague and ambiguous in current usage" (1946:36), coined the expression "lansign systems" for sign-sets of the kind in question, and proposed (as it turned out, to no avail whatsoever) to call the individual members of these systems "lansigns." The foundations for a semiotic linguistics were laid by Peirce himself (see also below); they were seldom better understood and complemented than by the American philosopher Joseph Ransdell (1980; for an American linguist's assessment, cf. Rauch 1987; cf. also Michael Shapiro 1983 and Pharies 1985).

A highly unusual model for the fusion of the verbal with the nonverbal, called "semiotic extension" (1979:58–100) has been developed by the psychologist David McNeill (b. 1933). It consists of a daring and productive elaboration of some ideas of L. S. Vygotsky by way of Peircean sign theory. McNeill presents a sophisticated bifurcated model for the organization of action: first, the sensory-

motor idea must encompass the other content, which is "the information that differentiates (specifies) the speech program which is
accessed via the sensory-motor idea." Second, "the sensory-motor
idea must be related to the other content." As to the ontogenesis of
semiotic extension, McNeill shows (1979:237) how the object of an
indexical sign must simultaneously be regarded as "the sign vehicle
of an iconic or symbolic sign."[4]

After this abridged *tour d'horizon* of major resident linguists'
perspectives on semiotics, let me return to Pike and his book. A
contemporary, quintessentially American linguist, Pike engaged in
evangelistic activity on behalf of the fundamentalist Summer Institute
of Linguistics (the headquarters of which is located at Santa Ana,
California) and the Wycliffe Bible Translators. His interests have
ranged from phonetics to discourse structure, rhetoric, and semantics. Eventually, however, venturing out of these areas, "because
some of us need to explore this trail," he declared a wish "to show
analogies between linguistic structure and the structure of society
and of nonverbal behavior" (Pike 1967:6), thus attempting to satisfy
the need for a unified theory. In a word—which he nowhere em-
ploys despite his evident familiarity with Peirce's *Collected Papers*
and especially with the two main semiotic treatises of Charles Morris,
and despite his having published several articles in *Semiotica*—he
turned to semiotics.

Unlike, however, most of our aforementioned linguist colleagues,
Pike has actually attempted concrete semiotic anatomizations of
certain social events, rigid in form or ceremony, and "repeatable in
general type with recognizable recurring elements" (Pike 1967:72).
One of these was a keenly observed church service (1967:73–97),
another the "family breakfast scene" (1967:122–128), and a third a
football game (1967:98–119). The last mentioned has since been at
least twice surpassed: once by another American-born linguist and
accomplished sign-theorist, John Lotz (1913–1973), whose passion-
ate semiotic analysis of football games I had read and discussed
with him not long before his untimely death, but the manuscript of
which has not been located among his papers (Sebeok 1989b:231–
252); and second in a fascinating, all-embracing account of soccer
by the witty English ethologist Desmond Morris (1981). Pike's
distinction between official game and spectacle also found an echo

in Goffman's distinction between players and participants, in the latter's quasisemiotic study, *Encounters*, of several types of interactions (1961:36 n. 30).

Eugene Nida's (b. 1914) fundamental studies of semantic elements "on which others can build" were emphasized by Allen Walker Read (1973:174). Nida's semiotic studies, confined to the verbal level, are preeminently oriented to translation theory and its applications; they have continued in this domain, culminating in a volume on the componential analysis of referential meaning (Nida 1975).

In the light of the foregoing paragraphs, these alternative arguments, and more, could now be entertained: that the story of linguistics be subsumed as a vast chapter integrated within the far more comprehensive chronicle of general and applied semiotics; that linguistics, offering a window to the mind, is therefore a branch of the cognitive sciences (which may or may not be tantamount to semiotics); or that semiosis, inclusive of universal grammar, being a criterial attribute of our biological endowment, is part and parcel of the sciences of life; or else that the age-old inquiry into verbal signs, being so empirical and rigorously formalized, constitutes an autonomous discipline demanding independent treatment. For the purposes of this essay, I opted to exclude American linguistics as such, but to embrace those among our linguists, like Pike, who have made distinctive and seminal contributions to nonlinguistic semiotics. This does not contradict the dogma that all linguists are semioticians (not true vice versa); but some are clearly "more equal than others."

The incursion of trained linguists—or, much worse, those but half-baked—into other, nonverbal or syncretic, anthroposemiotic domains, has sometimes proved unavailing or counterproductive. Yet at other times the use and application of linguistic models has been of considerable heuristic value. Consideration of just one example of each kind of outcome may be enlightening.

The field called in some quarters "kinesics" illustrates the outcome when linguistic categories are arbitrarily foisted onto areas of human behavior where they have little or no appositeness. "Kinesics" has been defined as "a term in SEMIOTICS for the systematic use of facial expression and body gesture to communicate MEANING, especially as this relates to the use of LANGUAGE (e.g. when a smile vs. a frown alters the interpretation of a SENTENCE)" (Crystal 1980:200; the term is alluded to in passing, under the lemma "Nonverbal Communication," in the *Encyclopedic Dictionary of Semiotics* [*EDS*; Kendon 1986: vol. 2, p. 612]). Sanguine researchers who minted this term and strove to delineate its compass authoritatively in the 1950s (although Mallery, Efron, and Ruesch in this country, and a host of Europeans, had solidly preceded them in the study of body motion as a form of communication) acted on the conviction that the "exhaustive techniques of linguistics" (Birdwhistell 1970:xi) were germane. As David Crystal had, however, correctly pointed out, "It is highly unlikely that kinesic behavior has sufficient structural complexity, discreteness, or semantic organization to warrant its analysis in the same terms as linguistic behavior; and spurious terminological identity is best avoided" (1974:270). An even worse mistake arose from this group's naïveté about "exhaustive techniques of linguistics" (whatever that euphoric phrase might have meant): for they not only committed themselves to the unmotivated and, as it turned out, false assumption that the rest of bodily motion was organized much as is the output of the speech apparatus (i.e., consisting of an arbitrary coordination, out of a narrow selection of producible acoustic signals, of vocal signs with the entire *Umwelt* as their field of reference), but they chose a *particular* descriptive schema (the so-called Smith-Trager model), which was even then on its irreversible way to oblivion.

In quite another sphere of investigation, however—namely, in endosemiotics—the use of another linguistic model, to wit, of generative grammar, has proved extremely productive. The term *endosemiotics* (Sebeok 1985b:3; Sebeok Forthcoming; and below) was coined in 1976 for the study of semiosis in such subsystems of the body as organ assemblies, organs, tissue, cells, and cellular organelles; among other subfields, it encompasses what has lately come to be called "semioimmunology." Now one of the most profound biological puzzles, clearly a semiotic problem, of how an antigen is recognized and how a structure exactly complementary to it is then synthesized, has focused on the ability of the immune system to make a specific adaptive response to an indefinitely large spectrum of natural and humanmade molecules and to distinguish protein molecules fabricated by one's own body (ego) from almost identical proteins of non-ego (autoimmunity).

Some immunologists have characterized the repertoire of the B-lymphocytes as "complete," meaning that the immune system can form specific antibodies to any molecule existing in the world, including molecules never before confronted or even invented. This technical use of "completeness" brings to mind an adage of Wilhelm von Humboldt's, about the capability of languages to "make infinite use of finite means." Chomsky later adopted (but never explained) this adage; in his earlier writings he called it "creativity," or sometimes "open-endedness." Niels Jerne, in a 1984 Nobel address permeated with semiotic terminology, proposed this analogous idea: "The immense repertoire of the immune system...becomes a vocabulary comprised not of words but of sentences that is capable of responding to any sentence expressed by the multitude of antigens which the immune system may encounter." Further, he said, "as for the components of a generative grammar that Chomşky mentions, we could with some imagination equate these with various features of protein structures" (Jerne 1985:1,058). After elaborating these, he noted with astonishment that the immune system embodies a degree of complexity comparable with language and, more surprising still, that one cognitive system has evolved with, and the other without, assistance of the brain (which, by the way, strangely enough excludes lymphocytes). The context for the reexamination of the immune system in such terms began with the elaboration of the idiotype network theory of Jerne himself, who realized that its receptors and specific secreted products (antibodies) recognize not only the external world of antigenic determinants (epitopes) but also the antigenic determinants on the immune receptors themselves (idiotypes). In brief, Jerne's semiotic insight was that corresponding to most—perhaps all—of the epitopes of the external universe there are corresponding internal images, or iconic symbols, within the organism's immune system.

We see then from these contrastive little homilies about semio-immunology and kinesics that the application of one linguistic model or another in selected corners of semiotic concern may at times provide illumination, at other times yield no insight at all, or worse, temporarily mislead. (Most work in traditional zoosemiotics, for example, has been based, in America as elsewhere, on the twin fallacies that animal signaling systems were in some vague sense the evolutionary antecedents of language and that the latter evolved for purposes of communication [discussed in Sebeok 1987c]).

If linguistics as a whole is to be excluded from this account, what about other massive logocentric endeavors, notably literary semiotics? For "many poetic features belong not only to the science of language but to the whole theory of signs, that is, to general semiotics" (Jakobson 1960:351). As far back as 1974, Richard W. Bailey and Seymour Chatman had already compiled a twenty-page bibliography under this specific rubric for this country and Canada alone; and indeed, as René Wellek says in his incomparable compendium of American criticism during the first half of this century, many "in the United States aim at an all-embracing structure of universal poetics and finally at a science of semiotics." (1986:156). Robert Scholes has fearlessly ventured in just this direction by way of a series of lively practical demonstrations of semiotic technique, with a glossary of semiotic terminology attempting to knit the loose ends of his book together (1982).[5]

Since midcentury, until at least the advent of the era of so-called "post-structuralism" (i.e., "deconstruction" and the unfortunately designated "pragmatism"), there has appeared a veritable avalanche of explicitly or implicitly semiotic works that bear on textual matters. And, concomitantly with—or perhaps despite—the coming of these novel approaches, whole fresh semiotic subdisciplines have sprung up, with a distinctively American flavor or at least with a strong input from the Western shores of the Atlantic, outlining many semiotic approaches to discourse (in the narrow sense of the term). Here are just a few samples:

- semiotics of the theater, comprehending both the playscript and the spectacle text, with other performance elements (Carlson 1988);
- puppetry, which "integrates many semiotic streams, codes, and channels," including "colors, costumes, gestures and body movements, dance, music, physical traits, and staging, as well as language" (Sherzer and Sherzer 1987:1–2; see also the 1983 special issue of *Semiotica* on "Puppets, Masks, and Performing Objects from Semiotic Perspectives," vol. 47);

- the analysis of narrative strategies employed in everyday conversations (Tannen 1984; L. Polanyi 1985) or in specialized conversational interactions, as between doctors and patients (West 1984);
- semiotic approaches to ethnomcthodology, a specialized discipline usually classified with the social sciences, utilizing text and talk, indeed, its own system of signification expressed in its own poetic idiom (Flynn 1990);
- the nature of medical descriptions in terms of a hierarchical model of information (Blois 1984);
- legal semiotics, in which a semiotic theory of narrativity may usefully be deployed (Tiefenbrun 1986; Kevelson 1988).

How to deal with such matters here without getting bogged down in a morass of specialization? What, for instance, is one to make of the protean American critical pluralist and philosophical synthesizer Kenneth Burke (Hymes 1968; Wellek 1986: chap. 14)? Burke (b. 1897) bristles with modern technicalities, drawn from, among many other fields, semiotics. In his suggestive essay, "What Are the Signs of What?" (Burke 1966:359–379), further clarified elsewhere, he argues, in an antinominalist stance, that things are the signs of words, not the other way around, and that language is symbolic action (Heath 1986: chap. 4). The system of symbolism he invented resembles nothing as closely as Ernst Cassirer's concept of symbolic form (1953–1957), although Burke thinks Cassirer (like Bergson) is more "Scientistic" (i.e., post Kantian), while his own views are more "Dramatistic" (i.e., in an older scholastic tradition of Medieval realism) (Burke 1966:23).

In a proper compendium of American semiotics, one would want to sift writings like Burke's judiciously from those of less semiotically saturated *littérateurs*, so that one would presumably meet the standards of one of Eco's hypotheses for the makeup of a history of semiotics, requiring "an impressive re-reading of the whole history of philosophy, and maybe many other disciplines" (1983:80), notably, I think, the history of criticism. An encyclopedic undertaking of that magnitude cannot, however, be conceived short of a massive interdisciplinary collaborative endeavor.

Eco justly notes that "there are certain poets or novelists who have investigated the life of signs or sign-behaviour more lucidly

than many theorists did," and aptly alludes to Proust (Eco 1983:81).
From the American side, I would adduce here, first and foremost,
the case of our eminent author of half a dozen outstanding novels—
more reminiscent, some think, of Camus than of Proust—Walker
Percy (b. 1916).

Percy began to publish essays on semiotic themes in 1954 and
has continued to pay serious attention to such issues ever since;
fifteen of his philosophical essays, including "Semiotic and a Theory of Knowledge," were collected in *The Message in the Bottle*
(1981: chap. 11). On August 13, 1982, he facetiously wrote me: "I
am figuring that since you venture into literary forms such as dialogues with Maeterlinck [cf. Sebeok 1986d: chap. 8], you can for-
give a novelist for trespassing into semiotics."

In 1980, Percy took a month off to participate *in statu*, as it were,
pupillari, in the First International Summer Institute for Semiotic
and Structural Studies, at the University of Toronto. He is thoroughly
comfortable in the pertinent works of Saint Thomas and Maritain,
Peirce, Cassirer and Langer, G. H. Mead and Morris, indeed, with
the contemporary semiotic scene here and, in increasing measure
since 1986, in the Soviet Union. While his own contributions to
semiotics flow outside the academic mainstream and, as such, have
gained him but modest scholarly renown, they are original and
interesting. (They have been analyzed in detail by Weldon Thornton
and W. H. Poteat [Broughton 1979:169–218], P. L. Poteat [1985:
esp. chaps. 3 and 4], and with especial sensitivity by his fellow
physician Robert Coles [1978].)

Percy's essay "A Theory of Language" (1981:288–327) contains
a fascinating critique of transformational grammar. For one thing,
he proposes an alternative that "is founded on a general semiotic,"
which he defines, in his personal triadic manner, as "the science of
the relations between people and signs and things" (Percy 1981:307).
In the same essay, however, he also fastens upon and reviews
"Peirce's theory of abduction...as a valid and possibly useful strategy
in approaching language as a phenomenon" (Percy 1981:320). He
then goes on to contrast this pivotal Peircean concept with Chomsky's views of it (cf. Chomsky 1980:136, 139–140)—which Percy
judges "odd and...wrongheaded" (cf. Fann 1970; Eco and Sebeok
1983).

Structural and functional triads, as against dyadic couplings, seem to allure Percy (cf. "Toward a Triadic Theory of Meaning," 1981:159–188, 199), evidently inspired by Peirce's "radical theory of signs which undertook to give an account of those transactions in which symbols are used to name things and to assert sentences about things" (although he follows Morris as well as, with modifications, C. K. Ogden and I. A. Richards). He deems Peirce's efforts to have been "heroic and unavailing" (Percy 1981:187), but the latter adjective surely no longer describes the state of this affair. Rather prematurely and, I think, uncritically, Percy grasps at an idea proposed by the late Norman Geschwind, who allegedly uncovered in the cortex the neurophysical substrate for the triadic structure of the symbolic act (Percy 1981:326–327).

Intriguing to me is the opposition Percy draws (alas, after Ludwig Binswanger's existential analysis school of thought, not its semiotically far more sophisticated primary source) between *Umwelt* and *Welt*: he holds that the first-mentioned, constituting the environment of a sign-using (by which he means "nonspeaking") creature, contrasts with that of the world of a speaking organism in "that there are gaps in the former but none in the latter" (1981:203). The former, he says (by the way, erroneously overlooking the social dimension that informs such speechless creatures as killer whales, lions, wolves, the African great apes, etc.), "only notices what is relevant biologically," as opposed to human beings, who dispose of the "entire horizon symbolically." Thus "gaps that cannot be closed by perception and reason," he adds, "are closed by magic and myth."

In fact, all animals, humans included, do have their *Umwelt* (corresponding to Edmund Husserl's [1913: subsection 28] "my natural world-about-me"), that is, an internal model of a universe (*Welt*) "as is"; but humans have a *pair* of interlaced models, the hierarchically superior of which ("secondary modeling system" in Soviet semiotic parlance, or approximately Husserl's "ideal worlds-about-me") has an added syntactic component. This component alone enables the construction of an infinity of possible worlds (Sebeok 1986d:13–14; Sebeok 1988b). (I unearthed a letter from Percy, dated April 19, 1982, asking: "Tom, could you refer me to a statement in English of von Uexküll's notions about *Welt*, *Umwelt*, *Innenwelt*, und so weiter?")

Except for Percy's above-named pre-twentieth-century ante-cedents, and for G. H. Mead (who, alas, died in 1931, eight years before I began my studies at the University of Chicago), the course of semiotics in the United States is now beginning to edge into my life span's ken: among Percy's modern sources, beside my teacher Morris, I had known Cassirer (1874–1945), Maritain (1882 1973), and Langer (1895–1985). The former two are, of course, "U.S. semioticians" by co-optation only, and this in a double sense: both Cassirer and Maritain were born and worked mostly elsewhere; and semiotics was the central, long-term preoccupation of neither. These basics of their nearly contemporaneous biographies notwithstanding, both spent years in their adoptive country, where each wrote, or reworked, pieces of considerable import about semiotic topics.

I should like to impart fleeting personal glimpses of the pair of émigrés and of Langer here, the briefest of anecdotes, really, since much more rounded sketches of each of them, by those who knew them better, are available; and their contributions, at least those of the two men, have of late been pored over by many. Such vignettes scarcely portray semiotic theories or applications, but they illustrate the processes through which the ideas emerge and illuminate the people who impel them.

In 1981, on Friday, April 10, having barely landed in Hamburg, where I had flown to take part in the Third German Colloquium of the Deutsche Gesellschaft für Semiotik, I received a phone call from Klaus Oehler, the organizer, my friend and host, asking me to accompany him immediately to a wreathe-laying observance beneath a bust erected in memory of Ernst Cassirer. This piece of sculpture stands in the foyer of the University of Hamburg *Philosophenturm*, where Cassirer had been professor of philosophy (occupying the same chair that Oehler, the foremost German specialist on Peirce, now holds) from 1919 until his dismissal and departure for Oxford and then to Göteborg in 1933. Others at this ceremony included members of the Board of the Deutsche Gesellschaft für Semiotik and a scattering of senior American semioticians. I was taken aback when I was unexpectedly called upon to make some commemora-tive remarks, but it turned out that, fragile as this link may have been, I was the only one present who had ever come face to face with Cassirer.

I recounted that I had attended Cassirer's lecture in the fall of 1944 on "Structuralism in Modern Linguistics." He delivered this, at Jakobson's invitation, before the Linguistic Circle of New York, at the New School for Social Research, some weeks before his sudden death on April 13, 1945. Cassirer and Jakobson chanced to cross from Göteborg to New York on the same freighter, *Remmaren*, May 20–June 4, 1941. What I remember vividly even to this day is that these words, adapted from Genesis 27:22, pressed on my mind throughout Cassirer's lengthy lecture: "The voice is Cassirer's voice, but the hands are the hands of Jakobson." After his lecture, in the course of which Cassirer stressed the word *semiotics* (see above), Jakobson and I, in the company of a few others, dined with him. Both the linguist and the philosopher gave an animated account of their daily conversations aboard ship, and I concur that "these talks no doubt influenced [Cassirer's] interest and work on structuralism" (Krois 1987:30, 222–223 n. 86). On the other hand, I could never find any trace of Cassirer's reciprocal influence on Jakobson's thinking. Of the two, Jakobson, then at his cerebral pinnacle, was doubtless the dominant personality, although Cassirer was reputed to have been quite self-assured in public in his younger days.

Not long after Hitler had come to power, Cassirer's senior colleague, Jakob von Uexküll, read a paper tinged with the classic semiotic flavor of his *Umwelt-Forschung*, at a Hamburg Congress of Psychology, on a piece of research he had recently concluded on the cognitive maps of dogs. As these are constructed of and demarcated by scent-signs, he asserted that a dog takes everything located within its olfactory field for its property. Cassirer opened the discussion by recalling that Jean-Jacques Rousseau had said that the first man who erected a fence and declared, "This is mine," should have been beaten to death. "After the lecture of Professor von Uexküll we know," he then expanded, "that wouldn't have sufficed. It was the first dog which should have been beaten to death." This bandying about territoriality was attacked in next morning's *Völkische Beobachter* by Herr Goebbels himself, under the punning headline: "Ktereien eines deutschen Professors!"

A profoundly original idealist yet an empirical semiotician, Uexküll deemed Cassirer the greatest living German philosopher, one who shaped an entire generation of students in neo-Kantian ways of thinking. In his *Essay on Man* (1944), a condensed American reworking of his *Philosophie der symbolischen Formen* (1964 [1923–1929]), Cassirer's argument is avowedly, although metaphorically, based on Uexküll's biosemiotic principles extended into our world: human beings' acquisition of the "symbolic system," Cassirer contended, transforms the whole of our existence; accordingly, he designated humans *animal symbolicum* (1944:26).

Uexküll's impact on the "American" Cassirer (1944:23–24) was profound. Still, I am convinced that a careful study of the writings of the senior scholar will show that Cassirer (and generations of *his* followers) failed to grasp Uexküll's fundamental idea of the "functional circle" (a construct made up of signs arranged in a negative feedback circuit), as well as his innovative fashioning of a new pragmatic, sensory semiotics. Readers can verify this adverse judgment for themselves by reading the works of Uexküll; for further general particulars on Cassirer, who is currently undergoing a mini-revival in this country, see John Krois's splendid book (1987); and as to Cassirer's brand of semiotics, see Donald Verene's authoritative lemma (1986). (An edition of Cassirer's complete works, including many unpublished remarks on semiotics, is in preparation, under Krois's direction; see Krois's appreciation of Cassirer in the 1989 edition of *The Semiotic Web* [Sebeok and Umiker-Sebeok 1987–1989].)

When L'ecole libre des hautes études was founded in New York in February 1942, Jacques Maritain became its first vice president, then succeeded Henri Focillon in 1943 as its second president.[6] At the time, I was a graduate student at Princeton University, but during the same year I also commuted to give a course at the Free School and to audit many courses there. It was there that I got acquainted with this amiable and admirable, prolific and many-sided *spirituel*.

Although it is difficult for me to remember the exact circumstances over a span of forty-five years, I do recall the sexagenarian philosopher inviting me, with his customary graciousness, to accompany him early one morning on a stroll from his apartment at 30 Fifth Avenue through Washington Square en route to Mass at (I think) Saint Joseph's Church. He inquired about my studies during that walk. I responded by telling him something about my growing desire, instigated by Morris and reinforced by Jakobson, for exploring the doctrine of signs, especially verbal. That appeared to engage his interest. He asked me if I had read Jean Poinsot, a name that meant nothing to me. He then admonished me—as I later recounted in a piece in the *New York Times Book Review* (Sebeok 1986h)—to peruse the *Cursus Philosophicus* of "the profound doctor" Poinsot. I am sure I heard the name Poinsot for the first time in the streets of New York that day.

All this chitchat, however, meant little to me then. Its significance fell into place only some fifteen years afterward, in the context of my reading Maritain's "Language and the Theory of Sign" (1957). Although I had casually studied some of Maritain's demanding philosophical books at the Aquinas-saturated University of Chicago and in Princeton, I had no way of knowing then that, increasingly since the late 1930s, Maritain had been pondering the theory of signs deeply, and that he was just seeing through press an article, "Sign and Symbol" (1943), itself a revised English version of a 1938 article, "Signe et symbole," which appeared in the *Revue Thomiste*, a journal then unfamiliar to me. In 1956 he expanded this original French article, which in turn was republished in English the following year in a book edited by his friend Dr. Ruth Nanda Anshen. (For further particulars of this convoluted bibliographic yarn, see Deely 1986:139.)

In 1957, while consulting an article by Jakobson (chap. 9) in the Anshen compilation, I was amazed to find Maritain's piece on "Language and the Theory of Sign" in the very same volume (Anshen 1957: chap. 5). It provided the key to our conversation back in 1943 (also dovetailing with another I had, in the 1970s, with the Portuguese linguist Jos G. Herculano de Carvalho, likewise about Poinsot—but that story is extraterritorial). At the very outset of his meditation, Maritain struck to the heart of semiotics' epistemological mission: "No problems are more complex or more fundamental to the concerns of man and civilization than those pertaining to the sign. The sign is relevant to the whole extent of knowledge and of human life; it is a universal instrument in the world of human beings, like motion in the world of physical nature," adding that "signs have to do with all types of knowledge. They are of considerable importance in the psychic life of nonrational animals" (Maritain 1957:86–87).

I have always been perplexed that, as a serious contributor to semiotics, Maritain remained, in America and elsewhere, essentially unrecognized outside of his parochial tradition, and even within (e.g., Hudson and Mancini 1987 make no mention of him). Jakobson, his erstwhile confrere at the Ecole libre and his co-contributor to the Anshen volume, never cited him (as far as I know), either in his lectures or in any of his writings. In October 1948, Maritain gave a series of lectures at the University of Chicago (these were to appear, in 1951, as *Man and the State*), and returned for more lectures in 1956. Morris and Maritain apparently failed to meet; and neither seems to have been aware of the other (despite the fact that Morris had an article on mysticism in the ever surprising Anshen volume [chap. 11]).

The rich Dominican vein in semiotics (Deely 1988)—running from Thomas Aquinas, with his threefold emphasis on the *modi significandi*, the *suppositiones*, and the abundant use of semiotic concepts, to the vast elaboration and consolidation of the latter by Poinsot, and onward to the New World through Maritain to John Deely (1982) and a very few others—has been insufficiently mined by the general semiotics community here or abroad. That mother lode of pure gold is far from exhausted. Now that I myself have turned sexagenarian, I wish I had grasped Maritain's credo sooner and better, for I have become convinced that the tradition in which he labored harmonizes with and enriches what I have elsewhere termed the "major tradition" in semiotic studies (e.g., Sebeok 1989b:63)

Susanne Langer (1895–1985) has long been regarded as "the philosopher most influenced by Cassirer" (Krois 1987:12). Morris considered her, together with Wilbur M. Urban, a "follower" of Cassirer (1946:189), and she herself has told us as much: "In many years of work on the fundamental problems of art," she says she found Cassirer's philosophy of symbolic forms, however elusive, "indispensable; it served as a key to the most involved questions" (1962:58). In 1946, she translated Cassirer's little book *Language and Myth*, characterizing it in her preface as imbued "by a final flash of interpretive genius" (Cassirer 1946:x).

After World War II, because of her easily accessible, attractive paperback, *Philosophy in a New Key*, Langer became something of a campus celebrity, but her work, while never regarded as trivial, seldom seems to have been taken for more than "a point of departure" by other philosophers such as Morris (1946:50). Thus Charles L. Stevenson (1908–1979) dissected her arguments ascribing "a symbolic function to the arts," specifically music, "that other writers have often denied to them" (Henle 1958:202), and judged those arguments implausible (see Henle 1958: chap. 8). Stevenson tried to show, more generally (as Abraham Kaplan had earlier), "that the importance of the theory of signs to all the arts, rather than merely to those commonly classified as representational, is seriously open to question" (Henle 1958:210). Similar difficulties, he stated, "arise in *any* theory of signs" (Henle 1958:219), yet he concentrated his specific criticisms on Langer's views alone. Years later, Morris, while completely ignoring Langer's thesis, found Stevenson's arguments not compelling (1964:67).

In mid-May 1969, Langer was a featured speaker at a symposium held at the Smithsonian Institution, where I was also a guest. She read a paper titled "The Great Shift: Instinct to Intuition" (Eisenberg and Dillon 1971: chap. 10), the indicant concept of which turned out to be her assertion that language began—"with symbolic utterance" (Eisenberg and Dillon 1971:325). She held that "speech is not derived from animal communication; its communicative and directive functions, though all-important today, are secondary; its primary function is the symbolic expression of intuitive cognition" (Eisenberg and Dillon 1971:326; she made the same point in Langer 1962: chap. 2).

In other words, language evolved, in her view (though the terminology here is mine; cf. Sebeok 1986d:10–16) as a uniquely human modeling system. In spite of Langer's unfortunate oral delivery—she was tiny, dwarfed behind the lectern, and practically inaudible because of the placement of the microphone—I was enthusiastic about her talk (some participating biologists, I gathered, were, by and large, not) and told her so at one of the social functions we attended afterward.

It is fascinating to note a clue *in nuce*, lurking in her statement above on the primary function of speech, to Langer's equivocal position in American semiotics. On the one hand, her frame of reference was sharply at variance with those advocated by simplistic physicalist technicians (some of whom are mentioned in Demers 1988) who strove to pursue an illusory comparison of language and animal communication systems. Their prejudices formerly set the tone for researches in this area in America, but, even today, there are linguists who believe, contrary to Langer, that "the development of cognitive power and communicative ability...together, yielded language" rather than the other way around (Lieberman 1988:28). On the other hand, Langer's judgments are now seen as being in remarkable conformity on this issue with the outlook of the Moscow-Tartu group of semioticians (Sebeok 1988b) as well as, for instance, with Chomsky (see e.g., Chomsky 1980:229–230). This kinship is not at all surprising, considering Langer's intellectual lineage or the pervasive (although riven) impact of the neo-Kantians, via Wilhelm von Humboldt and Peirce or, as the case may be, Uexküll and Cassirer, on the parties involved.

The only comments known to me specific to Langer's "properly" semiotic project, which is said to focus "on the foundations of the theory of signs from within a highly differentiated philosophical matrix," are Robert Innis's ([b. 1941]; 1985:87–89). Clearly, however, Langer's work merits detailed reconsideration in the near future, especially in its implications for aesthetics.

Although Innis apparently believes that "Langer's position...bears remarkable similarities" (1985:89) to Nelson Goodman's (b. 1906) ideas of notationality and similarity, Goodman himself avoids such comparisons: "I am by no means unaware of contributions to symbol theory by such philosophers as Peirce, Cassirer, Morris, and Langer....I reject one after another...the views common to much of the literature of aesthetics" (Goodman 1968:xii–xiii).

Incidentally, while Goodman, like Kenneth Burke and Erving Goffman, has generally steered clear of the "semiotics" tag, he did agree to become a plenary speaker, with a speech on "Routes of Reference," at the Second Congress of the International Association for Semiotic Studies (Vienna, 1979). For eminent figures such as these, then, as in the weird sisters' riddling reply to Macbeth's query, "What is't you do?," semiotics remains "a deed without a name."

A common ingredient of our national experience with semiotics is what I hereby propose to call the Jourdain factor: "Good Heavens! For more than forty years I have been speaking prose without knowing it." This factor first intruded on my attention in Montreal, the week after Christmas 1964, where I addressed an International Symposium on Communication and Social Interactions in Primates. I began by proposing "to evaluate the structure of primate communication...against the background of other sign systems used by man...and elsewhere in the animal kingdom," and went on to introduce the term "semiotics" (Sebeok 1967b:363). After my presentation, a gentleman came up to me and said: "I have been doing semiotics for years without knowing it." After identifying himself as Harley C. Shands, M.D. (1916–1981), he invited me to lunch, which I accepted the more so since I recognized his name as the author of a book (Shands 1960) I had recently read with much enjoyment and admiration. Over the next decade or so, Shands became a frequent contributor to semiotics journals, and published three books in the Approaches to Semiotics series published by Indiana University Press.[7]

Medicine was among the most venerable semiotic specialties in Western tradition (Sebeok 1986d: chap. 4), but American clinical practice had drifted away from the other branches of sign interpretation. Although Shands was a very busy teaching and practicing cardiologist-turned-psychiatrist, the tempo of his writing increased amazingly once he felt that he had the well-defined readership in semiotic circles he told me he lacked among his medical colleagues; in this country, his written output was exceeded only by that of the San Francisco psychiatrist Jurgen Ruesch (cf. Baer [b. 1937] 1975:107–137).

The subtle influence of the personality and publications of Shands (whose contribution to the scientific status of psychiatry was best assessed in Baer 1975:81–105) eventually produced unanticipated reverberations in my life: as our friendship thrived, I began to study the *Corpus Hippocraticum*, the writings of Galen, and medical semiotics in general. The two of us coorganized a national symposium on medical semiotics at the Wenner-Gren Foundation's New York headquarters, and later we took part in an international conference on the "Semiotics of Anxiety," convened by Thure von

Uexküll, and sponsored by the Werner-Reimers Foundation in Bad
Homburg (Sebeok 1989b: app. 1). Directly as a consequence of this
symposium, I was stimulated to start developing the notion of the
"semiotic self." This endeavor eventually led me back to a long-
interrupted dialogue with Milton Singer (see Sebeok 1989a).

As, under Shands's guidance, I kept hacking away at the periphery of clinical semiotics, my interest in "vital signs" grew, and
in the course of time blossomed into one series of lectures, under
that same title, for The Johns Hopkins Medical Institutions (October
1–November 24, 1985), and then another for the Schools of Medicine, Nursing, and Liberal Arts at Indiana University–Indianapolis
(September 11–November 20, 1986). These visits brought me into
close and (I trust, mutually) productive contacts with many White
Coats—physicians, nurses, laboratory scientists—from whom I
learned a great deal about endosemiotic processes, the arts of subjective and objective interpretation (of "subjective" symptoms and
"objective" signs), and about the varieties of professional interaction
in clinical settings with fellow professionals and their patients.

Some years after meeting Shands, I met another extraordinary
physician, F. Eugene Yates (b. 1927), the UCLA medical engineer
who coined the term "pharmacolinguistics," later emended to
"pharmacosemiotics." Among his other foundational contributions
to the problem of self-organizing systems, Yates published two
important companion articles explicating the transition from kinetics to kinematics, showing that "science has been permeated with
semiotic issues all along" (1985:359; cf. Yates and Kugler 1984).
Yates, as well as the Washington, D. C., neurologist Richard M.
Restak (b. 1942), are two among an ever increasing number of
doctors, here and abroad, who are moving back toward their semiotic roots on various paths. The most significant semiotic studies
converge on specialties other than psychiatry, ranging from the
genetic code to the brain code, and dealing particularly with the
metabolic code and the immune code (for details, cf. Sebeok Forthcoming).

Yates's observation that science is being saturated by considerations of significance is amply borne out by the writings (especially
recent) of Niels Bohr's and Albert Einstein's student, the distinguished American quantum physicist and cosmologist John Archibald

Wheeler (b. 1911). His preoccupations with "physics as meaning" (1984:137) were clearly influenced by Peirce (as Wheeler has confirmed in personal communications to me). At the heart of Wheeler's "meaning-circuit model" of existence lies the postulation that semiosis in a community of observer-participants "past, present and future is brought into being by the machinery of the world. However, it goes on to interpret this very world of past, present and future, of space and time and fields, to be—despite all its apparent continuity of imagination, immensity and independence from us—a construction of imagination and theory and troweled and plastered over countably many elementary quantum phenomena" (from Wheeler 1987). In short, physics, in Wheeler's grand conception, is the offspring of semiosis, "even as meaning is the child of physics" (1984:123).

The Jourdain factor keeps reappearing in variegated guises, as the social anthropologist Mary Douglas (b. 1921) reminds us in her speculative essay (prepared, as a matter of fact, at Harley Shands's instigation) on "The Future of Semiotics" (1982:198). As far back as January 5, 1960, in his inaugural lecture for the College de France, Lévi-Strauss, as is well known, bounded the scope of anthropology so as to be tantamount to that portion of semiotics that linguistics has not arrogated for itself, a delimitation he amplified by affirming that, since human beings communicate through signs and symbols, for anthropology, which is a conversation among human beings, anything interposed between two objects is sign and symbol. In 1962, Margaret Mead, alluding to "face-to-face communication, multi-modal and complex, within specified cultural and social settings" (quoted in Sebeok et al. 1972:285), after the ethnographer Weston La Barre's report at the same conference (see Sebeok et al. 1972:191–220), made much the same proposal.

How these influential scholars budged semiotics, in the two ensuing decades or so, "from the periphery of exploratory anthropological concern into the core of the field," at least in Anglophone areas, was traced out by Jean Umiker-Sebeok (1977). "The best recent work in anthropology," Ivan Karp (1986:35) trenchantly confirms, "moves toward a semiotics of social situations." Milton Singer, alluding in his important book to the "tilt of culture theory to semiotics" (1984:48–52), argues for a "semiotic anthropology." While the phrase "semiotic ethnography" (Herzfeld 1983; Karp 1986:31) is found here and there, the neologism "ethnosemiotics" eventually began to prevail (MacCannell and MacCannell 1982: chap. 4), although this term soon acquired multiple meanings: it is now sometimes used as a term for the investigation of indigenous systems of meaning, but occasionally also in reference to the decoding of indigenous systems (Herzfeld 1987:199). Competing expressions, such as "symbolic anthropology" or "semantic anthropology" are sporadically advocated, but other American anthropologists, such as Elizabeth Mertz, Richard Parmentier, and their associates (1985), are content to continue, in clean-cut fashion, to employ "semiotics" without any redundant qualifying prefix.

Although, in this country, archaeology has lagged behind the rest of anthropology—including folklore, or folkloristics (McDowell 1986)—in receptiveness to semiotic models (for a general survey, see Gardin 1988),[8] this has changed of late: in the fall of 1987, a multinational conference was convened at Indiana University on "Symbolic, Structural, and Semiotic Approaches in Archeology," the proceedings of which are now in preparation for publication in 1991 by Indiana University Press.

It is likewise intriguing to follow the latter-day convergence (ambiguous, to be sure) of semiotics with such kindred, but arguably more conservative, disciplines as geography, practitioners of which, we learn, acknowledge the contributions of Cassirer, Langer, and other figures familiar to us (Foote 1985:164); and with history, which, we are told, provides "the materials and the evidence for a possible doctrine of signs that, rather than close in on itself, opens out toward the infinite" (B. Williams 1985:321; a special issue of *Semiotica*, on Semiotics and History, will appear in 1990). Too, semiotics, it is comfortingly averred, "provides the only logical base for rebuilding the field of sociology" (MacCannell 1986:195).

Eco's celebrated observation about semiotics—the discipline studying everything that can be used in order to lie—is paralleled on the level of international relations by the Goffmanesque works of Robert Jervis. In his 1970 book, Jervis laid the foundations for a semiotic theory of deception as an integral part of international relations, and went on to apply the concepts and principles he developed to nuclear politics, including strategic planning (1987).

The relevance of semiotics for war and peace studies is manifest from Jervis's intricate political analyses, which can, of course, be equally useful on national or parochial levels.

Considering the medical provenance of Western semiotics, Dr. Shands's "Aha!" response was hardly astonishing to me. More so perhaps was Mary Douglas's acknowledgment of the Jourdain factor. I was, however, taken quite unawares by Sidney J. Levy's opening remarks in his elegant keynote lecture at the First International Conference on Marketing and Semiotics (Umiker-Sebeok 1987:13–20), in the course of which he said: "If I am a semiotician, I discover that with the surprise of the fellow who was delighted to learn that he spoke prose" (Umiker-Sebeok 1987:13–20:13). In his conclusion, Levy spoke of an intellectual voyage, a "venture on the Semiotic Seas" (Umiker-Sebeok 1987:19), evoking a simulacrum of semiotics as "an adventure" on which our good neighbors from elsewhere like to embark. Indeed, it was Roland Barthes (1988:4) who, in a 1974 lecture given in Italy, conjured up the same image when he told his audience that, for him, semiotics was neither a cause nor a science, discipline, school, or movement, but "an adventure." Levy, whose J. L. Kellogg Graduate School of Management at Northwestern University boldly hosted this conference, is one of the world's authorities on marketing.

If, as some economists do, we picture the human mind as a "consuming organ" (Schelling 1984:343), we must ask: What does the mind consume? The apprehension driven home by the Conference on Marketing and Semiotics was that the mind consumes signs, and marketing (including advertising, product design, and other adjunct endeavors) is focally concerned with bartering not "objects" but the entities we familiarly call signs and symbols (cf. Mick 1986; see also Mick 1988). So can one consider marketing a species of professionally applied semiotics?

But what is "applied semiotics"? As far as I know, this construction originated with Charles Morris, who wrote (1946:220): "The application of semiotic as an instrument may be called *applied semiotic*." Semiotic(s) as a whole, he proposed, can be pure, descriptive, or applied; the latter, he specified, "utilizes knowledge about signs for the accomplishment of various purposes" (Morris 1946:353–354). This division was one in an array of strategic trichotomies posited by Morris. These became popular in other fields (including marketing) where such distinctions were severally turned to practical account, but commonly in a rather mechanical fashion.

A version was incorporated into the anonymous (but actually written by Roland Posner) 1979 programmatic introduction to the initial issue of the journal of the Deutsche Gesellschaft für Semiotik, which devoted a long paragraph explicating "Angewandte," or applied, "Semiotik," as opposed to "Allgemeine," or general, and "Vergleichende," or comparative, semiotics. The former is made to cover an enormous expanse of topics, which, in sum, seems to comprehend much of what Morris would rather, I suspect, have included under descriptive semiotics, that is, of what the majority of us semioticians actually do. One cannot be sure, because Morris's categories are, in this respect, not at all clear-cut.

A more refined schema appeared in the inaugural issue of the *American Journal of Semiotics* (1981) by the Polish logical semiotician Jerzy Pelc, who consecrates over four pages (27–31) to applied semiotics. This comes into play, he says, "when the method of interpretation is applied not to a single thing, event or phenomenon but to a certain complex thereof, a set forming a whole, particularly a systematized whole" (Pelc 1981:27). His first example is literature. Although his tripartition—theoretical, methodological, and applied—differs somewhat from the Germans' as well as from Morris's, this illustration, indeed all his examples, are virtually the same as the ones enumerated by the Germans. In 1988, Jean Umiker-Sebeok undertook the preparation of an *American Directory of Applied Semiotics*, covering the Western hemisphere and, eventually, the Old World too. Her project "seeks information about individuals, centers, businesses, and projects...which utilize the concepts, methods, and empirical data of semiotics for professional problem-solving in business, education, law, or medicine." Judging by the great number of responses returned as of September 1988, of the last four substantives "education" seems to have been widely and broadly interpreted by recipients of Umiker-Sebeok's questionnaire to embrace not only pedagogy but a wide variety of artistic and humanistic subjects normally taught in universities.

To put it mildly, then, there is little consensus about what constitutes applied semiotics. There are similar difficulties, of course, with "applied anthropology" and "applied linguistics" (to say nothing, *mutatis mutandis*, of applied physics, chemistry, biology, and the like), even though there are independent U.S. learned societies to accommodate the devotees of each. Their fields of application are generally domain oriented, although the domains are matters of taste. In anthropology, the fields of practice are most often educational, medical, or urban; in applied linguistics, the teaching and learning of foreign languages or of the mother tongue are central, but the field sometimes also includes a host of so-called "hyphenated" fields, such as psycholinguistics, sociolinguistics, and clinical linguistics, as well as the planning of national language policy. (Other factors can also complicate matters. I was recently asked to contribute an article on semiotics to an American anthology of applied linguistics on the editor's bizarre presumption that the former was a branch of the latter.)

At the 1986 meeting of the Semiotic Society of America, we organized a round-table discussion on "Presenting Semiotics to the Professions." The fields of application represented were business, education (both secondary and post-secondary), government, mass communications, medicine, nursing, law, and museology. The content of applied semiotics, it seems, emerged there by inductive enumeration of topics rather than by abstract.

The circumstances in which the products of application are manifested, at least in the United States, are usually threefold: policy, action, and, most of all, information (in the vulgar sense)— that is, semiotics as a "resource." Accordingly, I have asked myself, as others wanted to know: Can any work that I have done be considered unambiguously *applied* semiotics? Why so?

To begin with, I exclude from this rubric the entirety of my various semiotically informed writings on animal communication and text analysis, such as on the sacred discourse and *einfache Formen* of an ethnic group I studied in the Soviet Union; a logos of Herodotus' *History*; a film by Steven Spielberg; the Sherlock Holmes canon; the last words of our President Grant; experimentation (however crude) with forms of expression other than the monograph or essay to convey scientific knowledge (in dialogue, say, or in verse); analysis of particular sign categories such as "icon," "symptom," or "fetish"; Japanese monkey performances; and modes of artistic expression in the world of animals. I would also hesitate to include under applied semiotics the "to-be-continued" series of compilations on aspects of "unverbal" semiosis that Jean Umiker-Sebeok and I jointly launched about fifteen years ago, covering thus far speech surrogates as drum and whistle systems, aboriginal sign languages of the Americas and Australia, and monastic sign languages (Umiker-Sebeok and Sebeok 1976, 1978, and 1987, respectively).

There remains only one assignment I have undertaken that meets all three of my criteria for applied semiotics, to wit, a mingling of policy and action with information. This piece of research is reported in Sebeok 1984a and in 1986d under the title "Pandora's Box in Aftertimes." The policy concerned has been under consideration by the U.S. government, under the direction of the Department of Energy, for more than two decades: How to dispose permanently of high-level radioactive wastes? However, the successful isolation of such wastes over long periods of time does raise a subsidiary set of problems, such as how to ensure not only that the wastes remain unaltered by natural events and processes but also that they be unaffected by future activities of humans, whether direct (say, a breach of the depository facility with a concomitant release of waste) or indirect (i.e., offsite), not to mention war, terrorism, or sabotage. Any action of this nature would have a significant potential for increasing the radiological dose to our descendants from the repository.

To deal with this potential, a Human Interference Task Force, with a wide range of expertise among the members (political science, sociology, environmental sciences, law, nuclear regulation, nuclear engineering, anthropology and archaeology, psychology, public policy, materials science, climatology, to name only some) was created by the Department of Energy in 1980, and I was soon coopted to represent semiotics. This committee was charged to prepare and submit a report to the U. S. Nuclear Regulatory Commission, via the Department of Energy. The report presenting the view and recommendations of the entire task force was submitted in September 1981. My views were also expressed in a report to the Bechtel Group, which had originally engaged my services for this exercise in applied semiotics. As I later remarked, my personal report addressed the specific problem: "designing a reasonably fail-safe means of communicating information about the repository and its contents, such that the system's effectiveness would be maintained for up to 10,000 years" (Sebeok 1986d:149–150).

I have often been asked why I agreed to serve on this Task Force. Three principal considerations played a part in my decision to do so. First, being the father of three daughters, I have a personal stake in the information-transfer system of chemically coded messages that determine the development of future generations of organisms. Second, as I contemplated the historiography of semiotics (including linguistics), I realized that semioticians have concentrated either on diachronic tasks (historical linguistics, ritualization, etc.) or on synchronic tasks (communication and signification, etc.) (see Sebeok 1989b: chap. 2) but never before on the shape of things to come. A stint in futurology offered something of a challenge. Third, from the outset, I looked at this exercise as being one indubitably in "applied" semiotics. Some important implications of this third criterion were severally foregrounded by the ten other contributors to a special issue of the German journal *Zeitschrift für Semiotik* (Posner 1984) devoted to communicating with future generations.

Before leaving for now the topic of applied semiotics, let me divulge one wholly unforeseen turn of events, making semiotic application doubly sure: the MoMing Dance Company, directed by Washington, D.C., choreographer Liz Lerman for the Dance Exchange, advertised among its coming attractions in 1987 twin performances, titled "Atomic Priests: Coming Attractions" and "Atomic Priests: The Future." Developed by Lerman and the company, the libretto is in large part based, "with music by Mike Vargas and [*the*] Henry Purcell," on my "Communication Measures to Bridge Ten Millennia," in which I proposed, as I had in my original report, an "atomic priesthood" charged with the long-term responsibility of monitoring human interaction with nuclear wast depositories. A friend at the University of Chicago, Michael Silverstein, who chanced to see the Lerman piece enacted, wrote me that "it was quite a moving experience." A review in the *Village Voice* characterized it as "a chilling and engrossing piece, made even more so by the vivid performing of everyone involved" (Jowitt 1987:97); and another reviewer, in the February 1988 issue of *Dance*, thought it looked "like a post-holocaust *Star Trek*. The people we see range from their twenties through their eighties and evolve in occupation from business-suited twentieth-century bureaucrats to mysterious elders executing rituals in a clearing in the distant future. Pictographs intending to warn serve mainly to tantalize, and priestesses distribute a deadly host. The elders...teach the young survivors to dance by guiding their bodies, as a Balinese teacher would." Thus far, I have been able to view the show only on tape (courtesy of Ms. Lerman): I found it to be a pair of soberly satirical pieces, cleverly blending more or less verbatim citations from my text with original music and dance, rendered with wit and gentle humor.

As I mentioned above, Morris (1946:219, 353), following a terminology suggested by Rudolf Carnap (1942:12–15), contrasted applied semiotics with two other kinds, one of which he named "pure." Morris went on to explain that pure semiotic(s)—an expression seldom encountered nowadays—"elaborates a language to talk about signs" (p. 353). If anyone qualifies as having spun pure semiotics it was surely Charles Sanders Peirce (1839–1914), for whom the notion of applied semiotics (at least in the senses illustrated above) would have been absurd, if only because "there is no absolutely definitive semiotic analysis of anything" (cf. Ransdell 1986:679). American semioticians all but universally, and foreign semioticians increasingly, espouse Peirce—whom Max Fisch has called "the most versatile intellect that the Americas have so far produced" (in Sebeok and Umiker-Sebeok 1980b:7)—as their undisputed *fons et origo* of the doctrine of signs. Peirce is also said to continue "to be the most original mind that the United States has yet produced,...more nearly like Leibniz than any other American philosopher with respect to the range, variety, and ingenuity of his intellectual contributions, and...the founder of what is still this country's most distinctive philosophical movement" (Nagel 1982:303). In short, the Peircean paradigm now reigns.

Lamentably, however, Peirce has in addition become a rather conspicuous figure of hagiology. He has a learned organization named in his honor, which has published a journal since 1965: the *Transactions of the Charles S. Peirce Society*. Subtitled *A Quarterly Journal in American Philosophy*, it publishes many articles on semiotic—or, to be precise, *semeiotic*—topics.[9]

Fig. 1-3
Charles Sanders Peirce, ca. 1875. (Official Coast Survey photo,
courtesy Peirce Edition Project, Indianapolis)

The domestic and foreign secondary literature about Peirce and
his voluminous writings, either published or still in manuscript, not
only is staggering but accretes at an almost exponential rate. Much
of this literature appears to be exegetical in character, and—since
Peirce was a polymath of extraordinary scope—merely tangential to
semiotics. Despite the long span of its composition between 1857
and his death, Peirce's monumental opus is topically fragmentable
only at the risk of losing vital affinities within the whole.

Carolyn Eisele has drummed into many of us the lesson that, for
one thing, "the key to understanding the connections between his
diverse undertakings was his mathematics" (in Dauben 1982:314),
and that, more specifically, his mathematics "contains much materi-

al of the first importance for semiotic" (in Ransdell 1986:6, 4). Indeed, as Joseph Esposito (1980:ix–x) correctly observed, Peirce "was to a considerable degree a *systematic* philosopher," who conceived of his calling "as an ensemble of investigations." The entire ensemble is subsumed within the framework of a tripartite "General Semeiotic" (consisting of speculative grammar [i.e., philosophical, theoretical, or "pure" grammar], critical logic, and speculative or philosophical rhetoric, sometimes dubbed methodeutic).

In recent times, cis-Atlantic books and essays tangent to semiotics tend to be reverentially peppered with citations from Peirce. Like the little old lady from Jersey City who went to see *Hamlet* on Broadway for the first time and reported disappointment because the play seemed to her to be little more than a string of hackneyed expressions, these Peircean *obiter dicta*—my all-time favorite being the one about "this universe is perfused with signs, if it is not composed exclusively of signs"—delude by virtue of their easy conversance.

Take as one example of Peirce's now well-nigh ubiquitous icon/index/symbol trichotomy. As I have previously insisted (Sebeok 1989b:110–111), such categories "can scarcely be understood when wrenched out of the total context of [Peirce's] semiotic." For they are but one set among a veritable cascade of triadic relational structures subsumed under firstness/secondness/thirdness: qualisign/sinsign/legisign (cf. Short 1982); rheme/dicisign/argument/, I/thou/it (cf. Singer1984); abduction/deduction/induction (cf. Eco and Sebeok 1983); mind/matter/God, language/expression/meaning; object/sign/interpretant (the latter further cloven into immediate/dynamical/final) (Sebeok, in Deely et al. 1986:35–42); possibility/actuality/necessity, unity/plurality/totality; and so (with many variations) on and on. At the core of Peirce's sem(e)iotic, one finds not at all, as is sometimes polemically claimed, the sign, but sem(e)iois (cf. Fisch 1986:330; Morris, Eco, Rey, and Landowski later hold comparable beliefs), unless the sign has been antecedently defined in terms of sem(e)iosis. But then the essence of Peirce's notion of sem(e)iosis involves irreducible tripartitions in relationship or action, which require a comprehensive rather than a piecemeal appreciation of such categories.[10]

Recognition and advocacy, as far back as 1952, of Peirce's

pioneering role in structural linguistic analysis, especially in the domain of linguistic operations with meanings, was among Roman Jakobson's many great merits. While Jakobson continued to give perspicacious glimpses of Peirce as a genuine forerunner of modern linguistics, he left elaboration to others. Accordingly, this topic became the theme of my 1975 presidential address to the Linguistic Society of America. At least two books by other American scholars (Michael Shapiro 1983 and Pharies 1985) later took the subject up again in more, yet still far from exhausting, detail. The fullest treatment to date is Joëlle Rhétoré's immense University of Perpignan dissertation, *La linguistique sémiotique de Charles S. Peirce* (1988), currently being translated into English for publication.

Beginning in 1878, in his famous "How to Make Our Ideas Clear," Peirce began to develop his "pragmaticist" view of meaning, according to which the meaning of a message is the behavior it induces, its truth-value depending on whether that behavior has consequences beneficial to the interpreter. It turns out that Peirce's view of meaning is in excellent conformity with the theory of evolution, particularly as regards the linkage between the individual and his or her *Umwelt*. In my opinion (and, in this area, there are only opinions), his is the only satisfactory theory of meaning in the murky history of semantics so far.

From the outbreak of World War I to about the death of George H. Mead in 1931 (b. 1863), semiotics in the United States was at a low ebb. Peirce-as-a-semiotician vanished from view, to be revived only in England in the early 1920s through the good offices of C. K. Ogden and I. A. Richards. He began very slowly to resurface here when his *Collected Papers* started to appear, followed by Morris's generous although limited endorsement: "His classification of signs, his refusal to separate completely animal and human sign-processes, his often penetrating remarks on linguistic categories, his application of semiotic to the problems of logic and philosophy, and the general acumen of his observations and distinctions, make his work in semiotic a source of stimulation that has few equals in the history of this field" (1946:290; reinforced in Morris 1970:18–22, 40–42, 55–56).

It was, of course, not Peirce but the pragmatist Mead who, through his lectures and unfinished manuscripts, influenced Morris at the outset, although later Morris came to perceive a significant, because independent, convergence between the two. Morris (1970:35) stressed that "Mead's analysis of the gestural sign (whether linguistic or nonlinguistic) made fundamental the behavioral nature of the interpretant toward which Peirce's semiotic had developed." Mead—unlike Peirce (cf. Short 1982:308 n. 10)—had a technical theory of meaning, which was triadic in character, involving "gesture, adjustive response, and resultant of the social act which the gesture initiates" (1934:80, and chap. 11), but, according to Morris (1970:36), "Mead's most important contributions to semiotic are his behavioral analysis of the language symbol and his elaboration of the key role of such symbols in the development and maintenance of the human self and the higher levels of human society."

In passing, it should be noted that Mead's views played a decisive role in the development of the sociology of symbolic interaction (including Goffman's formation—after all, he too studied at Chicago). And this is as good a place as any to mention the fascinating book by Hugh Duncan (1968), with its portentously double dedication: to Kenneth Burke, Master Symbolist of Our Time, and to George Mead, Founder of the Chicago Tradition in Symbolic Analysis; as well as a collection of essays by Herbert Blumer, which likewise rely chiefly on the thought of Mead, "who, above all others, laid the foundations of the symbolic interactionist approach" (1969:1). Nor should one forget the voluminous writings, as an offshoot of this same tradition, of Victor W. Turner, a Scotsman who taught at Chicago too, from 1968 to 1977, and who argued that "the relationship between symbolic behavior and social life was semiotic" (Babcock and MacAloon 1987:7); it was the "distinctive and influential feature of his symbolic anthropology that it was a 'grounded' semiotics" (meaning, I suppose, "empirically grounded") (Babcock and MacAloon 1987:11).

Semiotic(s) as such began to transpire publicly and acquire a measure of definition in this country only in 1938, with the publication of Morris's *Foundations of the Theory of Signs* (reprinted in Morris 1971:13–71), although its author progressively, after the early 1920s, commencing while training with Mead, immersed himself in the theory of signs. But, even in his twilight years, Morris

Fig. 1-4
Charles Morris. (Photo courtesy University of Florida Archives)

identified with Peirce, who, he said, felt himself to be only "a pioneer, or rather a backwoodsman, in the clearing and opening up" of semiotics. Morris felt essentially the same way about his own work (1971:8). In the ensuing years, the global impact of Morris, accrued through his books and teaching (although he remained a prophet with least honor at his own institution in Chicago) was impressive—how much so was borne in on me vividly in the course of my later travels in Asia and Europe, especially in Japan and the Soviet Union. In 1953 an excellent, informative, substantial book by the Italian (but Texas-linked) semiotician Ferruccio Rossi-Landi appeared about Morris's life and works, praising and displaying his *mentalità enciclopedica e classificatoria* (Rossi-Landi 1953:26).

Another subtle interpreter of Morris was the German (but American trained) philosopher Karl-Otto Apel, who wrote about Morris's semiotic(s) in 1959 and in his critical introduction (1973) to the German translation of Morris's 1946 book, *Signs, Language and Behavior*. These publications underscored the fact that Morris was, by and large, always more appreciated abroad than in this country (although some dissertations about him, by Barbara Eakins in 1972 and Richard Fiordo in 1974, were produced on campuses in Iowa and Illinois).

I want to add one diagnostic observation to what I have said about Morris in my "Vital Signs" (chap. 2): as the reputation and stock of Peirce have risen, those of Morris have declined in proportion. This is because Morris explicitly embraced behavioral psychology. Interestingly enough, Mead's theory of reciprocal, behavioral expectations is inconsistent with behaviorism, and closer to the standpoint of Peirce. Note how these two intersecting curves of this contemporaneous pair delineate the ascent of the cognitive sciences and the descent of behaviorism as well.

Morris made no direct contributions to either descriptive or applied semiotics. He defined the former (1946:353, 219) as semiotic(s) that "studies actual signs," giving as examples statements about "what signs signify to certain persons, how signs are combined in a specific language, the origin, uses, and effects of specific signs," and so forth, such statements, or ascriptors, constituting "a natural science" in contrast to logic.

In this respect, as in many others, Roman Jakobson (1896–1982), my second teacher in semiotics (see Sebeok 1989b: chap. 13), was the converse of and complement to Morris. When he landed in America (in June, 1941, as I mentioned, in the company of Cassirer), Jakobson already had half a lifetime's accomplishments in several branches of this domain behind him. Yet Eco did not exaggerate when he wrote that "ransacking Jakobson's immense bibliography to seek out an item explicitly devoted to semiotics may be disappointing," and that "despite his frequent use of the word 'semiotics,' some of the pages which have most influenced the development of this discipline fail to mention it" (1987:111, 112). The reason, Eco assumes, Jakobson never wrote a book on semiotics is that "his entire scientific existence was a living example of a

Quest for Semiotics" (1987:112). He was, in fact, "semiotically biased from his early years" (1987:113).

Fig. 1-5
Roman Jakobson. (Photo courtesy University Press of America)

The conceptual basis for Prague school theory, as F. W. Galan has demonstrated, was semiotics, its advent in 1934 effectively marking a final break with that of Russian formalism (Galan 1985: chap. 4). While some of this movement had its roots in a native Czech semiotics of art, most of it stemmed from Russia (Mikhail

Bakhtin's views among others) and Saussurean linguistics. The Prague school structuralists, Galan notes, "were eager to test the tools of semiotics analysis on material from the...arts—film, theatre, the visual arts, music and even ethnographic artifacts like folk costume" (1985:82). In the creation of this semiotics aesthetics, Jakobson rapidly took a leading role; in due course, it came to constitute a large part of the baggage that he eventually imported to this country. (Jakobson's first of many lectures at Indiana University took place in 1944 and was titled "The Theory of Signs." For an account of this event, which was flavored by Old World aestheticism, and burdened, moreover, by the speaker's thick Russian accent, see chapter 3 of this book.)

Initially, Jakobson was interested in Morris, but their relationship failed to flourish, because perhaps Jakobson's buoyancy was incompatible with Morris's Zen placidity, or perhaps because of profound differences in their respective traditions. The one thing they certainly shared was a focus on Peirce, and I have some reason to believe that it was Morris who first drew Jakobson's attention to Peirce. At any rate, as I recount in my essay "Vital Signs," by 1952, Jakobson was deeply engaged, to the point of a ruling preoccupation, in Peirce's "visionary theses" and "vast program, which even today answers the needs of modern thought" (Jakobson and Pomorska 1983:154). Jakobson's consistent and characteristic tenet, which he upheld to the last, was that the "number and range of *concrete* objectives that present themselves to semiotics argue for their systematic elaboration around the world. However," he cautioned, "one should reject all the unsuitable efforts of sectarians who seek to narrow this vast and varied work by introducing into it a parochial spirit" (Jakobson and Pomorska 1983:158; italics mine). We all know who the "sectarians" were that he put the rest of us on guard against, and where their headquarters were and are located to this day.

I was one among his pupils whom Jakobson encouraged "to try semiotics," which, by the early sixties, "was no longer an impossible dream; it was," Eco confirms, "the result of a successful quest" (1987:113). In other words, while Jakobson made no direct contributions to pure semiotics in Carnap's and Morris's sense, he was responsible as no one else before him for animating, both here and abroad, a large gamut of topics in descriptive semiotics (most particularly in the domains of language and several of the arts; cf. Jakobson and Pomorska 1983:152).

In his lecture during the 1952 Conference of Anthropologists and Linguists (the proceedings of which are recorded in Lévi-Strauss et al. 1953), Jakobson also declared his engagement with communication engineering; in particular, he seemed for some years to be under the spell of Claude Shannon and Warren Weaver's mathematical theory of communication (1949). This interest induced him, in 1960, to become deeply involved in a "Symposium on the Structure of Language and its Mathematical Aspects," where he cited Shannon in support of his statement about the "semiotic definition of a symbol's meaning as its translation into other symbols," referring to Shannon's definition of information as "that which is invariant under all reversible encoding or translation operations," or, briefly, "the equivalence class of all such translations" (*Structure* 1961:251). This was a neat way to bring under one umbrella Peirce's interpretant, Jakobson's translation theory, and Shannon's information theory. However, Jakobson's interest in information theory (as well as cybernetics) cooled considerably over time, and, except for remnants of fossilized terminology, it appeared to leave no permanent trace. Nor is any trace visible in current American semiotics overall.

I was singularly fortunate in having Morris and Jakobson as my two immediately successive companion guides through the thickets of semiotics. Both the Denver-born Morris, soaked in logical positivism and the scientific empiricism of the Vienna Circle, and the Moscow-born philologist, who spent the second half of his life ensconced among our Ivy League institutions, had quintessentially capacious and cosmopolitan outlooks. While Morris became increasingly concerned with questions of axiology, most notably in 1964, Jakobson grew ever more interested in mathematics and the natural sciences, especially in their mutual relations with semiotics (1974: chap. 3).

In the meantime, descriptive semiotics has been pursued on other fronts. For example, the Prague school's studies of the arts (which, as mentioned above, were enumerated, though not exhaustively, by Galan as film, theater, the visual arts, music, and ethnographic artifacts) have been enthusiastically continued by specialist

practitioners in this country and elsewhere. I have already alluded to
semiotics of the theater and of puppetry. Let me briefly touch upon
the remaining four, and mention some related matters, starting with
musical semiotics.

One of Morris's students from his seminar the year after the one
I participated in was Leonard Meyer (b. 1918), who became one of
this country's foremost musicologists. Meyer's work displays the
influence, among others, of Peirce, Colin Cherry, and Chomsky
(see, e.g., Meyer 1967:261–262). It is pervasively concerned with
modes of signification, which he calls the formal, the kinetic-syn-
tactic, and the referential, insisting that "any account of musical
communication that pretends to completeness must find a place for
all three" (1967:43). Although semiotics is only implicit in Meyer's
distinguished body of writings, it has constituted the pivot of Robert
S. Hatten's (b. 1952) work since 1982, when he defended his erudite
and programmatic dissertation, "Toward a Semiotic Model of Style
in Music: Epistemological and Methodological Eases," at Indiana
University, concluding that "whereas semiotics exhausts style, style
does not exhaust semiotics, which must ultimately embrace the
vastness of music as meaning" (Hatten 1982:213).

An inexplicable hiatus on the American scene is semiotics of
the opera, a form of great interest from Eastern and Western Europe
to Japan but curiously ignored in the United States. Perhaps the
most complex of syncretic objects, involving the literary, musical,
and scenic arts, with inputs from a still wider array of codes (as
noted in Sebeok 1985b:79), this area of concentrated international
researches at this time deserves the careful attention of young scholars
in this country as well.

On the other hand, semiotics of the dance, including the ballet
(see Marianne Shapiro 1981), directly linked not only to music but
also to nonverbal communication and to explorations of notational
systems, is an area that does flourish here (see Hanna 1986). An
innovative genre of interest has been an extension of semiotic
techniques of analysis to the art of mime, ranging from Marcel
Marceau to Pilobolus and Mummenschanz (see Royce 1987).

Another complex syncretic art form and an important early
testing ground for descriptive semiotics, the cinema, continues to be
as extensively plowed here as elsewhere (see Williams et al. 1986).

As to what Galan calls "the visual arts," modern semioticians tend to also take account of forms not usually considered "high arts," embracing, to be sure, drawing, painting, etching, and sometimes photography (à la Svetlana Alpers, Roland Barthes, René Lindekens, Christian Metz, Susan Sontag, and, more specifically, David Tomas 1982, 1983, and 1988) but also cartoons, comics, and such exotic practices as tattooing (Parry 1933; Glynn 1982:131–132) and other kinds of body scoring and cosmetic decoration (Morris 1977:222–225, 317). Sculpture, the plastic arts in general, and/or architecture may be included as well. I take all such forms to fall under what Meyer Schapiro (1970:488) has called "the art of representation constructs," involving elements such as the prepared surface, the boundaries, the positions and directions, the format of the image-sign, and so forth. In 1984, *Semiotica* devoted a special issue (52:3/4), guest edited by Mihai Nadin, to "The Semiotics of the Visual: Defining the Field."

Semiotics of the visual arts, perhaps more than other branches, has traditionally dealt in dialectic fashion with such core problems of semiotics as art and illusion, the artist and his or her subject (or model), and the relation between art and its societal context.

The role of semiotics in painting is, moreover, controversial in an interesting way with respect to the notion of conventionalism in pictorial representation, engaging, on opposite sides, sophisticated scholars such as Ernest Gombrich (1981) and Nelson Goodman (1968). Christine Hasenmueller (1984:335) fastens on the classic question whether the resemblance between images and the world is natural or conventional, and stresses that Gombrich's resolution, that resemblance is rooted in empirical parallels, as against Goodman's position of extreme relativism, "is crucial for semiotics." Richard Wollheim (1987:361 n. 23), too, sharply distinguished recently between two views, calling them "mainstream semiotics" (descending from Peirce) and "radical semiotics" (practiced by Goodman but also by György Kepes and Rosalind E. Krauss in this country). Wollheim claims to have "no particular dispute" with semioticians of the former persuasion, but only with the "[radicals] who hold that all signs, including pictures, are conventional."

Works on the semiotics of sculpture, in the orthodox sense, are rare, excepting discussions of the plastic characteristics combined with the ritual transformations wrought by masks (Crumrine and Halpin 1983; see esp. chap. 16 and p. 209 for a discussion of their symbolic function and "semiotropic effect"), totem pole or canoe carvings, and other decorative arts of Northwest Coast Indians (codified extensively in ethnographic accounts). Some semiotic aspects of the arts of floral arrangements and bonsai may also be studied under this heading.

By contrast, architectural semiotics, properly considered "a facet of a broader area of inquiry generically termed visual semiotics[,]...is integrally related to the semiotic study of the nature, functions, usage, and ideological status of cultural artifacts of many kinds— from megalopolitan formations to graphic notation" (Preziosi 1986:44).[11] Architectural studies have proliferated, in "a rich and complex mélange," in North America as in South America and elsewhere, representing "developments out of (and implications for) general semiotic theory" (1986:45).

Galan lastly refers to "ethnographic artifacts," especially—in tacit but obvious reference to the pioneer analyses of P. G. Bogatyrev, suggestively amplified by Henry Glassie (1973)—to "folk costume." Indeed, there exists a fair amount of literature on the semiotics of clothing (not enough, in English, in the fertile field of application of semiotics to uniforms, yet see, e.g., Jay Mechling [1987], on the semiotics of Boy Scout uniforms), including a 1981 book by the American novelist Alison Lurie, who entitled her opening chapter "Clothing As a Sign System." Many works explore the semiotics of bodily artifacts (Golliher 1987),[12] as well as a wide variety of fascinating corporeal extensions, such as the gardens (Casalis 1983) or culinary practices (Loveday and Chiba 1985) of the Japanese.

Kenneth Foote reviews four characteristic aspects of semiosis of the perdurable material expressions, as opposed to the dissipative aspects of vocal signs and other kinds of nonverbal ones, informally launching a kind of "distinctive feature analysis" (as this kind of exercise is called by linguists), which could usefully be generalized much further to remaining types of semiosis (1988:245–246; I gave one example of this in Sebeok 1985b:29–30, to wit, in reference to a comparative analysis of the advantages and disadvantages of channels used for communication in and across all species and inside the body). Foote relates the use of objects in semiosis to "human action in sustaining memory, and with effacement of memory" (1988:263), which is particularly pertinent to the notion of the second, or so-called semiotic, self (Sebeok 1989b: app. 1; amplified in Sebeok 1989a).

Scholars in our domestic workshops have also enriched the literature of semiotics with philological articles, treatises, and editions dealing with ancestral figures, eras, or movements. *Semiotica* on occasion publishes special issues along these lines. Two recent representative collections, both edited by Americans, dealt with "Semiotica Mediaevalia" (vol. 63, nos. 1–2, ed. Jonathan Evans) and "The Classical [i.e., seventeenth-century] Sign" (vol. 51, nos. 1–3, ed. Susan W. Tiefenbrun).

Among noteworthy products (in English) by a single author or editor (or a pair of editors) that have lately come to my attention, I would like to highlight three (but see also G. Weltring's 1910 thesis [republished in Hanke 1986] of the *semeion* in Aristotelian, Stoic, Skeptic, and Epicurean philosophy). Chronologically, the earliest among this trio is the edition of Philodemus of Gadara's *On Methods of Inference* (1978), edited by Phillip Howard De Lacy and Estelle Allen De Lacy. Most of this unique work, which presents the Epicurean view of semiosis, was recovered from a papyrus, and is here presented with the De Lacys' excellent translation and commentary. Having already mentioned above, as well as reviewed elsewhere (Sebeok 1986h), John Deely's extraordinary (therefore controversial: see Deely 1988) edition, with his translation and interpretive commentary, of Poinsot's *Tractatus de Signis* (1985), I need not dwell on its merits again. In a different genre, there is David Wellbery's (1984) *tour de force* study of the (primarily) German Enlightenment in its pre-Kantian phase reinterpreted in the light of modern semiotics, from which he then draws valuable insights to yield a perspective on our contemporary semiotic preoccupations.

There are, of course, numerous insightful American essays of a philological character (too many to list; in general, consult the *EDS* [Sebeok 1986c]). Among those historical figures or groups of interest to, or variously claimed for, semiotics we find: Augustine, Bachelard, Berkeley, Buber, Collingwood, Dewey, Heidegger, Hobbes, Hume, Locke, Lull, Mallarmé, M. Polanyi, Reid, J. Royce, Suarez, Wittgenstein, and the Conimbricenses, to name but a few.

II.

The university is perfused with signs, if it is not composed exclusively of signs.—Peirceonal communication

From this shifting kaleidoscope of people and ideas—the names and labels that take shape, shimmer, dazzle, although ofttimes fade away—I would like to turn next, albeit briefly, to the organizational aspects of semiotics, the external expressions that have molded its development in teaching and research in the United States.

We know something about Peirce's seminars at Johns Hopkins from 1879 to 1884, for instance from Joseph Jastrow's enthusiastic account: "The fertility of his resources imparted a breadth to his treatment that brought the student to a constant leadership of a rich mind. His knowledge never gave the impression of a burden, but of strength. His command of the history of science was encyclopedic in the best sense of the word....[His] sense of masterly analysis accomplished with neatness and dispatch—all seemingly easy, but actually the quality of the highest type of keen thinking—remains as the central impression of a lecture by Professor Peirce" (Jastrow 1916:723)—and more of the same.

Jastrow, as well as Christine Ladd(-Franklin), John Dewey, and Thorstein Veblen, participated in Peirce's seminars. We are, alas, ignorant of the semiotic complexion of these seminars. It has been asserted that Allan Marquand (1853–1924) was Peirce's sole Ph.D. candidate (in 1880). Marquand's dissertation dealt with "The Logic of the Epicureans," based on the Philodemus fragment; he also read a paper on this same subject at a meeting of the Metaphysical Club at Johns Hopkins (January 13, 1880), for which Peirce was the commentator of record. Unfortunately, Dewey's dissertation on Kant has vanished. Perhaps the most enduring monument to Peirce's students is the 1883 volume he collected, *Studies in Logic, By Members of the Johns Hopkins University.*

In my essay "Vital Signs" (see chap. 2 of this book), I state my belief that "the very first sequence of courses in semiotics, so labeled, in any curriculum anywhere" was offered by Charles Morris, beginning in the late 1930s, at the University of Chicago. In that same article I identify the only classmate of mine (of a handful) I can still remember: the teenage mathematician Walter Pitts, who became Warren S. McCulloch's collaborator (and tó whom, McCulloch wrote, he was "principally indebted for all subsequent success" [1965:9]).

I think that only three of us—the prolific science author Martin Gardner, the musicologist Leonard Meyer, and I—survive from among Morris's Chicago seminarians. When Morris moved to the University of Florida, he discontinued his semiotic seminars, and the teaching of a subject thus identified in university catalogs ceased until the alas now forgotten Ethel M. Albert briefly revived the practice at Northwestern University in the early 1970s, before her untimely death. Nowadays, the teaching of semiotics is commonplace in American institutions, sometimes in distinct departments, such as at Rice University, sometimes in other programs, such as at Brown and Indiana universities (cf. Rauch 1978; and Sebeok 1989b:272–279). Brown University, for example, has for decades offered an undergraduate concentration in semiotics through its Center for Modern Culture and Media.[13]

A decade ago, an exciting vision of Paul Bouissac (University of Toronto) was realized by the creation of the International Summer Institute for Semiotic and Structural Studies. Its basic purposes are to provide graduate and postdoctoral students and others with a set of courses and seminars in the various branches of semiotics, and to foster interdisciplinary exchanges by bringing together, for a reasonable length of time, specialists who share a common interest in the advancement of semiotics. The institute has typically alternated estivally between Canada and the United States (with occasional hibernal excursions to India and Brazil). In this country three institutes have been hosted at Indiana University (in both Bloomington and Indianapolis), and one each at Northwestern University and

Vanderbilt University.

In passing, I should allude to the International Semiotics Institute, formally established in Imatra, Finland, in July 1988, to consolidate pedagogical resources worldwide and to facilitate the movement of students among different institutions that offer semiotics courses in whatever guise. According to present plans, the day-by-day functions of the institute are to be carried out through over half a dozen regional centers, among them the North American Center, located at Indiana University.

It should also be recorded that a sophisticated course of instruction in semiotics was introduced in the mid-1960s at the elite Brookline (Mass.) High School for sophomores, juniors, and seniors, under the leadership of Donald W. Thomas (1976). The curriculum is supported by four readers especially designed for these classes. This project still continues, although it is unclear at this time how far, and with what success, it has spread beyond Massachusetts.

The idea to form a Semiotic Society of America (SSA) was initially propounded at the First North American Semiotics Colloquium, held at the University of South Florida on July 28–30, 1975 (see Sebeok 1977b). The following year, September 24–25, the society's initial meeting took place at the Georgia Institute of Technology, in Atlanta, with over one hundred registrants. The most important piece of business conducted was the adoption of the society's constitution, essentially as it was drafted by Allen Walker Read. The SSA has held over a dozen annual meetings since (frequently with rump sessions of the Charles S. Peirce Society), peregrinating from the East (Buffalo, Providence, Reading) to the West (Denver, San Francisco, Snowbird), the Midwest (Bloomington [bis], Cincinnati, Indianapolis), the Southwest (Lubbock), and the South (Nashville, Pensacola).

Proceedings of these meetings have been published since 1976 (with a hiatus from 1977–1980), chiefly on John Deely's editorial initiative, lately in volumes approaching 800 pages. Other serials of the SSA have included the now fugitive issues of the *Bulletin of Literary Semiotics*, replaced by *The Semiotic Scene*, finally replaced in 1981 by the *American Journal of Semiotics* (*AJS*) (first coedited by Irene Portis Winner with Thomas G. Winner, then by Dean MacCannell with Juliet Flower MacCannell). The *AJS* is now the society's, and therefore the United States', official learned publication in semiotics.[14]

Approximately thirty books have appeared to date under the series title Advances in Semiotics, published by the Indiana University Press. This series includes both of the principal, complementary anthologies designed for beginning students in the United States: Innis (1985) and Deely et al. (1986). Plenum Press brings out another series, Topics in Contemporary Semiotics; among its volumes to date is that by Krampen et al. (1987), often used as a companion volume to the preceding pair of readers. In 1986, Plenum also published in a single volume *The Semiotic Sphere*, featuring twenty-seven chapters on the state of the art around the globe.

The Semiotic Web, a continuing series of yearbooks under the imprint of Mouton de Gruyter, began appearing in 1986. Both the *Sphere* and the *Web* are produced at Indiana University's Research Center for Language and Semiotic Studies (RCLSS), under the editorial care of the undersigned and Jean Umiker-Sebeok. *The Encyclopedic Dictionary of Semiotics* was likewise prepared at the RCLSS, with the collaboration of a six-member international editorial board, and was published in Mouton's Approaches to Semiotics series.

III.

Que sera, sera.—Jo MacKenna (Doris Day) singing to Hank (Christopher Olsen) in Alfred Hitchcock's 1955 film, *The Man Who Knew Too Much*

At the outset of this essay, I incautiously pledged "to cautiously extrapolate from the known to the unknown," or in other words to speculate yet again on *Dove va la semiotica*?—in other words, where is semiotics, particularly semiotics in the United States, headed? Thus did Gianfranco Marrone (1986:149–151) pose the question to me and several other colleagues during interviews he conducted in Palermo, Sicily. Curious myself, I later attempted to seek a consensual answer elsewhere (Sebeok 1986e), and later still, if both succinctly and tentatively, to supply one myself (Sebeok 1989a).

Whereas modern practitioners of semiotics probe the perpetual and the universal, or, short of such lofty pursuits, are content to dwell on and reassess their past, our distant cousins—the oracles of Greece, the haruspices of the Italian peninsula, the augurs of Rome—like today's host of psychic readers, strive to prognosticate the future. Their perceptions, illuminations, predictions, their "pseudo-semiotic divinatory techniques" (Sebeok 1985b:28), risk being embarrassed by time (unlike the soothsayers in *Julius Caesar* and the witches in *Macbeth*, who did turn out to be right—but those were figures of fiction).

In cosmology, our ability to predict the future and retrodict the remote history of the universe hinges on a crucial discovery, made in 1929 by Edwin Powell Hubble, the American lawyer turned astronomer, which makes it possible to relate in a systematic manner the shift in the spectral lines of distant galaxies to their distances, or, briefly, size to age. This paradigmatic model of the expanding universe may be pictured as a theoretical laboratory in which the beginning, the present, and the destiny of our universe are seen not only as in flux but as radically different, and in which the energetic world of elementary particle interactions can be seriously investigated. In fact, the 1965 detection of microwave background radiation left over from the initial hot fireball of the Big Bang helped sustain the theory in most dramatic fashion.

Forecasts about the shape of semiosis to come, too, depend on which "paradigmatic model," or theoretical gambit, one chooses for one's frame of reference. Inconveniently, we have nothing as solid as Hubble's constant to lean on. But for me the sign science has always seemed to be a branch of the life science, and semiosis the most pervasive, indeed, criterial fact of all life on earth. The pluralistic laws of biology, which are not, to be sure, equivalent to the universals of classical physics, yet are high-level generalizations all the same, should therefore be applicable to semiosis. In short, it is seen as a teleonomic process. Thus, the explanation of any semiosic "fact" can be modeled only in the form of a historical narrative.[15]

We have inherited from Jakob von Uexküll (Sebeok 1989b, chap. 10) a consistent and elaborate doctrine of signs. Its significance lies in a seamless amalgamation of semiotics and biology, especially zoology. Two of the most salient features arising from this synthesis are the elucidation of, first, the nature of the coupling between an observing organism and an observed organism; and second, the mechanisms of mutual influence, or, more precisely, inviolable interdependence, between signs and behavior. This coalescence, synopsized and depicted by Uexküll's celebrated model of the "functional circuit" whereby every organism constructs its own subjective *Umwelt*, originated on earth with the evolution of the first cell.

Nothing exists for any organism outside its bubblelike private *Umwelt* in which, although impalpably to its observer, it remains, as it were, inextricably sealed. The behavior of every organism— "behavior" being defined as the trafficking by signs among different *Umwelten*—has as its basic function the production of "unverbal" signs for communication, and first of all for communication of that organism with itself. The primal sign relation in the ontogeny of an organism is therefore realized as an opposition between *ego* and *alter*.

This elemental binary schism subsequently brings to pass the second semiosic dimension, that of *inside* vs. *outside*. It is this secondary opposition that enables the organism to "behave," namely, to enter into relations or link up with other living systems in its surroundings. The coupling of the observed with the observer is thus, by definition, a phenomenon situated in this second dimension, where every "outside" becomes a denotatum (Morris 1946:347), a perceptual cue of an "inside." In other words, no "outside" exists beyond the impenetrable periphery of the *Umwelt*.

Jakob's son, Thure von Uexküll (1987 *et alibi*), has shown that whereas the functional circuit is based on a dyadic model for the generation of signs, for its productive function it is based on a triadic model, incorporating the equivalent of an interpretant. This double-track modeling posits the theory at once in both the binary (Saussurean) and the triadic (Peircean) traditions. It thus neatly reconciles the major with the minor semiotic traditions (even though the German neo-Kantian scientist, who was by profession a theoretical and experimental biologist, knew of neither).

The equivalent of the Peircean interpretant, in this conception, is to be found in the specific character of the receptor in question. The frame and the way in which the bifacial aspect of signs—

aistheton and noeton, signans and signatum, sign vehicle and designatum, etc. (Sebeok 1985b:117–118)—unfolds are dictated by each organism's biological needs (such system needs usually being called "homeostasis"), as spelled out by J. von Uexküll in considerable detail, especially in his hermetic *Theoretical Biology* (in German: 1973 [1928] [1920]), so wretchedly translated into English under C. K. Ogden's eccentric auspices (1926). Only via this semiosic operation can an organism attain the goals of its behavior.

Note an important consequence of this model: suppose that a behavioral segment, say, in a chimpanzee, is registered by an observing psychologist as a sequence of signing gestures to humans or other chimpanzees, and is interpreted by the psychologist as a string of communicational sign-vehicles. That behavioral segment then has to be, in the first instance, a product of that observer's subjective *Umwelt* (Sebeok and Umiker-Sebeok 1981; Sebeok 1987c). In fact, what may constitute a "sign" in the *Umwelt* of the observed organism is inaccessible to the observer. The solution to this seemingly intractable dilemma, according to J. von Uexküll, presupposes that the would-be observer of the behavior of another organism begin by analyzing his or her own *Umwelt* before productive observations of the behavior of speechless creatures can be undertaken. It is by way of such a comparative analysis that we are led straight into the heart of semiosis in our human world.

Another kind of *Umwelt* theory was independently invented in 1943 by K. J. W. Craik, who hypothesized that "the organism carries a 'small-scale model' of external reality and of its own possible actions within its head" (1967:61), and that the essential feature of thought is "not propositions but symbolism" (1967:57). Craik's hypothesis has many surprising features, among which is his version of semiosis (1967:50–51), or of a kind of action cycle; for him, the Peircean interpretant becomes roughly coterminous with "translation" plus "reasoning," the basic materials for which he glimpses in inorganic nature: "it is only the sensitive 'receptors' on matter, and means of intercommunication...which are lacking" (Craik 1967:59).[16]

After this short detour, we can return to some general considerations about future trends in American semiotics, though attempting nothing so foolish as a blueprint. The sad fact must be registered, to begin with, that the contemporary teaching of semiotics is severely, perhaps cripplingly, impoverished by the utter, frightening innocence of most practitioners of semiotics about the natural order in which they and it are embedded. The terminal reasons behind this impoverishment were sketched out in C. P. Snow's Rede Lecture, given in Cambridge, England, in 1959. These teachers of semiotics are, as Snow complained, by absence of training, tone-deaf over an immense spectrum of intellectual experience: "As with the tone-deaf, they don't know what they miss" (Snow 1959:15). Semiotics is too important to be left in the hands of the "semiotician *ordinaire*" (this phrase being Sidney J. Levy's unduly modest title, in Umiker-Sebeok 1987:13), for it will surely shrivel and wither unless this lesson sinks in. (For a recent, semiotically informed compensating effort, see Paulson 1988).

This is a good place to bring to mind again that our titans—Peirce, Morris, and Jakobson—were thoroughly, if diversely, seasoned in the scientific trends of their time. For many years Peirce called himself a chemist, but he had also written papers in mathematics, physics, geodesy, spectroscopy, and experimental psychology, among other fields. Joseph Jastrow (1916:724) made a point of noting about an 1883 paper of Peirce's that "the trend was biological, the product required the schooling of discipline and the inspiration of genius."

Morris's definition of semiotics is always and especially worth repeating. The scope of semiotics, he affirmed, encompasses "the science of signs, whether animal or human, language or non-language, true or false, adequate or inadequate, healthy or pathic" (Morris 1946:223); and as Jakobson remarked, in the perspective of biology, semiotics encompasses "the science of life which embraces the total organic world. The different kinds of human communication become a mere section of a much vaster field of studies" (Jakobson 1974:44).

These were essentially programmatic declarations, but they are being implemented daily, bit by bit, in laboratories all over the United States (and, of course, abroad as well). The results of such researches will certainly mold, continue to enrich, and inform our semiotics to come. Let me mention, if sketchily, some particulars. (For further details, see Sebeok Forthcoming.)

First, one practical chore that needs to be addressed by our students is either to define rigorously or to discard altogether from semiotic discourse such run-of-the-mill vocabulary items as "information" or "communication," on the one hand, and, on the other, a host of *ad hoc* neologisms scattered through various recent theory-tied analytical dictionaries and similar aids for would-be beginning semioticians. Robert Wright provides a persuasive model of clarity for the former in his chapters "What is Information?" and "What is Communication?" (1988: chaps. 9 and 17; see also Wright 1989). Terminological chaos remains, however, a painful, special scandal of our generation of semioticians that needs urgently to be ameliorated. (For some preliminary ventures in the rectification of terms, see Sebeok 1985b:156–164; and, for a more authoritative, though not necessarily always definitive, source see the relevant lemmata in the *EDS* [Stanosz 1986 and Moles 1986]).

Semiosis is by no means unlimited (save perhaps in a metaphysical sense). Interpretants certainly had a demarcatable beginning on the protocellular level (Fox 1988:89–92), and, unless they carry on in robots and reproducing von Neumann machines, they will cease with the extinction of life. Terrestrial semiosis—we don't know if there is any other—began in the Archaean Aeon (up to about 3,900 million years ago) and flourishes in the microcosmos, among the prokaryotic bacilli, cocci, and spirilla. All bacteria contribute to and draw benefits from a common gene pool. They form teams intertwined by localized semiosic processes. But the single most momentous fact about them is that they are not discrete organisms at all: together they "constitute the communications network of a single superorganism whose continually shifting components are dispersed across the surface of the planet," and as a body, they interact with eukaryotes in unremitting, complex global commerce (Sonea 1988:40).

Microsemiosis is thus by no means confined to exchanges of signs in localized teams and throughout the biosphere but takes place abundantly as well in prokaryotic interactions with eukaryotes (organisms with nuclei that can be thought of as masses of DNA). Each bacterium is "part of a much larger network—a network that in some sense resembles human intelligence" (Sonea 1988:45).

The eukaryotes notably include plants, animals, and fungi. We eukaryotes serve our ancestral prokaryotes as both habitats and supplementary means of transportation. To do so efficiently, signs must continually flow between us, the colonized, and our invisible colonizers. "As tiny parts of a huge biosphere whose essence is basically bacterial, we—with other life forms—must add up to a sort of symbiotic brain which is beyond our capacity to comprehend or truly represent" (Margulis and Sagan 1986a:152). At present, such, to be sure, is the case. But one of the most exciting challenges for our students will be to uncover precisely how signs are dispersed throughout the bacterial ensemble (a view aptly called the "unifying theory of intercellular communication" [Roth and LeRoith 1987:51]), to grasp semiosis on a planetary scale, and to make plain the proper place of the language-endowed animal enfolded within the vast, inaudible autopoietic biota.

Semiotic notions, it has been perfectly clear for some years, have increasingly illuminated certain areas of basic biological research. As I deal with several branches of endosemiotics elsewhere in more detail (Sebeok Forthcoming), it must suffice here to enumerate, with a few comments, some of these prospective research opportunities:

- The genetic code, notably the far-reaching similarities in structure between it and the architectonic model underlying the verbal codes of all languages (Jakobson 1974:49–53);
- The immune code, now widely regarded (in a frontier field dubbed either semioimmunology or immunosemiotics) as exhibiting not merely the properties of any semiotic system but rather of one functioning in the manner of an open-ended generative grammar (Jerne 1985);
- The metabolic code, an early study of which revealed Peircean thirdness, or symbolicity in the technical sense, functioning at the interface of certain extra- and intracellular events (Tomkins 1975);
- The neural code, as studied under the aegis of a new discipline called "neurocommunications."

It is worth noting, too, that the endocrine system and the nervous system, the two principal retes for the flow of communication within our bodies, are both specialized descendants of one common ancestor. Many of the molecules that served as messengers during the prokaryotic phase have maintained their essential structure even when their semiosic functions have changed over time. This explains many coincidences in semiosic processes throughout the five Superkingdoms (cf pp. 161–62 in this book), as well as why endocrine messengers turn up so often in exocrine systems (as the gastrointestinal tract, the bloodstream, and the axon).

In 1975, a young UCLA biochemist, the now deceased Gordon Tomkins, published a paper, now a classic of empirical semiotics as well, in which he established that the cyclic AMP (adenosine monophosphate) molecule is a symbol, a general sign in the precise technical sense of Peircean thirdness, in that it "represents a unique state of the environment." Robert Wright has recently affirmed that this molecule has all the attributes required for pragmatic meaning: there is a palpable "symbol...; something in the environment that the symbol represents...; and something alive that, upon processing the symbol, behaves so as to reconcile its well-being with that environmental condition (by heading elsewhere)" (1988:104). As evolution has progressed, cyclic AMP has hardly changed at all in meaning: it begins in *Escherichia coli*, within the human digestive tract, then searches for a more congenial environment when carbon is depleted; it provides social coherence in some species of hungry slime mold; and it is a common second messenger in humans, denoting different things in different contexts (Wright 1988:197). Tomkins has, in short, unveiled the ancient origin of the symbol, not essentially different in function from the symbols of human society. This line of research must be continued and expanded to other semiotic entities.

In fact, the phylogenesis of semiosis is now fairly well understood in its general outlines, although, of course, innumerable particulars need to be ascertained and elucidated in the years ahead. Semiosis emerged on earth with the appearance of primordial cells (some would argue for meaning inherent even in the DNA molecule and in viruses, but this is doubtful). It informs the microcosmos and the macrocosmos, leading to the universal evolution of language-as-a-modeling-system in the genus *Homo* and its manifestation as speech as a communicative device in the adult form of our species, *sapiens* (Sebeok 1986d: chap. 2, *et alibi*), followed by other actualizations of language, such as a sporadic assortment of speech surrogates and script and the accelerating technology of the organizational revolution (sketched in Beniger 1986).

Likewise, we are coming to understand the ontogenetic principles of semiosis in some species (e.g., some birds), including notably our own. Colwyn Trevarthen's elegant ethological researches on the unfurling of the semiosic powers of infants, especially in their early dyadic interactions with their mothers, are a giant step in this direction (cf. 1987).

The above are but a few critical domains of fundamental science, where that intersects with the sign science, and where sensitive semioticians of tomorrow could well make productive contributions.

How animals communicate (zoosemiotics; Sebeok 1968, Sebeok and Ramsay 1969; Sebeok 1972; and Sebeok 1977a) has been of considerable interest to workers in semiotics since the early 1960s, including the special problems of how the speechless creatures communicate with humans and vice versa (Sebeok 1988a [chap. 5 below]). The latter, however, is an area especially laden with misconceptions precisely when it is practiced solo by would-be inquirers untutored in semiotics and glaringly innocent of linguistics (Sebeok and Umiker-Sebeok 1981; Sebeok 1987c).

There is a growing tendency to look at animal groupings, notably insect societies, as information-processing systems; these groupings, especially semiosis in honeybee colonies, has not escaped the attention of computer scientists interested, as many nowadays are, in parallel processing. While each individual bee converts signs in serial fashion, we now know that the colony operates as an ensemble in "parallel." Members of the profession, viewing the human brain as an integrated social structure, have much to learn from this novel way of looking at zoosemiosis (cf. Seeley and Levien 1987).

On the other hand, how plants communicate (phytosemiotics) is a question that came seriously into the purview of semiotics less than a decade ago. We now know that phytosemiosic processes are enwrapped in zoosemiosic ones, which are thus hierarchically superior as well as more complex (T. von Uexküll 1987:5–6), and we understand why this must be so (see chap. 5 below). We also know why human cells understand the molecular messages of plants: for "many of the chemicals that served as messengers during the unicellular phase have maintained their essential structure, even as their communicative functions have changed" (Roth and LeRoith 1987:54).

Messages (besides, of course, materials like food) are produced by plants, transformed by animals, and dissipated by fungi (mycosemiosis). The complexities of zoosemiosis are thus logically consequent on the intermediacy of animals as transforming agents in this transmission loop. Messages that decay as a result of fungal action are eventually recycled in plants and animals; or, as we might say, the molecules are refabricated into novel strings of signs through the acquisition of further interpretants. The cycle of semiosic growth, maturity, and dissolution goes on and on.

How humans signify and communicate (anthroposemiotics) is the huge and multifarious field of inquiry, a world of our own intellective construction, imaginatively furnished with objects and events, that normally and routinely preoccupies most semioticians. This whole world is made up of intricate if only partially shared systems of signified content, tools with which each of us learns to establish liaison with our fellows by way of an ever-shifting mixture of verbal and nonverbal signs.

Messages are the proper subject matter of semiotics (cf. Sebeok 1985b:1), as they are for evolutionary biology, providing "the only connections between life now and life a million or a billion years ago" (Cairns-Smith 1985:28 and chap. 2). But, according to some, they also constitute the proper subject matter of all social and behavioral sciences as well. For, as Norbert Wiener argued three decades ago, "the social system is an organization, like the individual, that is bound together by a system of communication" (1948:24). Furthermore, "society can only be understood through a study of messages and the communication facilities which belong to it" (Wiener 1950:9). The social production of meaning entails "the possibility that sign systems might program social control," as James Beniger (1986:90) notes in his discussion of semiotics in his remarkable book on the origins and present state of the Information Society. Explorations of this topic, that is, the impact of the semiotic standpoint on "the control revolution," and the multiple ramifications of that impact, will no doubt intensify (although, or perhaps because, Margaret Mead stressed that continuing work on semiotics "should take place not in the context of power and manipulation" [in Sebeok et al. 1972: 286]).

Wiener presciently added to his thesis that "in the future development of these messages and communication facilities, messages between man and machines, between machine and man, and between machine and machine, are destined to play an ever-increasing part" (1950:9). His foresight provides one of the most intriguing opportunities for the semiotician on both the near and distant horizon in the hybrid field called cybersymbiosis, but which I prefer to think of as cybersemiosis. By this term I refer to those arenas of human sign action where either the message source or the message destination is not a life form but an electronically driven robot (a vision fleshed out in Margulis and Sagan 1986a and 1986b; cf. Sebeok 1988c) or a commingled composite of human and manufactured parts. Computer technology and robotics offer engrossing openings for the alert semiotician of today and tomorrow at these exciting frontiers of biotechnology.

I have tried at various times to inject concepts from catastrophe theory into semiotics (cf. Sebeok 1986d:25–26), following René Thom's germinal ideas, and building on those of Jakob von Uexküll, Peirce, himself a great mathematician, and others. Jean Petitot-Cocorda (1985), in Paris, succeeded admirably in reinterpreting Jakobsonian structuralism in these terms, but only a handful of American scholars have followed. Myrdene Anderson (Sebeok 1986d: chap. 3) and Floyd Merrell (1982:156 n. 10), both at Purdue University, are exceptional in this regard. Unfortunately, few of our semioticians are able to handle the mathematical concepts and operations.

A new project, also inspired by Peirce, providing a semiotic analysis of mathematical signs (including particularly of "zero" as a key to the naively naturalistic links between systems of representation and the "reality" they are assumed to stand for) has recently been launched by Brian Rotman (1987 and 1988); the effects of Rotman's fascinating, and I think undoubtedly productive, constructivist efforts have yet to become plain.

The name of Joseph Jastrow (1863–1944) has appeared several times in this essay, but no one thinks of this student of Peirce as a semiotician. He is usually mentioned as the first American Ph.D. (1886) in psychology. "Mr. Peirce's courses," he once remarked, "gave me my first real experience of intellectual muscle. Though I promptly took to the laboratory of psychology when that was first established by Stanley Hall [a student of William James, Hall (1844–1924) founded and promoted organized psychology as a science and profession in America], it was Peirce who gave me my first training in the handling of a psychological problem" (1916:724). (This problem was, in fact, a new way to determine the difference in limen, that is, the point of just noticeable difference in discriminating a sensation, a subject on which Jastrow published an early paper jointly with Peirce.) Jastrow became best known as a popularizer of psychology and a dedicated skeptic (as well as, incidentally, a sharp and cogent critic of Freudian theory). It is Jastrow the skeptic who chiefly interests me in this context.

Jastrow wrote several remarkable books of a skeptical cast. His *Fact and Fable in Psychology* (1900) featured chapters on topics ranging from "The Modern Occult" to "The Psychology of Deception," from hypnotism and spiritualism to "A Study of Involuntary Movements." In his *Wish and Wisdom* (1935) he had an excellent chapter on animal "geniuses," notably recounting the tale of the notorious Clever Hans, the horse able to "count" ("a simple fact, though a clever stunt," Jastrow 1935:205), and the hilarious case of Lola, the dog who kept a diary and rapped alphabetic messages with her paw onto her trainer's palm. These were two among other illustrations of "how a simple humanizing error in observation under a prepossession can compromise rationality, as wish diverges from wisdom" (Jastrow 1935:213)—as, unfortunately, it still does, although now tending to star apes and diverse species of marine mammals (cf., e.g., Sebeok and Umiker-Sebeok 1981; Sebeok 1986a).

These days, the indispensable and unending efforts of "skeptics"—a vocation, actually, of exceptionally dedicated scientists, philosophers, conjurers, and others—are being carried forward on a systematic, institutionalized basis by the (Buffalo, New York–based) Committee for the Scientific Investigation of Claims of the Paranormal, which now maintains an international network of "skeptics," and which publishes an outstanding journal, *The Skeptical Inquirer*. Its pages are filled with up-to-date articles precisely of the type pioneered by Jastrow.

Inspection of these articles and related "skeptical" books and publications reveals a pervasive resemblance to certain fundamental semiotic writings. This similarity should occasion no surprise to those acquainted with the *Treatise of Human Nature* (1739–1740) of the acute Scottish skeptical philosopher, David Hume (1711–1776). Hume transformed the notion of "sign" into the notion of "cause" (1739–1740, bk. 1, pts. 4 and 7; 1748, sec. 12). Interestingly enough, Alexander Bryan Johnson's thought was clearly linked to Hume's, while he was at the same time savagely critical of his illustrious predecessor, as well as of John Locke, accusing both of failing utterly to understand the nature of language. Yet also, as I noted early in this essay, the congruence of Johnson—who declared: "I am the first philosopher who has gone deeper than language" (Todd and Blackwood 1969:xvii)—with Wittgenstein, the quintessential modern Pyrrhonian skeptic or, for that matter, with the second-century Pyrrhonist Sextus Empiricus, the astute critic of Stoic theories of knowledge and of signs, is both surprising and quite remarkable.

Hume's influence on Peirce (and, via Peirce and James, on Jastrow), on the one hand, and on the contemporary "skeptical" movement, on the other, can hardly be overestimated.[17] Suffice it to point here to Eugene F. Miller's splendid demonstrations (1979 and 1986) of the way Hume went about reducing causal relations to what his predecessors had understood to be natural indicative signs. In sum, the consanguinity of these grand and, after Hume, indeed twinned, movements of our day—semiotics and skepticism—needs further careful exploration and documentation.

May I, in conclusion, gratify a hobby of mine, which I see as deeply implicated no less in semiotics than in the modern skeptical attitude? Skepticism is an activity that can boast of the finest connoisseurs of conjury, including Morris's student Martin Gardner. The youthful Charles Morris himself, in 1911, declared that he wished to adopt conjury as his career, a profession about which he produced, even as late as 1966, a quasireligious poem portraying such stage acts as "the pantomimes, the gestures, the replicas…mimes of the Great Magician" (Sebeok 1981b:85).

A detailed analysis of magic acts, for instance as exposed in Dariel Fitzroy, or "Fitzkee's," trilogy *Showmanship for Magicians* (1943), *The Trick Brain* (1944), and *Magic by Misdirection* (1945), reveals that the principles on which magical illusions are constructed are, on far deeper levels than is commonly allowed, identical with those of pure semiotics. Whether or not Morris was explicitly aware of these, he and others have surely grasped them intuitively. In the Renaissance, the man of science was still the magus. While, over the centuries, the professions of semiotician and illusionist necessarily diverged, the academic personality remains forever the doppelganger of the entertainer.

It was therefore delightful to have been present when Naomi Baron delivered her presidential address to the Semiotic Society of America in October 1987, in Pensacola, Florida. She demonstrated the first serious comprehension, as far as I know, of this by no means trivial area of prospective research. Baron's further formation, in her paper, titled "When Seeing's Not Believing: Language, Magic, and AI" (1988), of a vinculum with linguistics at one end and work in artificial intelligence at the other hints at the promises inherent in this line of inquiry.

As Jaron Lanier remarked, "We really have to create a world of illusion in order to deal with the physical world, because we don't have omnipresent sensory capacity...People really want to believe in reality" (in Wright 1987:9). In the last paragraph of my essay "Vital Signs" (chap. 2 below), I already have dared to call attention to this central—and now I would add, perennial—preoccupation of semiotics with "an illimitable array of concordant illusions." I here repeat that the overriding mission of semiotics is and will be "to mediate between reality and illusion," to penetrate to the illusion behind reality, in back of which will be discovered yet another reality, of a more intense texture. For, as Philodemus (1978:6.1–14), reporting Stoic arguments against Epicurean semiotics, queried in the first century B.C., "Why will the apparent any more be a sign of the non-apparent than vice versa? Besides," he added, "if indiscernibility obtains we will no longer have one thing apparent and the other non-evident."

Notes

1. The evident fact that both of these previous assessments were written by women who are themselves productive in the field underlines a fact worth pointing out, if parenthetically: that the global—including American—semiotics enterprise, prior to the late 1960s, was shockingly barren of female participation. Steiner's and Kevelson's articles too are bereft of references to women.

Still, this baleful situation has radically changed and continues to improve in several important ways. To adduce only two examples: both of the initial assistant editors of *Semiotica*, edited in the United States from the beginning (1969–), were prominent women scholars, Josette Rey-Debove and Julia Kristeva. Three of the presidents thus far of the Semiotic Society of America, founded in 1976, are well-known women professors, namely Irmengard Rauch, Naomi Baron, and Bennetta Jules-Rosette.

While women now populate much of the semiotic prospect, the virtually total absence of black faces from and contributions to meetings and publications, here as well as in Europe, remains odious.

2. Another case in point: two participants in the Bloomington conference (1962) later became presidents of the Semiotic Society of America, established fourteen years afterward; four of them of the Linguistic Society of America; and two of them of the Modern Language Association.

3. In a more detailed survey, I would want to take account at least of Grinker (1956) and of two series of conference proceedings, both sponsored by the Josiah Macy, Jr., Foundation: ten volumes on Cybernetics (ended in 1955), and four on Group Processes (ended in 1959).

4. Before leaving this section on linguists, let me add that four presidents of the Semiotic Society of America since its founding in 1976 were professional linguists, and one—Henry Hiż—came close (in order of service: Hiż, Allen Walker Read, Irmengard Rauch, myself, and Naomi Baron).

5. Once more, for the organizational record: three of the thirteen presidents thus far of the Semiotic Society of America can be reckoned literary semioticians (Thomas G. Winner, Michael Riffaterre, and Jonathan Culler).

6. Let it be avouched up front that the glaring omission of Jacques Maritain from the *Encyclopedic Dictionary of Semiotics* was in no way due to editorial negligence but to the last-minute dereliction of the would-be author of the entry. Luckily, this embarrassing gap has now in part been filled by Deely's paper, "Semiotic in the Thought of Jacques Maritain" (1986).

7. Shands was also the sixth person, and the first physician, to be elected president of the Semiotic Society of America, but he died two months after assuming office.

8. A distinguished folklorist, Richard Bauman, was president of the Semiotic Society in 1981.

9. Notoriously and ruinously, semioticians—or, in Rauch's rendering, "semiotists" (e.g., 1987)—have not yet reached unanimity as to their self-designation or the name of their field of endeavor. Thus, dedicated Peirceans

proudly identify their totem group by their unyielding use of *semeiotic*; Fisch (1986:322) even stresses that Peirce "never" used *semiotics*, although he evidently did compose that very lemma *sub voce* in the *Century Dictionary* (Whitney: pt. 19, p. 5, 486). Morris consistently used *semiotic* but permitted the publication of his collected writings on the theory of signs in a series titled *Approaches to Semiotics* (see my terminological note to Morris 1971:9–10). In like manner, Saussureans generally display their colors under the banner (when in English) of *semiology*, even though the master's better-suited, although for obscure reasons unsuccessful, coinage *signology* (Engler 1968:46) was also available (cf. Lady Welby's *significs*; for other *signum*-derived words, see Sebeok 1987a). No matter how leaky these instances of academic jargon may be, the denotation of each is the "same." But each harks back to a different tradition and, being overburdened by complex emotional resonance, carries different connotations. Dialectal divisions of this nature are, of course, confusing for the public and have impelled some practitioners to concoct (even as recently as in Landowski 1988:79–80), and then attempt to impose, *post hoc* divergences in denotation. *Semiotics*, with its foreign-language cognates, now appears to have the best chance for survival (see further Sebeok 1985b: chap. 2). (It is interesting that Jonathan Culler [1986: chap. 4], for example, heads the section of his book that deals with Saussure's *semiology*: "Semiotics: The Saussurean Legacy.")

10. Although there is no substitute for reading Peirce's original texts, there now exist several excellent accounts of Peirce's doctrine of signs, or major aspects of it, among which I would single out four from North America: Savan (1976), Short (1982 and 1988), and Ransdell (1986); for the beginner, Sebeok and Umiker-Sebeok (1980b) might in addition be helpful (and see also Sebeok 1981a, 1985b, 1986d, and 1989b).

11. Donald Preziosi, a linguistically adept archaeologist, was president of the Semiotic Society in 1985.

12. At this writing a colloquium on "The Body and Clothing as Communication" is being planned for ISISSS '89 (the International Summer Institute for Structural and Semiotic Studies, Indiana University—Indianapolis).

13. The *American Journal of Semiotics* devoted an entire issue (vol. 5, no. 2, 1987) to "Semiotics and Education," highlighting recent trends in this area in the United States.

14. Regional or local organizations have sprung up here and there. The largest among these is the Semiotic Circle of California, which had its third meeting in 1988.

The Fifth Congress of the International Association for Semiotic Studies is scheduled to be held in the United States in June 1994, to be hosted by the University of California at Berkeley.

15. For the best treatment known to me of both the explanatory and the nonexplanatory functions of models in biological theory, see Beckner 1959: chap. 3. Among those models particularly pertinent to semiotics, compare his discussions of the evolutionary model associated with the names of McCulloch

and Pitts, and of the feedback models of W. R. Ashby and the cyberneticists. On the uses of biological models in semiotics, see Sebeok 1986d: chap. 3, and on models more generally, see chap. 6 below.

16. Craik never mentions either Peirce or Uexküll, but he knew at least the 1923 version of *The Meaning of Meaning*, and, oddly, mentions Mrs. Ladd-Franklin (Craik 1967:108).

17. I intend to pursue this fascinating comparison elsewhere.

From Peirce (via Morris and Jakobson) to Sebeok:
Interview with Thomas A. Sebeok

by Susan Petrilli

Q: What are the main factors that contributed to your intellectual formation?

Sebeok: My most autobiographical piece is the essay called "Vital Signs" [see chapter 2], which you are in the middle of translating into Italian and which tells how I came to semiotics. In other words, first through Ogden and Richards, then through Charles Morris, and then, of course, the main influence in my life was Roman Jakobson. It was, in fact, through Morris on the one hand and through Jakobson on the other that I came back to Peirce.

Q: When did you meet Jakobson?

Sebeok: I met Jakobson in August 1941 in the house of Franz Boas in New Jersey, and, of course, it was love at first sight. I became his first American student, and I wrote my Ph.D. dissertation essentially

This interview, held in English, took place in Urbino, Italy, on July 21, 1987, where Thomas Sebeok gave a series of lectures from July 20–23 at the Centro Internazionale di Semiotica e Linguistica. Susan Petrilli originally translated the interview into Italian and published it under the title "Da Peirce (via Morris e Jakobson) a Sebeok: I segni di un percorso" (*Idee* 2, no. 5/6 [1987]:123–132). We thank her for permission to publish this interview for the first time in English. Petrilli is the translator of Sebeok 1989b [1979], *Il Segno e i suoi maestri* (Bari: Adriatica, 1985) and Sebeok 1986, *Penso di essere un verbo* (Palermo: Sellerio, 1989). She has also edited and translated into Italian the work of Charles S. Peirce, Victoria Lady Welby, Charles Morris, and (into English) Giorgio Fano and Gérard Deledalle.

under his influence. I kept in touch with him throughout his life. He was my friend until the day he died.

Q: How is it that while the general tendency in the United States is to shift from one university to another, you have spent your whole academic career at Indiana University in Bloomington?
Sebeok: I'm a very exceptional person at Indiana because most Americans go from one university to another throughout their lives. I have stayed in the same university for forty-five years, a very long tenure. Indiana University created a center for me [the Research Center for Language and Semiotic Studies], of which I have been chairman since 1956. It's a very long time, thirty-one years, during which I've had Indiana as my headquarters.

Q: In the United States do people migrate from one university to another by choice?
Sebeok: In America, normally people migrate not entirely out of choice but to get a promotion or financial advantage. You are teaching in one place and another invites you. But in my case my university has been good to me and I never saw any reason to leave. I've always been very happy in Bloomington. My entire teaching career has been there and at the same time, as you will see from my vita, I've been teaching in very many places while traveling.

Q: What relations do you have with Italy? How did your first contacts begin?
Sebeok: I went through gymnasium (high school) in Hungary. There, at least from the fifth year onward, I had to study a third foreign language. Latin and German were compulsory, and I chose Italian as my third language. As a matter of fact, I will say this for the first time for the record: I did so well in Italian that one day I received a medal from Mussolini. It was brought to me by the Italian ambassador to Budapest, who later became a professor here in Italy. And when I met him many years later, I said to him, "Do you remember giving me a medal from Mussolini?" He said, "Ssshhh!" So my Italian contacts began then. Even earlier my father owned a villa in Abbazia or Opatija, which is now in Yugoslavia. So I know the Trieste region very well. I used to spend every summer in Abbazia

together with my father, my mother, and so on. My Italian contacts go very far back.

Q: And what about your contacts at the intellectual level?
Sebeok: My intellectual contacts with Italy began through linguistics; I'm a linguist by training and I know a lot of Italian linguists fairly well. And of course I've been a friend of Umberto Eco for at least twenty years. I met Ferruccio Rossi-Landi much later—I can't remember the year exactly. In any case, Rossi-Landi and I became very good friends. I've also known Cesare Segre for a long time and quite love him. Then there's Gianfranco Bettettini and others....

Q: Is it possible to reconcile Charles Morris's behaviorism to his science of signs? We know today about the crisis of American behaviorism, especially that which concerns language, through Noam Chomsky's own criticism of it. However, Morris's semiotics continues to be important at the level of epistemology. How can we explain the continued validity of Morris's semiotics despite its connection with behaviorism?
Sebeok: I'm interested in this question, which is actually quite a long story. I met Morris in 1936 at the University of Chicago. He was an extremely nice man, one of the nicest human beings I've ever met. He was a Zen Buddhist, just a man of extreme kindness. I think I'm one of his two or three living students.

Q: Who are the others?
Sebeok: So far as I know, there are only two living students. One is the mathematician Martin Gardner. He went off in mathematics but was in Morris's seminar in semiotics the year before I was. In the next year I was in the seminar. Everybody else from that year is dead now. The year after there was the great musicologist Leonard Meyer. So I think that Martin and Leonard and I are the only living people who studied with Morris at Chicago. You see, Morris was the very first person in America, and, so far as I know, anywhere, to teach a course actually in semiotics. It was called Seminar. He repeated it two or three times. And then he left Chicago and went to Florida and never taught semiotics again. There are other students of Morris but not in semiotics.

Now, in 1938, Morris wrote his brilliant monograph on semiotics, which had nothing to do with psychology. Subsequently, between 1938 and 1946, he discovered behaviorist psychology; I always felt that this was a great mistake. I think he made two mistakes: the first was to align semiotics with psychology. I felt that this was irrelevant. Second, he made the mistake of aligning himself with a particular kind of psychology, which at that time was of course very hot, behaviorist psychology, in particular of the kind practiced by people like Clark L. Hull and Edward C. Tolman. He also became very friendly with a man called C. E. Osgood, with whom I once wrote a book myself [Osgood and Sebeok 1965 (1934)]. Often I would say to Morris, "I loved your 1938 book and I think it was much more important and much better than your 1946 book." He was a very nice man and always said: "Well, you're entitled to your opinion. I don't agree with you; I think the 1946 book is very important because, precisely, it aligns you with psychology." Now, your question stated that behaviorism has essentially declined. I will add that it has declined in a way that has ruined Morris's book too, because behaviorist psychology simply doesn't work, and so Morris's semiotics of that time simply doesn't work.

I want to point out an interesting parallel to this in semiotics. Ray Birdwhistell invented something called kinesics which is a kind of method for analyzing nonverbal gestures. It's interesting to see that Birdwhistell made an absolutely parallel error. He said that all nonverbal behavior is organized like language, and that therefore the method of analysis of gestures must be based on linguistic work. Not only is this absolutely unmotivated—there's no reason to think that nonverbal behavior is organized like verbal behavior—but Birdwhistell also made a second mistake. He aligned himself with a rather old-fashioned linguistics, one which was very behavioristic and no longer works. It was called the "Smith-Trager model." Nobody in modern times has ever heard about it. The Smith-Trager model of syntax was totally displaced by other modern models. Birdwhistell, in effect, has coded thousands of pieces of photographs and drawings and so on, that can no longer be used because the model is dead. The same thing happened with Morris, you see. He described semiotics in terms of a behaviorist framework, and since that behaviorist framework disappeared, so did that book. In my opinion, it is not worth much any more. However, I must say that not everybody agrees: Roland Posner, for example, thinks very well of that book.

But I think it is no longer interesting. Besides, there's another thing. The more Peirce is discovered, the more Morris falls into obscurity—except for his 1938 book, which, as I've said, is very good.

Q: From semiotics centered upon human society there has been a development in the direction of zoosemiotics: what is the role today of zoosemiotics in the field of the human sciences?

Sebeok: It's clear that semiotics has two aspects: the study of the verbal (that is, linguistics) and the study of the nonverbal. However, what most semioticians untrained in biology don't understand is that semiotics of the nonverbal is an enormous field that includes not only human nonverbal behavior, which is about 99 percent of what human beings do, but also an entire vast world of millions of animals. In addition, it includes plant semiosis and other kinds of semiosis, such as those occurring inside the body—for example, the genetic code, the immunological code, and other internal mechanisms. So, just in sheer quantity, nonverbal semiosis overwhelms the verbal. However, the verbal, of course, is of very great importance for this little corner of the globe that human beings occupy and operate in. So, in that sense, I would say that a complete semiotician has to study both verbal and nonverbal semiosis. It is simply not possible to restrict one's semiotic interest to humans without neglecting 99 percent of the world. Ninety-nine percent of nature, I feel, consists of things other than human.

Q: In your book *I Think I Am a Verb* [1986d], as throughout the rest of your scientific production, you speak of continuity between the animal world and human beings.

Sebeok: Well, of course there's a continuity in the sense that there's evolution. Human beings are a product of evolution, and the genus *Homo* has invented this very interesting code, the verbal code, but this exists only in the genus *Homo* and the few species that the genus *Homo* comprehends. Of course there's continuity because all the world is connected.

Q: At the level of interpersonal communication, use of the verbal characterizes hominids, whereas the nonverbal...?
Sebeok: The nonverbal, I'd say, is the criterion of life. All life functions with nonverbal signs. Human life functions with two kinds of signs, nonverbal and verbal.

Q: We could say that nowadays there is a return to the semiotics of Charles Sanders Peirce. What relation can we establish between Peirce's semiotics and René Thom's catastrophe theory?
Sebeok: It's very interesting to discover, if you read anything by Thom, that he quotes very few people. And as I recall, other than technical mathematicians, he quotes really only three people: Heraclitus, the ancient Greek philosopher, Peirce, and Jakob von Uexküll. So, René Thom has read Peirce; he is very much aware of Peirce, and he has reanalyzed some of the basic concepts of Peirce, including the so-called icon-index-symbol relationship in terms of catastrophe theory. I would say that catastrophe theory, in a way, grew out of Peircean semiotics. After all, Peirce was a great mathematician. As a matter of fact, he specialized in the same kind of mathematics Thom specializes in, that is, in topology. Thom published an article [1980] in *Semiotica*, an extended commentary on Peirce, which is not usually included in his collected papers. So René Thom is extremely sophisticated, and his work is in a way a further development of Peirce, as I said in *The Sign and Its Masters* [Sebeok 1989b].

Q: Do you think we could speak of a development in informatics at the technological level, on the one hand, and, on the other hand, of stagnation at the level of artificial intelligence, which also concerns language (language learning and teaching, translation, etc.)?
Sebeok: That's a matter of opinion! You know there's a new book on this subject by James R. Beniger (1986), who describes what he calls the "information society." Peirce and semiotics play a part in this book, which is then carried forward to modern informatics, artificial intelligence, computers, and so on. It is a very authoritative and interesting book that I recommend highly. However, I would like to add one more thing. In the future one can expect more and more conversions between human beings and machines. There's a

whole new field that produces organisms called *cyborgs*, that is to say, animals enhanced by machine parts. For example, genetic engineering is largely based on the combination of mechanical devices with living creatures. I think eventually one can look forward to a new form of evolution that will produce these organisms that are half organic and half machine. This is a utopian concept, but I think it's coming. For example, think of a person with an artificial heart, an artificial limb, and so on. This kind of evolution will continue, so eventually there will be these curious, half-organic, half-inorganic things. Human intelligence in general is already enormously enhanced by computers. You can do with computers what you could never do before, if not in quality, then certainly in speed, but also I think in quality. It is only a matter of a few years before computers, satellites, and other robots—in other words, robotics—will no longer be a separate thing, but combined with organic processes. I think that is the way the future works.

Q: What do you think of theories that explain the origin of verbal language by presupposing a gestural language?
Sebeok: Well, I've written a paper on that called "The Origin of Language" (Sebeok 1986f). The heart of the argument is—and I think this also explains why research in this field has become stalled— that one has to make a sharp distinction between language, on the one hand, and speech, on the other. As long as language and speech are confused, there can be no progress. My argument is that language appeared approximately two and a half million years ago in a sequence that paleontologists call *Homo*. The first known species to appear is called *Homo habilis*. Brain development continued through *Homo erectus* and so on—it was an evolutionary adaptation. But language must not be thought of as a communicative device; this is a fatal mistake. Language is a modeling device. All animals have mental models or mental representations of the world. Language is also a modeling device, a mental representation of the world which, however, is different from all the animal models in that it has a feature that linguists call syntax.

Now, with syntax human beings are able to disassemble the model as if it were made of Lego building blocks. You can reassemble them in an infinite number of ways. With syntax you can take sentences apart and hook them together in different ways. And just because humans have this ability they can produce not only worlds in the way in which animals produce them, but they can produce possible worlds, which is always the argument of Gottfried Wilhelm von Leibniz. Leibniz said that there are infinite numbers of possible worlds. So with this kind of syntactic model you can produce an infinite number of parts: every historian makes a past, which is just a model; you can imagine a future, like science fiction—you can imagine any number of science fictions; you can make scientific theories; you can create lyric poetry; you can imagine death; you can talk about unicorns, which only human beings can do. Now, having evolved this interesting modeling mechanism, *Homo sapiens* emerged two million years later (which is very recently, about 400,000 years ago). Around that time it became possible to externalize language and to put it in the linear form we call speech. At that point—and this is not *adaptation* but *exaptation* (cf. pp. 183–84 in this book)—when language was externalizable as speech, it became also a device for communication, and this device enhanced the nonverbal capabilities that humans already had. We can also express ourselves nonverbally by our faces, our eyes, our hands, body posture, and many other ways. Now, we are able to do two things: nonverbal and verbal. But this became possible only when language turned into speech and that, I think, is a very recent development of about 500,000 years ago. That's the argument of my article.

Q: So language is, if anything, the potential capacity of speech.
Sebeok: Speech presupposes language, but language does not necessarily imply speech. There are many creatures that have language but no speech.

Q: In language learning theories, the role of the icon has often, I think, been overlooked. How important is the icon, not only in language learning theories but also in robotics and, therefore, in models of artificial intelligence constructed on the basis of theories of language learning?
Sebeok: Yes, this is not absolutely true. There was a conference held at Stanford University in the 1960s on models. Chomsky was one of the principal speakers. Everything becomes quite clear when you

look at what a model is: a model is an *analogy*. It's a miniature, as it were, a mental representation of something. Now, a model is presumably linked to the thing it represents by analogy, by similarity. Consequently a model can be defined as a sign with a very heavy iconic value. For the model to work, it has to have some similarity to the object it represents; how much similarity is another question. It's possible to have very little similarity: for example, the mathematical formula $A + B = C$ is the icon of a relationship, and the A, B, and C can stand for almost anything. There is not necessarily similarity, but there has to be an analogy between the formula and what the formula stands for.

Similarly, language in some sense models the universe and has to have, therefore, an iconic relationship to the universe. Now, as Jakobson wrote in a famous article called "Quest for the Essence of Language," which appeared originally in a journal called *Diogenes* (1965), there are cases when language is very iconic. For instance, Jakobson's example is that Julius Caesar said, "*Veni, vidi, vici,*" instead of "*Vici, vidi, veni,*" because the former is an iconic representation of what Caesar really did. First he came, then he saw what had to be seen, and then he conquered. He couldn't say it in the opposite order because that would have been nonsensical. So this sentence is very iconic. And, for example, if I ask you, "How do you get from Urbino to Bari?", you will obviously say that you go here, and here, etc. If I write down what you say and look at the map of what you have described, it will be an iconic representation of the relationship of Urbino and Bari. It would be completely crazy if you give it backward or sideways: the description has to be iconic or else it would be very confusing or a joke. So there are some highly iconic linguistic situations. Paolo Valesio offers us some examples on a sound level, a phonological level. Other linguistic representations are iconic but not so obviously. Jakobson's other example is the comparative degree, as in the case of big, bigger, biggest. Jakobson's point is that as you go from the big to the comparative bigger to the superlative biggest, the forms become longer or at least not shorter. So the intensity of the comparison is reflected in the number of phonemes.

Q: My last question is the following. Peirce makes a distinction between three genres of similarity: graphs, metaphors, and images. On the other hand, I don't think he makes a distinction between the different types of similarity. For example, Ferruccio Rossi-Landi distinguishes three: analogy, isomorphism, and homology, which may be indifferently represented through images as much as through metaphors or graphs. Once we say that the icon and, therefore, similarity play a fundamental role in the development of language as well as in the development of knowledge, we perhaps need to ask ourselves whether we should specify the type of similarity we are dealing with. Why is it, for example, that for Rossi-Landi similarity as analogy or as isomorphism does not contribute to the development of knowledge but, instead, to assimilation, and consequently to the loss of diversity and alterity between objects being compared? If anything, it is instead similarity as homology, which does not compare individual things but models, determining abstractions, that plays a role in the development of knowledge.

Sebeok: Well, of course you're right. Peirce said that there were three kinds of icons, or *hypoicons* as he called them: *visual images* (and most people have jumped to the conclusion that that's the only kind of icon there is, but of course that's incorrect); *graphs*, which play a very large role in Peirce and in his theory of "existential graphs," a mathematical theory elaborated by Peirce that is enormously important and a very powerful tool in mathematics; and *metaphor*, only mentioned by Peirce—he never did anything with it. Now, since Peirce there has been an enormous amount of literature on different kinds of icons and on what iconicity means, with no conclusive statement. I think it was developed in a very interesting manner by René Thom, and, of course, I've written about iconicity—so has Eco. I think Rossi-Landi simplifies things a little. In my opinion there are not only three kinds of icons but many others. For instance, Eco has written on the mirror, the mirror image. What kind of icon, if at all, is a mirror image? And there are other notions, for example, not only isomorphism, but twins. Let's take a look at yet another case: if you have a million black Volkswagens, what is the relation between one Volkswagen and the other Volkswagen? If you look at a forest of Volkswagens, you cannot tell which is an icon of which. What is the icon, what is the original? Of course you can say, as some people do, that the original is the blueprint of the mathematical formula that is in the machine that produces all the Volkswagens, and all the Volkswagens are icons of this abstract mathematical engineering formula. Rossi-Landi is correct in pointing out the complexity and that there are many kinds of icons that may have had quite different influences on the mind. But, as I see it, there are not only three kinds of icons; there are many more. Of course, the one that seems to interest people obsessively is the metaphor. Every day a new book comes out on the metaphor, most recently by an American called George Lakoff [1987]. There's also an excellent book by Paul Ricoeur (1978). So metaphor, which is a kind of super-icon, seems to be of great interest to people. But I think it's only one kind of icon.

CHAPTER TWO

Vital Signs

When a physician sets out to evaluate a somatic system, he relies on established procedures drawn from accumulated biomedical knowledge—his personal long-term memory store, supplemented, when necessary, by a literature search—which leads to the formulation of hypotheses that become progressively narrowed with increasing specificity. "Abduction," said Charles Sanders Peirce, "makes its start from facts, without, at the outset, having any particular theory in view, though it is motivated by the feeling that a theory is needed to explain the surprising facts....The mode of suggestion by which, in abduction, the facts suggest the hypothesis is by resemblance—the *resemblance* of the facts to the consequences of the hypothesis" (1931–66:7.128; see further Sebeok and Umiker-Sebeok, in Eco and Sebeok 1983:18–19 and passim). The generation of clinical hypotheses is based on cues (Elstein et al. 1978:279–280) or on the use of indicators of disease (Fabrega 1980:125), or, more exactly, on a Gestalt-yielding composite of reported (subjective) symptoms and observed (objective) signs—in a word, diagnosis. Faced at the start with an ill-defined problem, the physician progresses toward a solution by selective cue acquisition, according to a plan—delineated by Hippocrates and Galen—that facilitates and will perhaps result in the identification of a certain state of affairs in terms of a set of coherent defining characteristics. Since this abductive operation, which is a facet of memory organization and retrieval, is but poorly understood, it is hardly surprising that even experienced physicians will differ in style and substance as to their inferential ability and so sometimes construct dramatically dissimilar prognos-

---

A slightly revised version of the presidential address to the Semiotic Society of America, delivered to the Ninth Annual Meeting in Bloomington, Indiana, on October 12, 1984. The address was originally published in the *American Journal of Semiotics* 3 (1985):1–27, and reprinted in Sebeok 1986d.

tic models.

When a patient initially encounters a licensed physician (or surrogate medical technician functioning under a physician's authority or direction), a so-called "general survey" ensues. This rapid scan of the subject's apparent state of health, summed up from an array of verbal and nonverbal signs that are transmitted mainly via the auditory, optical, tactile, and olfactory channels, is followed by a compulsory registration of three or four factors which, together, are called *vital signs* (or merely, as nominalized attribute, *vitals*): the pulse rate, respiration, and blood pressure, with temperature being frequently added. The accurate recording of these values provides indispensable, integrated data for the abductive sequence and continual heuristic evaluation supervening. (For the assessment of vital signs, particularly suited tools have even been designed and are wontedly kept handy: the stethoscope, the sphygmomanometer, and the thermometer; see Barber and Dillman 1981: chap. 9.)

In Peirce's pragmatism, what I am is what I do, and what I do is tantamount to what I signify. This is clearly the implication of his famous dictum, "Man is an external sign," or, as he amplified, "My language is the sum total of myself" (5.314; cf. Sebeok 1989b:61–73). Transmuted into Peirce's nomenclature, a vital sign—namely, its recorded value—must be indexical, "by virtue of being really affected" by the object denoted, and because it is actually modified by the object in some respects (2.248). "The value of an index is that it assures us of positive fact" (4.448). Or, as René Thom (1983:267) later put it, with a Gallic touch, "the index is always an actant which is, or has been, in contact with its object, if it is not actually a part of it." Finally, as Roman Jakobson (1971b:347) noted (interchanging "symptom" with "sign"), "the acceleration of pulse as a probable symptom of fever is, in Peirce's view, an index, and in such cases his semiotic actually merges with the medical inquiry into the symptoms of diseases."

A human body is thus an inextricably complex text that has been encoded and determined by the combined action of nature and nurture (or that minuscule segment of nature some anthropologists grandly compartmentalize as culture). This text may at once be utilized and referred to. It perdures through life by unremittingly giving off streams of signs, among them, imperatively, the vitals.

Any elucidating interpretation of a consecution of such signs comprises a message referring to a code; it is therefore a duplex overlapping structure, which, as Jakobson (1971b:65–70), pointed out, is cast in the autonymous mode. Maurice Merleau-Ponty (1964:65–70), in a brilliant disquisition on signs (which deserves to be better known than it seems to be), elevated the level of discourse by telling us to see the term "body" as designating

> a system of systems devoted to the inspection of a world and capable of leaping over distances, piercing into the perceptual future, and outlining hollows and reliefs, distances and deviations—a meaning—in the inconceivable flatness of being.... Already in its pointing gestures [viz., indexical signs] the body not only flows over into a world whose schema it bears in itself but possesses this world at a distance rather than being possessed by it...the primary operation which first constitutes signs as signs, makes that which is expressed dwell in them through the eloquence of their arrangement and configuration alone, implants a meaning in that which did not have one, and thus—far from exhausting itself in the instant at which it occurs—inaugurates an order and founds an institution or a tradition. [p. 67]

The fall of 1984 marked my forty-first year at Indiana University, and nearly the span of my entire career in scholarship as well. Over these four decades and more, I have delivered countless lectures and seminars on a variety of academic topics, which, since the early 1960s, have tended to cumulate with an upsurge in semiotics rather than, as formerly, in linguistics as such or elsewhere at its periphery. Accordingly, I feel that I have earned the *appanage*—which, having "bread" at its etymological core, is a natural accompaniment to any banquet such as ours, and which surely harks back at least to a Socratic feast held in Athens in the year 416 B.C., where the conversation centered on the vital signs of life and love, and is therefore still remembered—as the president of an American learned society to preempt this perhaps only remaining opportunity to indulge in personal reminiscences, comment on the institutionalization of our common cardinal concerns, and then to prognosticate about the direction in which we may be headed. It remains to be seen whether your response to me will be the same as that of Phaedrus the Myrrhinusian, at the symposium in the House of Agathon, to Eryximachus the physician: "I always do what you advise, and especially what you prescribe as a physician...and the rest of the company, if they are wise, will do the same."

An abiding responsibility of a physician is to validate his professional credentials—you find appropriately reassuring documentation to this effect hanging on the walls of most consulting rooms.
Props such as certificates help set the stage, define the situation, or,
in Paul Bouissac's (1976:190) happy phrase, provide "the semiotic
key" to the interaction to follow. Highlights of my intellectual
genealogy might help convince my captive audience that I am experienced and, conceivably, an "authority." The keying should elicit
your collective reaction not to my message as such, but to the
message as encoded in terms of your traditions, including expectations and attitudes you yourself have brought with you to this
dinner. The role of the receiver (listener or reader), in what nowadays might be dubbed a cognitive framework, was foreseen by
Peirce and substantially fleshed out afresh by Umberto Eco (1979,
especially chap. 7).

My first fumbling outreach toward the theory of signs, and of
their influence upon human life and thought in numberless unexpected ways, dates from 1936, the year that I encountered the fourth
edition of *The Meaning of Meaning* (Ogden and Richards 1938),
that flawed patchwork of a masterpiece of which Charles Morris
(1971:337) was to pronounce a decade afterward that it continued
the development of the British empiricist line of analysis of signification "in terms of a psychology which progressively became indi-
vidualistic and sensationalistic." The work of C. K. Ogden and I. A.
Richards has also been called "as seminal as the *Origin of
Species*....Ogden and Richards were concerned to give shape to the
pattern of thought, to chart the psychological and the metaphysical,
which is like navigating without a compass. Their achievement was
to construct a compass. It was imperfect and in many ways crude,
but it was a compass" (Anderson, in Florence and Anderson
1977:238). Many Cambridge undergraduates of that period, certainly, devoured and debated this book; as a compass it served to point
me in several directions at once, but, to begin with, toward Ivor
Richards himself. This self-declared materialist and neo-Benthamite
was, at the time, the most eminent Fellow of Magdalene College,
where I was sent up for 1936–37 as an unripe undergraduate, and
where I sought out the Guru of Cambridge—I think the epithet was

coined by Basil Willey, of Pembroke—at the Pepysian Library. Richards's explosive semantic energy—his vitality—and his eventual development of new critical devices that he later came to call "speculative instruments," subtly influenced my views of linguistic instability and diversity and focused my interest on the controls exerted upon meaning by context—the very themes Richards was to dwell on in one of his several wise contributions to the 1958 Conference on Style, held at Indiana University and sponsored by the Social Science Research Council's Committee on Linguistics and Psychology (Sebeok 1960:241–252). (During the week of the conference he was our guest in Bloomington, and the two of us regenerated our acquaintanceship of more than twenty years.[1])

My critical interests, during the intervening decades and after, took a radically different turn, as I have summed up elsewhere (Sebeok 1974a). I might enlarge on them here, however, by quoting from an autobiographical fragment by one of the acutest and most accessible teachers of criticism and literary history, at the University of Chicago, that I was ever inspired by, the Scotsman David Daiches (1971:35–36):

> I liked my Chicago students and made friends with many of them. Some are now distinguished professors, a fact which can cause me embarrassment as well as pride. In 1957 I was lecturing at Indiana University and there met Thomas Sebeok, the linguist, who as a mature graduate student, refugee from Europe, had attended my classes at Chicago. He is older than I am, and as he has grown older acquired an air of venerable wisdom which I have never been able to achieve. Professor Sebeok seized my arm at the party when I appeared and proceeded to introduce me to a number of people with the formula, 'I'd like you to meet my old teacher.' People turned expecting to meet a wizened old man: I was in fact forty-four at the time. When they saw me, they concluded that this was some esoteric joke of Sebeok's and it proved difficult to explain that he was in a sense telling the truth.

I opt to cite this passage less to round out my portrait of the semiotician as a young man than to supply one more illustration of the devious workings of the Clever Hans effect upon the mind's recall; not only was I not "a mature graduate student" at the time but a struggling junior, and the actuarial fact is that I was born in 1920, Professor Daiches in 1912!

I gained my first ghostly glimpse of Peirce from a generous summary of his account of signs reprinted in appendix D of *The Meaning of Meaning* (Ogden and Richards 1938), where it was reproduced "by the kindness of Sir Charles Welby," (p. 279) who, together with his wife, Victoria, seems to have been friendly with the ubiquitous polymath C. K. Ogden. I never met this remarkably erudite, eccentric man, but became responsible, in 1967, for the reprinting of his astonishingly prescient essay, *Opposition*, with a newly commissioned introduction by his erstwhile collaborator I. A. Richards.

Another figure I first encountered through the pages of *The Meaning of Meaning* was Bronislaw Malinowski, lately come back, exhausted, from the Trobriand Islands. "After our first four hours of discussing Theory of Signs and the fundamentals of Reference," with Ogden, Richards reported (Florence and Anderson 1977:104), Malinowski suddenly announced that he had to rest. "Had Ogden a sofa available: and some high quality pornography? He needed to quieten his mind"—an affection for which I have a lot of fellow feeling! Nowadays, Malinowski is seldom discussed in a semiotic ambiance, although the second volume of his *Coral Gardens and Their Magic* was, in my view, a major effort at a synthesis of verbal and nonverbal encounters; as he wrote in 1935, "Please remember that the integral role of gesture in speech is quite as important to the understanding of an utterance as the one or two significant movements of indications [read 'indexical signs'] which replace an uttered word" (Malinowski 1965:26; cf. Sebeok 1989b:50). Malinowski's kinship with George Herbert Mead, and especially with John Dewey's concept of experience and nature—the distinguishing characteristics of which are to be located in the type of language and communication that humans have developed—is worthy of note, and surely merits further explication beyond the well-known attempts of J. R. Firth, Meyer Fortes, and Edmund Leach (in Raymond Firth 1957; cf. Malinowski 1965: vol. 2, pp. 59–60, n. 1). Let me just add that I was sufficiently aroused by this rare but seminal work, in the early 1960s, to borrow Fred Eggan's copy, and to insist that it be reprinted in my (now defunct) series, the Indiana University Studies in the History and Theory of Linguistics (published by Indiana University Press).

I have, on occasion, remarked that the real influence of *The Meaning of Meaning* lay less in the text than in the five appendices and the two supplements (which altogether occupy almost a third of the volume). It was supplement 2, written by a physician, which—as I look back half a century—decisively influenced my perduring perception of semiotics in its multiform relationships to the art of medicine; more broadly, to the life science; and more widely by far, to the science of nature. I shall return to this *idée fixe* presently.

In the late 1930s, at the University of Chicago, Charles Morris began to offer a series of seminars devoted to the theory of signs, which must have been the very first sequence of courses in semiotics, so labeled, in any curriculum anywhere. Martin Gardner participated in the first (Sebeok 1978c), and I in the second, along with the late Walter Pitts, who, even in his teens (he was about fourteen years old at the time), was a scintillating mathematician and delightful oddball. After each seminar, Pitts and I fell into the habit of going out for coffee to discuss Morris's colloquia and a stream of oddments. I clearly recall what Pitts once told me: "Semiotics, you see, according to Morris, is, like Gaul, divided into three parts." "Go on," I prompted. "That's all there is to it," he sighed, and soon afterward left Chicago (where "I had nothing more to teach the faculty!") for MIT. There, he began to collaborate with Warren S. McCulloch on several epochal papers, which remain, to this day, of pivotal consequence for general semiotics.

At this point, I should confess that although I have collaborated, in sundry ways, with a dozen or so prominent psychologists of my generation—Roger Brown, John B. Carroll, Paul Ekman, James J. Jenkins, George F. Mahl, George A. Miller, Robert Rosenthal, Charles E. Osgood (and became, in fact, in 1954, coeditor and coauthor of *Psycholinguistics* with the last)—I had audited only a single formal course in that subject during all my graduate years, but that with no less a personage than B. F. Skinner. He became a visiting professor at the University of Chicago in the summer of 1940, where he gave an early version of his later-to-become-famous—or infamous—William James Lectures, delivered at Harvard University, on verbal behavior. Chomsky and Jakobson intensely disliked his eventual book, and I was amused to read of my own reaction, as reported in Skinner's autobiography (1979:249), to the Chicago lectures:

I had plenty of material on literature and language, but for the first time I ran into criticism. When I said that a word that is only slowly recalled is pronounced more forcefully the longer the delay, two of my students measured the latency and loudness of responses to a list of questions and found that their subjects did not speak more loudly when it took them longer to answer. I should have specified the contingencies more accurately. It is only in a conversational setting, where a listener is waiting and one must say something, that a longer pause builds up more aversive situations from which one is more strongly moved to escape. An auditor in my course on language was Thomas A. Sebeok, already an accomplished linguist, and I had to watch myself when I strayed into that field, which was not close to my own. Tom arranged for me to speak to the Linguistics Club.

The researches of Robert Rosenthal must be singled out here. His ever-escalating discoveries concerning the Pygmalion effect and its obverse, the Golem effect, have such blood-and-guts implications for each of us that it is bewildering to me why a legion of inquirers fails to labor at this inordinately fecund interface between our field and experimental psychology at its most exciting. By "exciting," I wish here to suggest the palpable, or at least plausible, impingement and spillover from psychology into neuroendocrinology. It is precisely in the dynamism of the brain and the self-organizing properties of neural networks, driven, as they are, by experience throughout life, where the next and perhaps final frontier of semiotic inquest will find its be-all-and-end-all resolution (Sebeok and Rosenthal 1981:199–205).

· In the 1970s, I was overcome by a regrettable terminological exuberance, and began to wallow in a tumult of neologisms, among them the cheerfully anticipative coinage *psychosemiotics* (Sebeok 1985b:141; Sebeok 1989b:260), given currency by I. M. Ullman (1975) and others. The truth is that I don't really know what this portentous word means, save that it smacks of contentious reductionism. There is a difference, after all, between *psychosemiotics* and semiotics informed by psychology. This notwithstanding, since the heady years of *Psycholinguistics*, my interest in human psychology has steadily eroded, with, to be sure, notable areas of exception—see my work on Karl Bühler (Sebeok 1981b: chap. 5), Martin Krampen's (1981a) on Jean Piaget, and, of course, the monumental achievement of Jerome S. Bruner and his students in this country and of L. S. Vygotsky and A. R. Luria in the Soviet Union, to identify but a few relevant pacesetters. Recent work in animal psychology, especially as concerns the semiotic comportment of certain mammals, has proved so calamitously flawed (see Sebeok 1989b: chap. 5; Sebeok 1981b: chaps. 7–8) that research in that bailiwick is likely to stay moribund until the advent of a superlative theoretical mind comparable to Jakob von Uexküll's in scope and originality (see Sebeok 1989b: chap. 10; see also *Semiotica* 42:1–87), harnessed to that of an observer of the minutiae of animal behavior comparable to Heini Hediger's in insight and power.

Before leaving Skinner, I do want to affirm that our personal relations have always remained most cordial, especially since he became my affable neighbor during his tenure at Indiana University. Our concerns have diverged until quite recently, when he demonstrated that a pair of pigeons could accurately engage in sustained and natural conversation without human intervention, and that a pigeon can transmit information to another entirely through the use of symbols (Epstein, Lanza, and Skinner 1980). This piece of clever lampoonery decisively abrogates decades of high-priced pretentiousness, while it clearly attests to the uniqueness of language, but it does so, as it were, by an *argumentum a contrario per positionem*. I would also like to echo an observation of Jakobson's (1971b:670) about all forms of semiotic communication and communication in general (which are fused in a dialectic, by virtue of their exactly communal *renvoi*): that all the *signantia* and *signata* in their interrelations require first and foremost a purely semiotic analysis and interpretation, and that the "continuous efforts to substitute a psychological treatment" for indispensable semiotic operations are doomed to failure. I hold this sort of censure to be true *a fortiori* of sophistic and baleful Freudian and pseudo-Freudian junkets into the semiotic domain. Psychoanalysis is dying at its cocaine-dusted roots, so attempts to replant this mystical fabrication in our midst amount to mere desperate diablerie. Incidentally, I have often been asked to comment on the semiotic contributions of Jacques Lacan (1966), to which I usually respond by repeating what Robert Frost told Lincoln MacVeagh about Carl Sandburg: "He was the kind of writer who had everything to gain and nothing to lose by being translated into a different language."

In passing, let me also assert—leaving the documentation for a future occasion—that, in a parallel manner, *mutatis mutandis*, the failed marriage of semiotics with a jejune version of Marxism that even Marx himself would surely have disavowed—following a period of furious flirtations that climaxed in East Germany with Georg Klaus (1962) and in Russia with L. O. Rjeznikov (1964), but that are still iterated, here and there, at the periphery of Europe—has ended up a herring that I deem both red *and* dead. (Augusto Ponzio [1984] spells out the reasons for this judgment in compelling fashion and puts forth seven interesting arguments for a relationship of complementarity between semiotics and Marxism as an open system.)

If you have attended my humble pedigree so far, you will have discerned repeated referrals—as Jakobson (1980:22) preferred to render his French *renvoi*, a word by which he deftly captured and transfixed each and every sign process conforming to the classic formula *aliquid stat pro aliquo*—to our lodestar, C. S. Peirce. Peirce figured, however evanescently, in the work of Ogden and Richards, who influenced Morris, whose acquaintance with Peirce was earnest and far more extensive, although filtered through his idiosyncratic applications of behavioristic attitudes; Morris's "behavioral semiotic" has not much in common with Peirce's—John Dewey allegedly dubbed it "a complete inversion of Peirce" (Morris 1971:444), a judgment with which I happen to concur. However that may be, Morris fancied his position to have been "very close indeed to that of Peirce" (Morris 1971:446), and set me to reading assiduously whatever fragments of his semiotic were accessible at Chicago in the late 1930s.

By the early 1940s, I had become ensorcelled by Roman Jakobson (see Sebeok 1974b: Foreword, and chap. 3 below), whose indelible effects on my scholarly development became pervasive and overriding, although, I trust, never epigonic. I am thus unique in having undergone formal training by both the philosopher Morris and the linguist Jakobson. The two men were, of course, acquainted, but by no means intimate; I dimly remember the three of us dining together in a Manhattan café. They cited one another at practically no time; it would take a separate effort to account for their distressing mutual intellectual and temperamental aloofness.

Jakobson visited Bloomington on several memorable occasions, but the one event I want to single out here is the momentous—yet, in some important ways, oddly barren—Conference of Anthropologists and Linguists, in July 1952 (written up in Lévi-Strauss et al. 1953: cf. Lévi-Strauss 1986 for delightful recollections of his ten days in Indiana). The results of this conference were summed up in a tripartite report. From the point of view of anthropology, the *rapporteur* was Lévi-Strauss (1953:1–10), in an intoxicating paper that later (1958:77–110) became a passport to the architectonic apprehension of this world-class contemporary thinker. He also came to conclude in this same book (p. 399) that anthropology is not only closest to humanistic studies but that it aims to be a "science sémeiologique," because "elle se situe resolument au niveau de la signification," that is, it takes *meaning* for its guiding principle. By 1960, he expanded this view: "Nous conçevons donc l'anthropologie comme l'occupant de bonne foi de ce domaine de la sémeiologie que la linguistique n'a pas déjà revendique pour sien" (Lévi-Strauss 1973:18). It is difficult to be sure of when or how Lévi-Strauss arrived at this conception about the heart of his science, which I take to be the perpetual search for invariances in society and culture. Further, all human relationships are to be regarded as a function of Kantian categories (or the like), which all of us use to organize experience. This quintessentially semiotic procedure uncannily resembles Jakob von Uexküll's *Umweltlehre* when extrapolated from nature to culture through the media of chiefly verbal signs. When Lévi-Strauss arrived in Bloomington, he came with an already well worked out model of the properties of mind, as I well know, since I distributed the draft of his paper, then titled "Toward a General Theory of Communication." Yet his local exposure to Jakobson— by then, and especially just that summer, saturated with Peircean ideas—and to the strongly Saussure-impelled Louis Hjelmslev— during that very summer engaged in completing, on this campus, the first English rendition of his 1943 Danish monograph (Hjelmslev 1953)—could hardly have failed to touch him and perhaps caused him to sharpen and even reforge his model in some respects.

Jakobson was our other major *rapporteur*, and he spoke nominally from the point of view of linguistics, but more from the standpoint of the then-fashionable "theory of communication" (Lévi-Strauss et al. 1953:15–16), a partially fleeting *nom de guerre* for semiotics. At the outset, he observed that language "is an instance of that subclass of *signs* which under the name of symbols have been astutely described by [Y. R.] Chao [who, by the way, was another active participant in our conference]" (1953:12). Jakobson then went on to tell us:

> In the impending task of analyzing and comparing the various semiotic systems, we must remember not only the slogan of de Saussure that linguistics is a part of the science of signs, but, first and foremost, the life work of his no whit less eminent contemporary and one of the greatest pioneers of structural linguistic analysis, Charles Sanders Peirce. Peirce not only stated the need of semiotics but drafted, moreover, its basic lines. His fundamental ideas and devices in the theory of symbols, particularly of linguistic symbols, when carefully studied, will be of substantial support for the investigation of language and its relation to the other systems of signs. [Lévi-Strauss et al. 1953:12]

He then emphatically repeated that Peirce "must be regarded as the genuine and bold forerunner of structural linguistics" (Lévi-Strauss et al. 1953:20). To appreciate the force of Jakobson's *obiter dicta*, one must attend to the time of their delivery and the composition of his audience. He was not only the "first linguist to become aware of Peirce's relevance to the advancement of linguistic theory" (Michael Shapiro 1983:6; for a listing of other, successively later, reappraisals of Peirce by Jakobson, see Eco 1977:55 n. 3, to which should be added Jakobson 1980:31–38, revised from a 1975 oral presentation) but a seemingly quixotic adventurer into very hostile territory indeed. Intending no condescension, but after rereading again the third part of our report (this compiled by Voegelin and myself [Lévi-Strauss et al. 1953:22–67]), I really doubt if more than perchance a mere handful out of some forty scholars assembled had ever even heard the name of Peirce—let alone in the context of linguistics—or had an inkling of what the word *semiotics* denoted and connoted. At the risk of doing several distinguished colleagues of mine serious injustice, the only ones I can be sure of were Yehoshua Bar-Hillel and Rulon Wells, as to the identity of Peirce, and Chao, Hjelmslev, Lévi-Strauss, John Lotz, and Alf Sommerfelt, as to the associated technical terms. (This is not to say that topics we would now consider of salient semiotic import, especially to nonverbal communication studies, were not—if more or less casually—alluded to, by, for instance, Ray L. Birdwhistell and Norman A. Mc-

Quown [Lévi-Strauss et al. 1953:29, 57–58] and others.)

The 1952 Conference of Anthropologist and Linguists took place during the ignominious epoch Jakobson later characterized (1971b:594; cf. chap. 3 here) as a "stage of relative life of the U.S.A.," where the Archimedean battle cry prevailed: *Noli tangere circulos meos*! The American linguists present were especially inimical to and suspicious of this alien intruder in their Tory know-it-all midst, but Jakobson handled them, in his brilliant summation, with his accustomed graceful elegance. The goings-on have, as he put it, "a polyphonic structure," but he pledged to try "to be as objective as I can" (Lévi-Strauss et al. 1953:11). His master strategem—one he was later frequently to reemploy, with unpredictable outcome, when promoting other American autochthonous heroes, such as William D. Whitney, Franz Boas, Edward Sapir, and, even, when opportune, L. Bloomfield—consisted of deftly turning the table on his adversaries by proving to them that the ideas they deemed outlandish were, in fact, embedded in the bedrock of their own glorious patrimony, to which they were lamentably blind and deaf.

Playing the role of a conjurer pulling a rabbit out of a hat for this particular audience was a magisterial ploy with the added virtue of being genuinely heartfelt, although, alas, not readily substantiatable. Jakobson's intuitions were uncanny and his prophecies both foreshadowed and helped shape things to come. Unfortunately, to surmise that if the ideas of Saussure and Peirce, "both concordant and rival," could have been matched in the years following World War I, such a juxtaposition "would perhaps have altered the history of general linguistics and the beginnings of semiotics" (Jakobson 1980:33), is a scarcely verifiable "what might have been"—a historical romance.[2]

I remarked earlier that the aftermath of this conference was, in some respects, curiously sterile. In particular, I was alluding to its confounding lack of traceable impact on Hjelmslev. The Great Dane, as Jakobson insisted on identifying Hjelmslev, spent his entire summer in Bloomington, and, as far as I can recall, took a full and active part in our meetings when he was not closeted with his American admirer and temporary collaborator, Francis J. Whitfield, laboring on his distinctive brand of formalized structural linguistics, dubbed "glossematics." It would be out of place to track the short but Byzantine history of glossematics in all its Western ramifications, but a few of them may be worthy of mention. First, within Denmark itself, glossematics has virtually ceased to exist. Second, in North America, it occupies today a minuscule niche; its sole professors are Sydney Lamb (1981) and a handful of his students. In a spirited rear-guard defense of glossematics, Lamb (1981:24) argues that Hjelmslev "shows that the methods and concepts he develops can be extended to other systems not generally considered to be languages....The systems of this larger class that has language at its center he calls 'semiotics.' That is, a semiotic is a quasi language that can be illuminated by the methods developed in immanent [vs. transcendent] linguistics. And it turns out that every science is a semiotic."

The sorry fact is that the program so confidently advertised has never been carried out successfully in any domain of science, all the while leaving wide open the thorny questions of whether linguistics is a part of semiotics, semiotics is a part of linguistics, or that the *tête-à-tête* adjacency of this pair of substantives may well be of a different cognitive order entirely (cf. Sebeok 1989b:63). In the Germanic world, we must concur with Th. Kotschi's 1977 judgment (adverted to by Jurgen Trabant in Krampen et al. 1987: chap. 4) that glossematics as an important school of European structuralism, if ever countenanced at all, has sunk into oblivion. Trabant, who is a specialist in Romance linguistics and philology, argues that Hjelmslev must be fairly adjudged a founder of general semiotics, and this is indeed how he may have been perceived among certain Francophones, notably by (the early) Roland Barthes, and particularly so by A. J. Greimas and his adherents, who form the imposingly self-designated Ecole de Paris (Coquet 1982). Greimas and J. Courtés (1982 [1979]:167), for example, claim that "la théorie du langage, présentée par L. Hjelmslev, peut être considerée comme la première théorie sémiotique cohérente et achévée: elle a été un facteur décisif dans la formation de la sémiotique en France." This last pretense leaves one profoundly perplexed if one considers French semiotics in its entire rich range. Thus Hjelmslev's name is rarely even mentioned in—and does not figure at all in the bibliography of—Pierre Guiraud's best-selling *La sémiologie* (1971), or Gerard Deledalle's keen *Théorie et pratique du signe* (1979). Moreover, Hjelmslev was subjected to severe criticism by Georges Mounin (1970:99), who was of the opinion that "au fond la sémiologie en elle-même ne l'interesse pas." France's most creative figure in modern semiotic theory, René Thom, seems wholly unaffected by Hjelmslev, and, as if all this were not bewildering enough, Annette Lavers (1982:181–182), who takes it upon herself to trace Greimas's "sources of inspiration," excludes Hjelmslev, but includes Viggo Brøndal, his compatriot and arch adversary. I cannot help speculating about the course of modern Continental semiotics had Hjelmslev become sensitized, that hot summer in Bloomington, to Peirce. Perhaps, if so, the Semiotic Square associated with Greimas (1982 [1979]:29–33) might today be called the Semiotic Tricorn!

Before I bid farewell to glossematics, I should record that Hjelmslev was an extraordinarily erudite and charming gentleman, as well as a genial guest and host, with whom I loved to visit, especially at his home in Charlottenlund, Denmark. On the other hand, I found it unworkable to dispute glossematics with him, since its very formalization presupposed a limitless chain of antecedents and implicated an endless concatenation of consequents. So our social exchanges, *chez nous* or *chez lui* turned into little more than elegant academic gossip sessions, which, I believe, we both thoroughly enjoyed.

Perhaps I have dwelt at inordinate length on a parley that was orchestrated in this small university town in July of 1981, sounding a cacophonous medley of voices, some now, alas, stilled, others seldom, these days, raised. In part, I was simply carrying out Galen's prescription for anamnesis, the bringing of the past into focus (Sebeok 1984b:220) to build up a case history for etiology's sake. As Benjamin Miller (1978:380) explains, your "doctor or his nurse will ask a great many questions at your first checkup in order to learn every detail of your health background....This means he has to work like a detective searching for all sorts of clues." The probe for the vital signs is only stage alpha in the quest for a prognosis.

Perhaps, moreover, I should refrain from the dropping of names, since I am sympathetic to Paul Bouissac's (1976:372) Golden Legend prospect of the lip service we tend to pay the so-called fathers and forefathers of semiotics. But it behooves members of our profession to be mindful that names, that is, singular proper names, comprise a conspicuous subclass of indexical signs (Sebeok 1985b:138–140): they are senseful, if imprecise, but they acquire rigidity and take on specificity the more descriptions they are augmented by; the Bacons—Roger and Francis—exemplify this process close to home. Such names function, in Erving Goffman's matchless expression, as "identity pegs" (Sebeok 1985b:139) on which to hang descriptions, a capacity involving a universal metasemiotic operation. Besides, "name magic" may be one device by which we mortals fancy to exert control over the universe. And finally, as Peirce (4.568) put the matter in a nutshell:

> The first time one hears a Proper Name pronounced, it is but a name, predicated, as one usually gathers, of an existent, or at least historically existent, individual object, of which, or of whom, one almost always gathers some additional information. The next time one hears a name, it is by so much the more definite; and almost every time one hears the name, one gains familiarity with the object.

Since 1952, I have participated in an untold number of other deliberations, here, elsewhere in this country, indeed, all over the globe. To pick just one of the latter at random, I might mention the 1970 Jerusalem exploration of the elusive subject of pragmatics (Staal 1971:29–32), convened by the late Bar Hillel, the leading expert on indexical expressions, during whose eventually fatal illness Max Black became our master of ceremonies. To enumerate them all—let alone the names of all the participants—would be as entertaining as a recitation of the phone directory, but a passing mention of a few may help trace the long path we have traversed. In August of 1960, Lévi-Strauss and I coorganized a meeting in Paris titled "Analyse structurale et sémantique des mythes et de la littérature orale." Edmund Leach spoke often and with his usual witty eloquence. A slender but fascinating written resumé has been preserved (Leroi-Gourhan et al. 1964:643–647)—fascinating because the partakers included the cream of English anthropology. I learned only about six months after my return from Paris, in a tactful but *desolée* letter from my dear friend Geneviève Calame-Griaule, that the local low-tech operator of the recording device had installed the wire backward. I regret not only the lost words of the like of Raymond Firth, Anthony Forge, Meyer Fortes, Edmund Leach, R. I. Pocock, and all the rest but also that I thereby forfeited my only chance to have coedited a volume jointly with Lévi-Strauss.

Two conferences, both of them held at Indiana University, have to be alluded to in even the most minimal list for their inseminating effects on the flowering of semiotics. The earlier was the already mentioned 1958 Conference on Style, where Jakobson spoke on "Linguistics and Poetics" (Sebeok 1960:350–377), which, he later confided to me, became his single most often cited paper, and hence the most influential among a multitude. The other one was a congregation, in May, 1962, of sixty scholars of various persuasions, ruled over and harmonized by the indomitable Margaret Mead. "As we build a science of semiotics," she fatidically insisted (Sebeok 1960:279), "it will be necessary to assimilate...discrepant sequences of research experience. Some are hundreds of years old, some are extremely recent. Some result from the vicissitudes of systems of prestige, or methods of instrumentation, or local cultural hierarchies among the sensory modalities....Some result from accidents of professional interests or the availability of research funds at a particular period....Still others are the result of fashion in research" (See chap. 1 of this book for further remarks on this meeting).

In 1960–61, I spent the first twelve of what was later to amount to about twenty-six months of my life at the Center for Advanced Study in the Behavioral Sciences at Stanford University. This was a vintage year there for linguists, who included Jakobson, and for anthropologists, who included Leach, and perhaps a dozen or so others in both fields combined. For my personal unfolding, however, those months were a watershed for quite a different reason. In my undergraduate years, I received sound basic training in biology, particularly in genetics, which led me to agonize, in the 1940s, about my choice of career. World War II propelled me to clutch the verbal code rather than the molecular code, and that retained me for two busy decades. At Stanford, however, my yearning for nature became overwhelming, and, rather naively, I tried to catch up with a twenty-year stockpile of facts and trends in the life science. Soon realizing that my ambition was a pipe dream, I decided to, as it were, specialize on a single facet, and chose ethology in general and animal communication studies in particular; in those days the two labels, and comparative psychology besides, shared much the same referent. My preoccupation during that priceless period of freedom resulted in a book (Sebeok 1972), a conference report (Sebeok and Ramsay 1969), two cumbrous collections of papers (Sebeok 1968; Sebeok 1977b), coresponsibility with my wife, Jean Umiker-Sebeok, for a freshly launched series of volumes on animal communication, and my resting forever saddled with the word *zoosemiotics* and its equally obnoxious spinoffs. Eventually, it also landed us at the storm center of a foolish controversy (Sebeok and Umiker-Sebeok 1980a) about whether animals have language, to which the one-word answer is: No!

Eventually, after years of reflection, I concluded that semiosis is *the* criterial attribute of life, an axiom that I continued to build on throughout my "semiotic tetralogy" (Sebeok 1985b [1976]; Sebeok 1989b [1979]; Sebeok 1981b; and Sebeok 1986d) and in a number of shorter publications. I have presented hundreds of pages of arguments for this obsession of mine, which, however, fits comfortably within a neosemiotic tradition perspicuously maintained by Peirce, and is currently fostered, in a highly original fashion, by René Thom. Its most distinctive and explicit contributor was Jakob von Uexküll, that demiurgic but largely misunderstood creative genius of biology, whose best work dates from the first half of this century. Steeped as he was in the teachings of Kant, Uexküll's technical writings were enshrouded in a sometimes unduly opaque philosophical wrapping. His eldest son neatly condensed his conception of reality (or as Jakob von Uexküll termed it, *Natur*) in a revealing paragraph which I quote here both for its own sake and because it accurately stands for an opinion I still share. "True reality," Thure von Uexküll observed in his edition of his father's *The Theory of Meaning* (J. von Uexküll 1982), which "lies beyond or behind the nature that physicists, chemists, and microbiologists conceive of in their scientific systems[,] reveals itself through signs. These signs are therefore the only true reality, and the rules and laws to which the signs and sign-processes are subject are the only real laws of nature. 'As the activity of our mind is the only piece of nature directly known to us, its laws are the only ones that have the right to be called laws of Nature'" (in T. von Uexküll 1982:3). Peirce wrote the same thing to Lady Welby (see Hardwick 1977:141): "It is perfectly true that we can never attain a knowledge of things as they are. We can only know their human aspect. But that is all the universe is for us." And, in the footsteps of Jakob von Uexküll, the great French geneticist François Jacob (1982:56) put the matter most generally and, withal, most picturesquely:

> No matter how an organism investigates its environment, the perception it gets must necessarily reflect so-called "reality" and, more specifically, those aspects of reality which are directly related to its own behavior. If the image that a bird gets of the insects it needs to feed its progeny does not reflect at least some aspects of reality, then there are no more progeny. If the representation that a monkey builds of the branch it wants to leap has nothing to do with reality, then there is no more monkey. And if this did not apply to ourselves, we would not be here to discuss this point. Perceiving certain aspects of reality is a biological necessity; certain aspects only, for obviously our perception of the external world is massively filtered. Our sensory equipment allows us to see a tiger entering our room, but not the cloud of particles which, according to physicists, constitutes the reality of a tiger. The external world, the "reality" of which we all have intuitive knowledge, thus appears as a creation of the nervous system. It is, in a way, a possible world, a model allowing the organism to handle the bulk of incoming information and make it useful for its everyday life. One is thus led to define some kind of "biological reality" as the particular representation of the external world that the brain of a given species is able to build. The quality of such biological reality evolves with the nervous system in general and the brain in particular.

The principle that signs are the only true reality is generalized in Peirce's famous challenge that all this universe is perfused with signs, if it is not composed exclusively of signs (cf. Sebeok 1977a:v), and carried further by Thom (1983:264–276), when he depicts the dynamic of semiosis as "the very image of life," adding that the "voice of reality is in the significance of the symbol."

It appears from Leach's spirited Patten Lecture of October 1984 (see Leach 1984), presented at Indiana University,[3] that our respective positions on this constitutive issue are largely consonant. Leach stated: "I see no reason at all to believe that more than a very small fragment of reality out there could ever be registered by a human brain," and that "elements of real world structure can somehow be perceived...as patterns of interpretable signs." Certainly, this standpoint, which I have tried to succinctly instantiate, is akin to but by no means identical with either problematic idealism, often attributed to Descartes, or the dogmatic idealism ("immaterialism") Kant erroneously imputed to Berkeley.

To spell out my present opinion on the relations of semiotics to the idealist movement would require a monograph, such as the case of the giant rat of Sumatra, a story for which, as Sherlock Holmes announced, the world is not yet prepared. Let me just say that I reckon this problematic to lie in the innermost heart of the contemporary semiotic enterprise. In its essence, the enigma is equivalent to the multifaceted system of "ancient questions about the nature of the mental and its relations to the bodily" (Bunge 1980:xiii), or what is often discussed under the ticket of "mind and brain," in its many monistic and dualistic permutations (e.g., Eccles 1982:239–245). I have previously (Sebeok 1981b:13) declared that my personal bias inclines me toward that variant of the dualist-interactionist theory, maintained by J. Z. Young, which involves a principle of double coding and control. I defined "mind" as a system of signs which is, roughly, tantamount to Jakob von Uexküll's *Umwelt*, and "brain" as a system of signs displayed, for example, as a physical network, or structure, of neurons. The question to be investigated is how mental manifestation of the information in the mind is transcoded into our central nervous system, and vice versa. The solution must come from neuroendocrinology, and, once the solution is apparent, once the information engineering specifications are blocked out, much of what we call semiotics today, including notably linguistics, will become superfluous. This is my prognosis, in which readers can place as much confidence as they are willing to consign to their physicians.

Theoretic biology is a hot field, with important concerns of its own, tossed about in a *Sturm und Drang* at its own frontiers. Six of us (Anderson et al. 1984) have written a paper in which we attempted to construct a provisional framework compacting what appeared to us a number of new developments in the life science, using bricks and mortar made up of semiotic elements as our tools. We offered our paper as a target for critical discussion from which, we very much hope, some sort of reasonable consensus will emerge. Our article appears cheek by jowl with a pivotal guest editorial by Jean-Claude Gardin, Paul Bouissac, and Kenneth E. Foote (1984), concisely presenting ten interrelated theses that every practitioner of semiotics must make it his or her business to assimilate or take issue with, but which none can afford to ignore.

The domain of semiosis most assuredly extends over all terrestrial biological systems, bounded, at their lowest limit, by molecular mechanisms and, at their upper limit, by a hypothetical entity baptized, about 1979, *Gaia* (cf. Seielstad 1983: chap. 8; Anderson et al. 1984). There is a growing conviction, held by an increasing number of scientists in a surprisingly diverse array of disciplines, that life and its environment evolved together as a single tightly coupled system. James E. Lovelock, a gas chromatographer, Lynn Margulis, a geneticist, Lewis Thomas, a research physician, and others, including myself, have embraced this notion, perhaps gauchely named after the Greek goddess of the earth. Gaia, if it exists, is the largest living organism we know of, with devices for sensing the surrounding environment, undergoing internal metabolic changes and adapting to them, and regulating the entire megamachinery solely by way of precise and subtle message exchanges. This is a system informed, through and through, by sign action; therefore, we are responsible to be heedful, or at least mindful, of it, whether it is in a state of equilibrium—which is, fortunately, most of the time—or under threat of gross perturbation. This is so because we—I mean not just members of this profession but all members of the species—are an articulately conscious cog (very likely the only one) occupying this huge space vehicle.

The province of semiosis, I repeat, envelops life in all its manifestations: the diminutive Lilliputian islands of the molecular geneticists and virologists; Gulliver's middle-sized world, the theater most of us are familiar with, and in which the action—the sign action that is—unrolls from instant to instant; and the Brobdingnag demesne, hanging there in space, as a gigantic closed ecosystem named Gaia. But is this the end of the story? Does it make any sense to say that semiosis tempers *more* than this grand biogeochemical system in which are inalienably bound all the conjugated components of a unique set of planetary processes?

Since I gave a talk in West Germany, in the fall of 1981, in the

context of Peirce's cosmology, concerning the quasi-fallacy (as I
insist it is) that reality exists outside of us—touching, along the way,
on sundry deep conundrums about von Neumann's chain, on the
pair of paradoxes of Schrödinger's cat and Wigner's friend, and,
above all, on Professor John A. Wheeler's mind-blowing conception
of the participatory universe (M. Gardner 1983: chap. 19)—my
nagging doubts continued to both multiply and magnify. Possibilities for aligning physics and semiotics are slowly beginning to swim
into focus, and I forecast that the means of entry to the universe will
be found in the classic adage *Nosce teipsum*. The key is concealed
within ourselves.[4]

For me, this coming together was traversed mainly via two
paths. The first of these was called the anthropic principle, by
Robert Dicke, in 1961; it has since then been greatly extended by
Brandon Carter; and has now limpidly been elucidated by Paul
Davies (1980: chap. 8). The anthropic principle interested me because
it offered a rational explanation for the fact that we happen to be
alive at just the era when the age of the universe is equal to about 15
billion years, or 1.5×10^{10}, an enormous number that is dwarfed
when one considers that gravity is weaker than electromagnetism by
a factor of 5×10^{39}, or, to put it in another way, that this principle
provided an alternative to coincidence. There are only two interpretations possible of quantum theory as a framework for understanding the world as it is: either chance or choice. There exists a vast
array of universes, but, as far as we know, only one of these is
inhabited by creatures endowed with the semiotic capacity, on which
hinges all knowledge of existence and cosmology, and much besides.
A preordained ecosystem, a world tailor-made for its denizens, has
inevitably got to be a universe perfused with signs. Consequently, I
am strongly drawn to Wheeler's suggestion that the fundamental
physical constants, the nuclear and cosmological parameters, and
others, are constrained by the unbudging requirement that life evolve,
and that these constants are altered by our consciousness of them. In
brief, life modifies the universe to meet its needs, and accomplishes
this by means of sign action. (Incidentally, Max Bense [1984] came
to the identical conclusion, that the anthropic principle is a semiotic
principle, although I am at a loss to follow his dense yet exiguous
argumentation.)

The second path became patent to me in July 1984 during an exciting in-flight conversation with a wonderfully imaginative and endlessly knowledgeable medical engineer, F. Eugene Yates, concerning the leap from kinetics to kinematics—the study of motion exclusive of the influences of mass and force. His pathbreaking paper (Yates and Kugler 1984), in my estimation, heralds for us yet another spectacular vista to hurry in pursuit of.

In medicine, the word *syndrome* refers, collectively, to a rule-governed configuration of signs that are assumed to have the same cause. The cardinal point about the indexical signs I have been discussing is that each and every one of them points in the same direction. The body semiotic disembogues scores of encouraging vital signs that not only fit snugly with the basic sciences of nature but are appreciated by leading mathematicians and scientists of both inanimate and animate creation once they grasp what semiotics is truly about. Ten years ago (Sebeok 1974a:211), I characterized semiotics as a mode of extending humankind's perception of the world, and depicted its subject matter as "the exchange of any messages whatever and of the systems of signs which underlie them." I now have impressive progress to report: the central preoccupation of semiotics is an illimitable array of concordant illusions; its main mission to mediate between reality and illusion—to reveal the substratal illusion underlying reality and to search for the reality that may, after all, lurk behind that illusion. This abductive assignment becomes, henceforth, the privilege of future generations to pursue, insofar as young people can be induced to heed the advice of their elected medicine men.[5]

Notes

1. Reproduced below is most of Richards's inherently tantalizing last letter to me, handwritten about fourteen months before his death:

Magdelene College,   17 Feb 78
Cambridge, UK

Dear Professor Sebeok,
I am pained to say that—after all your most courteous and patient
correspondence and your sending the Peirce-Welby Correspondence [sic]
Book: *Semiotics* [sic] *and Significs*, I find I am having to be to you a total
disappointment. I have done more than a little exploring into the book, but
somehow the topics treated, the assumptions made and the tones taken by
both parties have become so remote from my present thinking that
anything I could write would be, I know, imperceptive and unfair.
Originally, it was C. K. Ogden who was interested both in Welby and
in Peirce, and I had hoped that I would be able to revive the curiosity with
which he infected me in 1920. But, alas, NO. (I will be 85 in a few days
time now and doubtless *that* is the real explanation of my inability.)
You would have had this apology far earlier but *influenza* has been playing
its part—happily well over now. I will gladly send the book back but hold
it for the moment in case there is someone this side of the Atlantic to whom
you would wish it to go. With real regrets,

Sincerely,
I. A. Richards

P.S. The Editorial Introduction (Charles S. Hardwick [1977]) is strangely
ill-informed. E.g. p. xxxi, he seems to know nothing to the point about F.
P. Ramsey (who virtually translated Wittgenstein's Tractatus and was
immensely indebted to C. K. Ogden from the time when Ramsey, as a
Winchester Schoolboy used to review the toughest things (Major Douglas
& Keynes etc., etc. for Ogden's *Cambridge Magazine*)...

2. An attempt at such a reconstruction constituted the thrust of my presidential
address to the Linguistic Society of America, delivered in San Francisco, on
December 30, 1975, under the title "The Pertinence of Peirce to Linguistics."
I never published this address because so much of it was necessarily speculative. When the monumental Peirce Edition Project, the *Writings of Charles S.
Peirce: A Chronological Edition* (see Peirce 1982; Peirce 1984), is brought to
an end, perhaps some future historian of twentieth-century linguistics and
semiotics ought to try again. The earnest endeavor of Michael Shapiro (1983:ix)
"to found a Peircean linguistics" has, so far, been met by a resounding silence.
3. Leach was both the guest of honor at the banquet at which I delivered this
speech (also entitled "Vital Signs") and, the same week, a Patten lecturer at
Indiana University. (For one of his two Patten presentations, see Leach 1984.)
4. "The Role of the Observer" was the title I gave to this invited lecture,
delivered on October 7, 1981, in Hamburg, to the third Semiotisches Kolloquim

of the Deutsche Gesellschaft für Semiotik. My paper remains unpublished, *mea culpa*, because the confluence of new theories of physics—known as "unified theories"— and the newest ideas in cosmology is an ongoing process about the outcome of which an outsider, such as me, can, at this juncture, surmise little of semiotic pertinence. The fact that the universe is evolving increases semioticians' chances for a useful contribution eventually, but not at a time when, to paraphrase a recent reflection by John A. Wheeler, increasing knowledge of detail is bringing an increasing ignorance of plan. The justification for the statement *Nosce teipsum* was superbly stated by Heisenberg (1955:29):

> The old division of the world into objective processes in space and time and the mind in which these processes are mirrored—in other words, the Cartesian difference between *res cogitans* and *res extensa*— is no longer a suitable starting point for our understanding of modern science. Science, we find, is now focused on the network of relationships between man and nature, on the framework which makes us as living beings dependent parts of nature, and which we as human beings have simultaneously made the object of our thoughts and actions. Science no longer confronts nature as an objective observer, but sees itself as an actor in this interplay between man and nature....In other words, method and object can no longer be separated. *The scientific world-view has ceased to be a scientific view in the true sense of the word.*

5. Like any other academic pursuit, semiotics is made up of an inner form, or intellective construct, expressed in an outer form, which takes on many traditional guises. The famous Saussurean comparison of language to a sheet of paper comes to mind: you can't take a pair of scissors and cut the outer form without at the same time cutting the inner form. One can well adapt Saussure's point (1972:157) that semiotics operates *"sur le terrain limitrophe,"* in other words, that it is not comprehensible apart from its social context, which has a compelling historical dimension as well. Vital signs of this kind, which were not even alluded to above, include organizations, such as the International Association for Semiotic Studies and its quinquennial congresses; many local societies, with annual, biennial, or occasional meetings, the largest of these being the Semiotic Society of America, conceived at the first North American Semiotics Colloquium, held at the University of South Florida in 1975 (Sebeok 1977b), and realized a brief fourteen months later at the Georgia Institute of Technology; and the immensely successful sequence of International Institutes for Semiotic and Structural Studies held, or scheduled to be held, at the University of Toronto, Vanderbilt University, Indiana University, and Northwestern University during the summer sessions of the Centro Internazionale di Semiotica e di Linguistica, convened every July for the past fifteen years. Corresponding to such sodalities, there are numerous book and monograph series, journals, and news outlets to accommodate all tastes. Last but not least, there are curricular configurations of diverse cast, some emphasizing teaching,

some research, and some both. While a complete report would fairly note those that have died and those that seem moribund, the morbidity rate is reassuringly small. The health inventory of semiotics was never more pleasing than in the mid-1980s.

CHAPTER THREE

Roman Jakobson's Teaching in America

> Socrates is an evildoer, and a curious person, who searches into
> things under the earth and heaven, and he makes the worse appear the
> better cause; and he teaches the aforesaid doctrines to
> others....Socrates...corrupts the youth...does not believe in the gods
> of the state, but has other new divinities of his own.—Plato, *Apology*
> (trans. Jowett)

In a foreword to a collection of some of my essays in verbal art, I
briefly recounted my first meeting with Roman Jakobson, on the
sultry twenty-seventh day of August, 1942, when we spent a long
afternoon absorbed in animated conversation in the garden of Franz
Boas's house in Grantwood, New Jersey. I recorded that, among
other topics, "he spoke to me at generous length about the highly
ingenious accomplishments of the Russian Formalist school and its
productive reformulations by the Prague Circle, stressing the close
ties of both with structural linguistics." I noted that our friendship
dates from that occasion, "as does my abiding absorption with the
study of the verbal arts" (Sebeok 1974b:vii–viii).

Now I have been honored with an invitation to comment on
Jakobson's "teaching" during his American period, that is, following his arrival and settlement in this country after his dramatic
hegira from Czechoslovakia, and then, successively, from Denmark,
Norway, and Sweden. Since teaching is a far more intimate expression
of scholarship than any formal publication can possibly be, this
narrative must necessarily be laced with autobiographical observa-

Reprinted, with slight revisions, from Sebeok 1989b [1979]. It originally
appeared in *Roman Jakobson: Echoes of His Scholarship*, ed. Daniel
Armstrong and C. H. van Schooneveld (1977).

tions; and since Jakobson's instructional activities are so vast in scope, I can generalize with confidence only from such glimpses of it as good fortune has bestowed upon me. These date, in the main, from the war years and immediately thereafter, while Jakobson was professor of general linguistics and of Czechoslovak studies at the Ecole libre des hautes études in New York City (1942–1946), then visiting professor of general linguistics (1943–1949) at Columbia University. I never attended his courses at Harvard University, where he served, from 1949 until his retirement in 1967, as professor of Slavic languages and literatures and general linguistics, nor at MIT, where he became Institute Professor in 1957. However, throughout this entire period, I heard him lecture on various other campuses on occasions too numerous to recall in detail. We have attended a good many conferences together, both in the United States and abroad. In particular, he has frequently been our guest at Indiana University. I recollect four of his sojourns with especial pleasure: his first visit to Bloomington during the war; his concluding report at the fortnight's Conference of Anthropologists and Linguists in July 1952 (Jakobson 1971b:554–567); his enthusiastic participation in the Conference on Style, in April 1958, in the course of which he delivered what may be his most often cited paper, "Linguistics and Poetics" (published in Sebeok 1960:350–377); and a sequence of lectures delivered here during the 1964 Linguistic Institute.

When Jakobson and I first met, I was a graduate student in transition on several levels: literally, from the University of Chicago (and utter penury) to Princeton (and the promise of relative affluence afforded by a splendid fellowship). At the same time, I was also intellectually at sea, thrashing about somewhere in the middle of the common Atlantic pool that J. R. Firth so eloquently delineated a few years later (1949). My early linguistic attitudes had essentially been molded by two men, neither of whom was at Chicago any longer: Manuel Andrade, who died prematurely, and Leonard Bloomfield, who reluctantly accepted a call to Yale in 1940. After their departures deprived me of their comfort and steady linguistic counsel, I read voraciously according to my own appetites, and thus came to discovery of the linguistic school of Prague and a glimmer of understanding of the distinctively Russian flavor the late Nikolaj Trubetzkoy and the very lively Jakobson had imparted to it, transforming its classical doctrines as these had sprung from native soil (cf. Vachek 1966).

When Andrade suddenly died, he had already "gone a long way toward developing a semiotically grounded linguistics, much farther than any studies yet made in this field," and his ambitious program "involved the building of the whole of linguistics upon semiotical foundations; he believed that in this way linguistics would obtain a metalanguage appropriate to the description and comparison of all languages" (C. Morris 1946:223). I was strongly influenced by Andrade's highly original views and their applications, but far from sufficiently equipped at the time to carry his project further, especially since his remaining notes and manuscript fragments were scarcely utilizable. In any event, no one else was much interested: he was ahead of his time in our prevailing linguistic milieu, and this pupil of Franz Boas is remembered today, if at all, only for his technical work on Quileute and several Middle American Indian languages.

Bloomfield, who became my next advisor, had just published a masterful essay proclaiming that "linguistics is the chief contributor to semiotic. Among the special branches of science, it intervenes between biology, on the one hand, and ethnology, sociology, and psychology, on the other: it stands between physical and cultural anthropology" (1939:55). In his classes and private sessions, however, Bloomfield refrained from discussing broad issues; his concern, no doubt rightly, was with imparting the formal skills required of any practicing linguist. It was at his pounding insistence that I was set on the path of specialization in Finno-Ugric languages and linguistics, despite the very nearly total absence of instruction in them within the Western Hemisphere, a circumstance that forced me into an autodidactic stance, yet one that ultimately led to the institutionalization of this field in America. Bloomfield's procedures, essential for training though they may have been, left me unsatisfied and restless, for they gave a disjointed, choppy, incomplete picture of linguistics. I could, therefore, understand, in some measure, why, some twenty years later, a new generation of linguists deemed it fit to set up a straw man in his name, selecting him as an emblem for a brand of inadequate behaviorism; Jakobson was, of course, perfectly correct in maintaining that "sur bien des points Bloomfield reste supérieur au mouvement qui se réclame de lui" (in Faye, Paris, and Roubaud 1972:47).

Such, then, in capsule form, was the initial state of my affairs when, at the age of twenty-one, I journeyed across the Hudson, from New York City, to seek out the cosmopolitan linguist, already acclaimed throughout Europe, but not yet acclaimed in America. I was sufficiently well acquainted with some of his writings to have aroused my curiosity to enlarge my knowledge in a face-to-face meeting. The afternoon turned into an intense tutorial, extending late into that summer evening, in the course of which two subjects were discussed in the manner of a Greek symposium, as it were, liberally interspersed, that is, with drink and food: Jakobson's apperception of phonological theory and his notions about poetic language. Although the phonemic principle was well known in America, and accepted even then by all modern schools of linguistics, Jakobson convinced me then and there that any further development of linguistic sound analysis must proceed by dissolving the phoneme into distinctive features, and that binary opposition can consistently be applied as a patterning device for the entire phonemic material. And while Bloomfield had instilled in me his conviction that "the artistic use of language by specially gifted individuals" enjoyed general favor as a substitute for the observation of language (1939:5–6), Jakobson opened my eyes and ears to the true, exciting potential of a poetics when practiced by a master of linguistics. This was, indeed, a propaedeutic experience leading toward the kind of holistic vista of the language sciences that I had been vainly groping for at Chicago. I therefore resolved to stay in close touch to learn more.

The first formal opportunity for doing so developed within the framework of the Ecole libre des hautes études, assembled under the auspices and on the premises of the New School for Social Research. Jakobson described the *école* as "a university founded by French scholars who were refugees from the Nazi occupation," where we "were teachers and students of one another" (in Mehta 1971:232), and where "dès le début les différences entre étudiants et professeurs se trouvaient abolies par le fait que les professeurs eux-mêmes allaient écouter les conférences de leurs collègues" (in Faye, Paris, and Roubaud 1972:34). Thus Claude Lévi-Strauss came to introduce Jakobson (and the rest of us) to structural anthropology, while

Jakobson opened the door for Lévi-Strauss (as he did for many others) to linguistics. I remember that both had the courtesy to come to my raw course on the history of the Hungarian language—my very first teaching assignment—whereas I attended as many of their lectures as my commitments to Princeton would allow. I tried never to miss Jakobson's packed seminars, after which we usually went to a nearby bistro to continue animated conversations about the topic of the evening.

It was at the Ecole libre that I heard Jakobson lecture for the first time, and I would like to refine here my impression of his platform style, which seldom varied whether he spoke in French (and he did in those times, in New York) or in any other language. I had once written of "the many-valued, unmistakably Jakobsonian, rhetorical stratagems that are sprinkled among the expository statements...there by tactical intent, at once to persuade and to seduce" (Sebeok 1965b:86). With conspicuous exceptions—his very carefully worded summation of the results of the Ninth International Congress of Linguists, which he read verbatim on August 31, 1962 (in Jakobson 1971b:593–602), was one—the lectures of Jakobson gave off an air of uncontrived happenings (in the semiotic sense of Winfried Nöth [1972:130–131]). He appeared to rely on miniature cue cards, consulting them mostly for melodramatic effect rather than for content.[1] He conveyed the feeling that he created, shaped, and edited his topic of the moment to express it in a rhythm best suited to his auditors' pulse; a Spanish newspaper report characterized Jakobson's 1974 Madrid lectures as harmonious musical performances directed by the lecturer and played by the audience. The overall effect was that his students—all of his audiences became students—were moved unusually close to him, to the extent of even becoming protective. One cannot help recollecting that Jakobson once professed in the Moscow School for Drama; he had kept in touch with a former actor of the Moscow Art Theater, and later made effective use of him (Sebeok 1960:354). I am strongly reminded of a passage in which Stanislavsky comments on his own methods: "To achieve a harmony...one needs more than outer, physical tempo and rhythm; one needs inner, spiritual tempo and rhythm. One must feel them in the sound, in the speech, in the action, in the gesture, in the movement, in fact, in the entire production" (1959:443). Sometimes a genuine improvisation replaced a "happening": when, shortly before Christmas of 1942, he received a cable from Copenhagen announcing the death of Viggo Brøndal, he substituted for his lecture an unforgettable, yet impromptu eulogy of his friend which deeply affected all of us present, although no one in the audience had ever met this important but remote personage of the Cercle Linguistique de Copenhague.

The ambience pervading and surrounding our group was international indeed: "Il y avait des gens qui passaient par là, qui venaient nous écouter ou qui venaient parler eux-mêmes. Toutes les langues possibles s'y mêlaient," Jakobson related in an interview (Faye Paris, and Roubaud 1972:34). Americans—both established scholars from Columbia and neighboring institutions and much younger ones, partially drawn from the Language Section of the War Department (then located at a New York address, 165 Broadway, which became the eponym for a heroic era in American linguistics)— were gradually attracted into Jakobson's orbit. (Somewhat disconcertingly, he was followed around, as well, by an indeterminate cloud made up of East European and Russian groupies, to whom he was unfailingly gracious and kind, although they did erode his time.)

Many of our crowd moved on with him to Columbia, where, in 1943, he offered an evening seminar on the topic of case systems, stemming from a trail-blazing monograph he wrote in 1935.[2] Each student in this seminar was assigned to analyze exhaustively the case system of a language of his choice, present his findings orally, then revise the presentation in the light of the ensuing discussion. I selected Finnish. The resulting paper became a chapter of my eventual dissertation, dealing with the form and function of several Finno-Ugric case systems. Although my Ph.D. degree was awarded by Princeton (in 1945), Jakobson served, to all intents and purposes— and with the enthusiastic concurrence of my chairman, Harold H. Bender—as my thesis supervisor; it was thus, and in this sense, that I chanced to become his "first American student." Incidentally, at Jakobson's behest, his monograph (1971b:23–71) came to forge an initial link between John Lotz and me, and in due course our lives continued variously to commingle with his, as mentioned elsewhere (Sebeok 1989b: chap. 14).

Jakobson's strictures on the work-in-progress of his students could be very telling: about one of my early papers, he gently hinted that he thought I had written it with my left hand; of another, he remarked that it seemed to him especially interesting for what I had left out. On the other hand, when a finished piece of work had gained his coveted approval, he would stand behind it with his full authority. While he generally tended to be reasonably equable and tolerant of criticisms leveled directly at himself—responding, usually, in due course, to a coherent set of them, without invidious identification (the "Postscriptum" to his *Questions de poétique* [1973] being a good example)—he would not countenance indirect attacks disguised as censure of his students. His loyalty to them—and, by his own count, "about a hundred of [his] former students are professors in this country" (Mehta 1971:232)—remained abiding and fierce; in cases such as James P. Soffietti's Columbia thesis on Turinese phonology, his defense could result in deplorably acrimonious clashes with colleagues like R. A. Hall, who, of course, perceived the polemic in quite different terms (R. A. Hall 1975:141–142). When, as sometimes happened, two of his former students collided, he would not, however, hesitate to take sides strictly on the merits of the case at issue (Jakobson 1971a:209), painful as that may have been. Little wonder, then, that generations of his disciples, down to the youngest, many of whom declared that they went to Cambridge for the opportunity of working under him, were steadfast in their allegiance, proclaiming "his ability to illuminate a question from various points of view" (Gribble 1968:7).

It would be seriously misleading to pretend that Jakobson's teachings were an instantaneous and resounding success in America. Far from it: they were roundly condemned by an influential cabal of autochthonous and lately naturalized linguists—mostly a generation or two older than mine—clustering around "165 Broadway." In a lecture delivered on December 27, 1974, as part of the Linguistic Society's Golden Anniversary Symposium on "the European Background of American Linguistics," he characterized his foes of this era by an abusively intended Aesopian epithet, *administrators*, which, however, was so veiled that it was widely misinterpreted. In truth, these men were mostly misguided chauvinists, afflicted with a hubris doubtless induced by the pressures and fears of an uncertain military conflict in the backdrop. Regrettably, the behavior of this small but powerful clique—which caused Jakobson and his friends untold anguish, to say nothing of economic loss—left a sinister stain on the otherwise magnificent tapestry of achievements of American linguistics of the 1940s. Fortunately, this dark episode was transpierced by brilliant shafts of light emanating from giants like Franz Boas and Leonard Bloomfield; their instant appreciation for Jakobson's decisive presence must be allowed to compensate for all the rest, which had better stay buried along with other, similarly motivated, wartime debris.

The affidavit against the teaching of Jakobson was much the same as the charges preferred by Meletus, summed up in the epigraph at the outset of this chapter. "This inquisition," Jakobson might have continued in the words of Socrates, "has led to my having many enemies of the worst and most dangerous kind, and has given occasion to many calumnies....There is another thing:—young men...come about me of their own accord; they like to hear the pretenders examined, and they often imitate me, and proceed to examine others; there are plenty of persons, as they quickly discover, who think that they know something, but they really know little or nothing; and then those who are examined by them instead of being angry with themselves are angry with me..."

In the fall of 1943, I took up permanent residence at Indiana University, where Harry V. Velten, Charles F. Voegelin, and I soon invited Jakobson to come for some lectures. Voegelin asked him to send some feasible topics, and was startled to receive a list of nearly one hundred titles. Jakobson arrived in Bloomington by bus, greeting me with the question, "Where are the Indians?" He spoke on the cultural and social history of Slavic languages (Jakobson 1968), several of which were then taught here intensively to Army personnel, and was then also asked to give an *ad hoc* talk in J. R. Kantor's seminar. Kantor was an extreme behavioristic psycholinguist who relished controverting with linguists (see Kantor 1936). For some reason, Jakobson chose as his seminar theme "The Theory of Signs," which, as far as I know, was his first presentation of semiotics in this country. He had hardly finished when Kantor bounded forward, shouting, "Why, that was nothing but medieval philosophy!" "Not at all," I remember Jakobson retorting, "it goes back at least to

Plato!"

So Jakobson continued to flourish, as he related to Philip Rahv, "now and then in hostile, and often in amicable contexts" (Jakobson 1972:18). For the summer of 1946, the late Stith Thompson organized the first Folklore Institute, assembling at Indiana University a highly interesting mélange of scholars of various ages. Among the welcome participants were Roman and Svatava Pírková Jakobson, who, as I recall, were driven out to Bloomington by Alan Lomax, who came to join his father, John A. Lomax.

During approximately the same weeks, the much more venerable Linguistic Institute was in session at Ann Arbor, under the inspired direction of Charles C. Fries. I happened to be among the members of the visiting faculty of the University of Michigan that summer, and so was George L. Trager, a well-known American specialist in Slavic languages, who, in 1944, had been the unfortunate recipient of a particularly savage review by Jakobson of his *Introduction to Russian*. Although the facts were beyond dispute, the tone of Jakobson's piece generated much resentment. It was the custom then to conduct during the institute weekly luncheon conferences, led chiefly by distinguished visitors. When Fries canvassed the faculty for nominations, I proposed Jakobson, but was first hooted down. However, I kept nagging away, and, with Voegelin's sympathetic support, finally prevailed upon Fries. I then fetched Jakobson from Indiana by car, and, on July 24, he addressed the assembled faculty and student body on "Comparative Metrics as a Problem of Modern Linguistics." Trager sat not far away in the audience.[3] Jakobson kept disarmingly referring—and, seemingly, deferring—to him as "my great and good friend," this unexpected warmth causing the victim (at least momentarily) to melt, and me irrepressibly to giggle. At any rate, and in spite of the novelty of the topic in linguistic circles of those times, his debut at the institute was, by all accounts, a *succès fou*. Fries thereafter turned into one of his ardent admirers, and Jakobson became one of the most sought after guests at Linguistic Institutes.[4]

The hallmark that stamped all but the most solemn of his public utterances was Jakobson's wit. He sprinkled his lectures with humorous asides, often calculated to point up the discrepancies between reality, with its shortcomings, and a state considered desirable by the speaker in temporary collusion with his listeners. Anecdotes about him could fill a modest-sized monograph; although I have always suspected that he secretly engendered most of them himself, such stories tend to take on a life of their own, becoming collective property much in the manner of his and Peter Bogatyrev's "Die Folklore als eine besondere Form des Schaffens" (in Jakobson 1966:1–15). Possibly the best known has to do with Jakobson's arresting accent. While his mastery of the grammatical and lexical resources of spoken English was elegant, and of its rhetorical effects superb, his pronunciation remained shockingly alien, giving rise to a remark most often ascribed to Jerzy Kuryłowicz (in Mehta 1971: 229), but, in fact, circulating in numerous variants: "Jakobson can lecture perfectly in six languages—unfortunately, all of them Russian." His proficiency in handling discussion was histrionic and, partly as a consequence, a lot of fun to watch. I was once chairing a lecture where he spoke for a scheduled hour or so to a large assembly of students. When the time came for questions, his mostly young audience were shy, and too overawed to speak up. After a few moments of awkward silence, Jakobson turned to me, holding his hand high: could he address a query to himself, he wondered? I nodded, he put his question, then went on to answer himself, thus expanding his lecture for another rapt hour. Some years ago, in the early 1960s, the director of the Newberry Library convened a meeting of a dozen or so linguists in Chicago, culminating in a convivial banquet, where we were called upon to relate "Jakobson stories" in turn, most of which I have now forgotten. What does linger in my memory is the spontaneous outpouring of affection with which the many hilarious incidents—true or alleged—were suffused. Not a trace of malice disfigured that glow. I remember remarking on that pleasant atmosphere to friends who walked me back to my hotel: I felt that, after nearly twenty years of searching, Jakobson, who was born on October 11 and hence jocosely fancied his affinity with Christopher Columbus, had found the symbolic Indians he vainly looked for upon his first alighting in Indiana, and they had finally made him their honored chief. After this mutual discovery, the benefice of his teaching continued to radiate serenely out of Cambridge, prompting even his callowest followers to proclaim that he had, indeed, "played a key role in the development of linguistics in

America," and to acknowledge that "he has a lasting, and often decisive, influence on our scholarly development" (Gribble 1968:7). The youth of America thus turned out to be luckier than the youth of Athens, whose elders succeeded in killing the man of whom Crito said "that of all men of his time whom [he has] known, he was the wisest and justest and best" (Plato's *Phaedo*, trans. Jowett).

Notes

1. Once I had to miss a class where Jakobson was to have dealt with glossematics, and, the next time, I asked him to lend me his notes. He handed me a small stack of cards. The top card read: "The dog." The rest were equally uninformative. Plainly, the secrets of glossematics were not concealed in that cache. Years afterward, the meaning of the legend on that card dawned on me— but that is another story, involving—to mention it only briefly—the various contextual meanings of the vocable "dog" in their relation to its general meaning.

2. "Beitrag zur allgemeinen Kasuslehre: Gesamtbedeutung der russischen Kasus," in Jakobson 1971b:23-71.

3. Jakobson subscribed to a journal edited by this man, and told me that one of his checks was cashed with the erudite endorsement *Pecunia non olet*.

4. Jakobson's stellar role in the 1952 session, along with a sensational performance by Lévi-Strauss (1963:67-80) was an especially memorable *tour de force*. A particularly distinguished group listened to his pivotal presentation that introduced fundamental semiotic concepts to an essentially native audience, most of whom heard the name of their turn-of-the-century compatriot, Charles Sanders Peirce, for the first time. As usual, time was to bear out amply his farsighted assessment (Sebeok 1975a). For a more detailed discussion, see chapter 2 of this book.

PART TWO

Semiosis and Method

CHAPTER FOUR

Is a Comparative Semiotics Possible?

Il y a un double mouvement une aspiration de la nature vers la culture, c'est-à-dire de l'objet, vers le signe et le langage, et un second mouvement qui, par le moyen de cette expression linguistique, permet de découvrir ou d'apercevoir des propriétés normalement dissimulées de l'objet, et qui sont ces propriétés mêmes qui lui sont communes avec la structure et le mode de fonctionnement de l'esprit humain.—Lévi-Strauss to G. Charbonnier, 1961

Même les sciences de l'homme ont leurs relations d'incertitude.—Lévi-Strauss

Many early anthropologists were certain that there were universal patterns of culture or universal categories which underlay all cultures; thus Adolf Bastian—who was, incidentally, a staunch critic of Darwinism—contended that, by general law, the "psychic unity of mankind" everywhere produced "elementary ideas" (*Elementargedanken*; cf. Hugo Schuchardt's [1912] concept of a linguistic *elementare Verwandtschaft*, derived directly from Bastian), which, responsive to different external stimuli, then gave rise to areal divisions and, at a further stage of evolutionary development, to cultural

The argument developed in this article was first presented in an impromptu talk delivered in January 1967, in a seminar held at the Collège de France, under the joint auspices of Claude Lévi-Strauss, Roland Barthes, and A. J. Greimas. The somewhat different version presented here constitutes chapter 1 of Sebeok 1968 and is also reprinted in Sebeok 1985b. It is reprinted here by permission of the Indiana University Press. Grateful acknowledgment is hereby made to the National Science Foundation for a Senior Post-doctoral Fellowship with tenure, in 1966–67, at the Center for Advanced Study in the Behavioral Sciences and the University of California (Berkeley), and for a Research Grant (GB-5581) awarded by the NSF Program in Psychobiology.

variation in history proper; compared to the basic laws, however, he considered the latter of subordinate significance (Lowie 1937).

Contemporary anthropologists have, on occasion, furnished partial lists of items that seem to occur in every human society known to history or ethnography, and have shown that, when some of these—notably language—are analyzed in detail, the resemblances among all cultures are found to be very numerous indeed: "For example, not only does every culture have a language, but all languages are resolvable into identical kinds of components" (Murdock 1945). On the other hand, while C. Kluckhohn (1953) has underlined that "linguistics alone of all the branches of anthropology had discovered elemental units...which are universal, objective, and theoretically meaningful," he has also questioned whether comparable units are, "in principle, discoverable in sectors of culture less automatic than speech and less closely tied...to biological fact." Whatever one may think about the underlying assumptions here about the nature of the relationships between the biological and the social sciences—I join with the view outlined by L. Tiger and R. Fox (1966) and endorse the research strategy it implies (cf. Glass 1967)—an unambiguous resolution of this apparent quandary emerges with the consistent application throughout cultural and social anthropology of the systems concept that is the cornerstone of all modern linguistics. This concept was pithily reformulated by Claude Lévi-Strauss (1962b) when, with the aim of disposing of such vague notions as "archetypes" or a "collective unconscious," he emphasized the validity of latent relational as against patent substantial invariance: "seules les formes peuvent être communes, mais non les contenus" (p. 121). The more general slogan of Gregory Bateson (Sebeok 1968: chap. 22), "The pattern is the thing," once more underlines what all linguists know, that any typology must be constructed by a rigorous elimination of redundancies from the systems assumed to be topologically equivalent. When viewed in this way, any two cultures are seen as superficially different representations of one abstract structure, namely, of human culture; and it is this isomorphism which accounts for the feasibility of communication across cultures. The search for universals thus once again turns out to be a search for the "psychic unity of mankind," that is, for the fundamental laws which govern human behavior.

In no domain has this search been more diligent—and, after several false starts, more productive—than in linguistics, beginning with Roger Bacon's dictum, "Grammatica una et eadem secundum substantiam in omnibus linguis, licet accidentaliter varietur." The early decades of the nineteenth century were suffused by a creative fervor as linguists of that era pursued their single-minded quest to consolidate and order the enormous quantities of concrete language data which had been amassed in the eighteenth century, chiefly under the impetus of Leibniz. Their engrossment with the diversification of language through time and with the concomitant reconstruction of extinct stages of languages by the comparative-historical method temporarily overshadowed, if never quite extinguished, an antecedent tradition of "philosophical" grammar with which the seventeenth- and eighteenth-century students of language were deeply concerned (cf. Sebeok 1966). As early as 1808, Friedrich von Schlegel—who was a pupil of George Cuviers, the founder of comparative anatomy—proposed a program of investigation animated by a biological metaphor which crudely foreshadowed the key notion of general ethology, that behavior unfolds with morphological growth and differentiation (as a consequence of genetic programming; see, e.g., Lorenz 1965): "Comparative grammar will give us entirely new information on the genealogy of language, in exactly the same way in which comparative anatomy has thrown light upon natural history" (Pedersen 1962). The rewarding preoccupation of the past century with problems of linguistic kinship left its scars on the striving for typology in that era, of which perhaps N. Marr's theory of stadialism—developed through the 1920s, as a misconceived Marxist and equally perverted scientific effort to correlate linguistic (especially morphological) types ordered as pseudoevolutionary stages, with psychological and societal stages arranged in parallel manner—was the last and most thoroughly discredited survival (Thomas 1957).

An initial impression of rich and seemingly inexhaustible diversity—assigned primacy by empirically inclined anthropological and other descriptive linguists of (roughly) the second quarter of our century—is now again being gradually superseded by the growing conviction of pervasive and significant invariance in the midst of surface variety. The history of linguistic thought has ever oscillated

between a predominant preference for data collecting and the view
that languages are separate objects to be described, compared, and
interpreted, as against a concentrated search for universals of language
and their defining properties. This latter goal—especially in its
contemporary development—necessarily involves an understanding
of the neurophysiological (Darley 1967) and the even more broadly
biological (Lenneberg 1967; Sebeok 1968: chap. 21) characteristics
of humans, their modes of perception, categorization, and transformations, in order to account for the behavior of this unique language-
using species and, more immediately, for the processes of linguistic
ontogeny. As V. Zvegintsev (1967:140) has insisted, the study of
language universals becomes meaningful "only when viewing them
as interconnected with other sciences, and the results of this study
acquire equal importance both for linguistic proper and for other
sciences."

The study of language universals—whether substantive, as
traditionally pursued (and as exemplified in Greenberg 1963 and
Greenberg 1966), or formal, as recently proposed by generative
grammarians (Katz and Postal 1964; Chomsky 1965)—reveals that
all known natural languages are relatively superficial variations on
a single underlying theme—what Wilhelm von Humboldt, in 1821,
explicitly recognized as "an intellectual instinct of the mind" (Cowan
1963)—a model which is, moreover, both species-specific and
species-consistent. The fruitless (but apparently still not altogether
resolved antithesis between "innate" and "acquired" categories of
behavior (cf. Hinde 1966) is reconcilable in our domain if we
assume that the universal glotto-poetic scheme (deep structure, intended as an approximation to the Humboldtian notion of "inner
form") is hereditary, while the environment contributes the behavioral variability (reflected in surface structures or "outer forms"). In
other words, the development of a normal neonate's faculty of
language, which presumably includes a set of the universal primes
of the verbal code, is wholly determined by the genetic code, but in
such a way that his or her identical genetic blueprint can then find a
variety of expressions in phenogeny through space and time. The
feedback from a human's environment to his or her genetic constitution, the interaction between human nature and culture, yields the
thousands of natural languages, but neither parameter can account

for more than a portion of the formative rules which led to their creation. The conclusions seem inescapable that the faculty of language—*le langage*—survived only once in the course of evolution, that its basic ground plan has remained both unaltered in and peculiar to our species, and that the multiform languages—*les langues*—concretely realized in human societies become differentiated from each other later on through the miscellaneous, more or less well recognized, processes of historical linguistics.

While language, in its several concrete manifestations, notably speech (but also in its derivatives and transductions, e.g., into script or electrical pulses) is, of course, the human signaling system *par excellence*, indeed, the hallmark of humanity (or, as Simpson [1966] put it, "the most diagnostic single trait of man"), it is by no means the sole method of human communication—only a particular, uniquely adaptive case. Other devices at our disposal, together with those properly linguistic, constitute an important part of semiotics, rapidly burgeoning into an autonomous field of research. The term *semiotic*, confined in earliest usage to medical concerns with the sensible indications of changes in the conditions of the human body, that is, symptomatology, later came to be used by the Stoics with a broader meaning and seems to have been introduced into English philosophical discourse by John Locke, in book 4, chapter 21, of his *Essay Concerning Human Understanding* (1975 [1690]). Locke considered the doctrine of signs as that branch of his tripartite division of all sciences "the business whereof, is to consider the Nature of Signs, the Mind makes use of for the understanding of Things, or conveying its Knowledge to others" (p. 720). For communication and for recording of our thoughts,

> Signs of our *Ideas* are...necessary. Those which Men have found most convenient, and therefore generally make use of, are articulate Sounds. The Consideration then of *Ideas* and *Words,* as the great Instruments of Knowledge, makes no despicable part of their Contemplation, who would take a view of humane Knowledge in the whole Extent of it. And, perhaps, if they were distinctly weighed, and duly considered, they would afford us another sort of Logick and Critick, than what we have been hitherto acquainted with (p. 721).

The real founder and first systematic investigator of *semiotic*, however, was the subtle and profound American philosopher Charles

Sanders Peirce: "I am, as far as I know," he observed, "a pioneer, or rather a backwoodsman, in the work of clearing and opening up what I call *semiotic*, that is, the doctrine of the essential nature and fundamental varieties of possible semiosis; and I find the field too vast, the labour too treat, for a first-comer. I am, accordingly, obliged to confine myself to the most important questions" (Peirce 5.488 [ca. 1906]). It is, incidentally, to Peirce that we owe the classification of signs into icons, indexes, and symbols, which (with some essential modifications) has proved to be of great utility in several recent studies of both human (Jakobson 1964; Jakobson 1965; and Jakobson 1967) and animal communication (Sebeok 1967c).

The unique place of *semiotic* among the sciences—not merely one among the others, "but an organon or instrument of all the sciences"—was stressed by Charles Morris, who proposed (1938) to absorb logic and mathematics, as well as linguistics, entirely into *semiotic*. Morris's trichotomy of *semiotic* into syntactics, semantics, and pragmatics has also proved generally very useful and particularly so in stimulating various approaches to animal communication (cf. Marler 1961 and Altmann's and Sebeok's chapters in Altmann 1967). "The whole science of language," Rudolf Carnap then reaffirmed in 1942, "is called semiotic," and, in 1946, Morris introduced further refinements that are valuable for mapping out the field of animal communication (Sebeok 1967a), such as the distinction among pure *semiotic*, which elaborates a language to talk about signs, descriptive *semiotic*, which studies actual signs, and applied *semiotic*, which utilizes knowledge about signs for the accomplishment of various purposes. The variant form *semiotics*—by analogy with *semantics* and its congeners, rather than with *logic* and its—seems to have gained currency on the initiative of Margaret Mead, as a term that might aptly cover "patterned communications in all modalities" (Sebeok et al. 1972).

As a scientific discipline, general semiotics is still in its infancy. When Ferdinand de Saussure postulated (in one version of his posthumously published book, 1967 [1916]) the existence of a science devoted to "la vie des signes au sein de la vie sociale," he further remarked that, since *sémiologie* (as he called it then; nowadays the French term is being increasingly replaced by *sémiotique*, because the former more commonly means "symptomatology") did not yet exist, no one could foretell what it would be like; one could be certain only that linguistics would be a part of it, and that the laws of linguistics would apply to it. Even today, semiotics lacks a comprehensive theoretical foundation but is sustained largely as a consistently shared point of view (Barthes 1964), having as its subject matter all systems of signs irrespective of their substance and without regard of the species of emitter or receiver involved. As M. R. Mayenowa (1967:59) has correctly observed, since the semiotic disciplines, excepting only linguistics, "are themselves of recent origin, more or less contemporary with semiotics, we cannot as yet be said to have developed adequate and universally accepted theories for sign systems, other than those developed in linguistics for the natural languages." It remains to be seen whether a general theory of semiotics can be constructed such that the problems and solutions relating to the natural languages can themselves be reformulated in an interesting way. At present, the trend continues in the opposite direction, that is, the descriptions of other sign systems tend to more or less slavishly imitate—despite occasional warnings, e.g., by Lévi-Strauss (1945)—and more often than not quite erroneously, the narrow internal models successfully employed by linguists. The literature of semiotics is thus replete with mere restatements rather than solutions of problems, and the need for different kinds of theory at different levels of "coding" appears pressing.

The total communicative repertoire of humans consists of two sorts of sign systems: the anthroposemiotic, that is, those that are exclusively human, and the zoosemiotic, that is, those that can be shown to be the end products of evolutionary series. The two are often confused, but it is important to distinguish the purely anthroposemiotic systems, found solely in humans, from zoosemiotic (Sebeok 1970) systems, which humans share with at least some ancestral species.

Anthroposemiotic systems are again of two types: first, language, plus those for which language provides an indispensable integrating base; and second, those for which language is merely— and perhaps mistakenly—thought to provide an infrastructure, or at least an analytical model to be approximately copied. Obvious examples of systems of the first type are furnished by any of the arts qualified, for this very reason, as verbal (Stender-Petersen 1949), where a particular natural language necessarily intervenes between the source of a message and its destination (cf. several articles in Lotman 1965 and 1967). Among such complex macrostructures, which may be considered secondary semiotic systems (cf., however, the discussion in Kristeva 1967), belong also forms (cf. T. Tsivian, in Lotman 1965) of normative etiquette behavior; as well as those assemblages of objects that humans have elevated to the status of sign systems as they have filtered them through their languages. Thus clothing serves at once a protective and a communicative function, and food satisfies both a need for calories and a craving for information: the nomenclature of fashion (Barthes 1967b) or of cooking (Lévi-Strauss 1962a) is the untranslatable *signans*, to be understood in relation to the use to which the objects are put in this or that society, in brief, to the corresponding transmutable *signatum*. (It is interesting to note in passing that clothing, in its duple function, is not a universal but that bodily adornment, constituting a system of signs with no evident protective function, is).

To the contrary, such is not the case when addresser and addressee are coupled, e.g., in the acoustic channel by music (Ruwet 1967), in the visual channel by chalk marks (internationally used by men's tailors), or in the chemical channel by manufactured perfumes (Sebeok 1967c): semiotic systems of this type, although uniquely human, do not imply any particular linguistic code. Myth and ritual, which function *in situ* as mutually redundant (although not necessarily homologous, cf. Lévi-Strauss 1956) components of a single culture complex, illustrate, in the sense implied here, typological opposites.

Zoosemiotic systems found in humans, *inter alia*, are sometimes classified under such labels as paralinguistics and kinesics (see bibliography of Hayes, in Sebeok et al. 1972), proxemics (Hall 1968), or simply in terms of the sensory channels used, as gustation for proximal and olfaction for distal chemical signaling (Sebeok 1967c), or tactile (Frank 1957)—more specifically, cutaneous (Moles 1964)—communication. Although there seems to be no compelling reason to assume, and some evidence (supporting intuition) to the contrary, that sign systems of this sort are languagelike in any but trivial ways—chiefly arising from the evident fact that they, like language, are classified as semiotic disciplines—they are often prejudicially modeled according to one fashionable theory of language or another. Thus kinesics, to take one glaring example (but others could readily be cited), was deliberately and closely drawn by analogy with a design considered temporarily serviceable by a dominant school of American descriptivists of the late 1940s. This adherence has severely constrained the presentation of a wealth of valuable data on body motion, as well as distorted, in consequence, the proper perspective on kinesics in the hierarchy of semiotic systems in general. The particularism of linguistics of the previous generation, already mentioned, has led even one of the acutest observers of human postures and movements, Ray Birdwhistell (e.g., 1963), to deny altogether the existence of universal gestures, and this in spite of Charles Darwin's (1872) empirical analysis of displays, including a thorough treatment of human expressions, and Birdwhistell's own avowed attitude when he first began to formulate a research strategy without the benefit of linguistics. As a matter of fact, and as one would expect *a priori*, recent pilot studies have confirmed that Darwin was quite correct in asserting that certain human expressions do occur cross-culturally and are probably universal: for instance, film documents of flirting girls from five cultures "show in principle the same type of facial expression and ambivalent behavior" (Eibl-Eibesfeldt and Hass 1967).

There are, indeed, compelling reasons for sharing Noam Chomsky's skepticism for studying animal communication systems, human gestures, and language within the same framework, unless one is willing to rise to a level of abstraction where there are "plenty of other things incorporated under the same generalizations which no one would have regarded as being continuous with language or particularly relevant to the mechanisms of language" (Chomsky 1967:73). To establish this level of abstraction is precisely the challenge of semiotics, but diachronic continuities are not material to the theory. William N. Tavolga (in Sebeok 1968: chap. 13) is also quite correct when he states that it is "erroneous to use the methods and theory developed for the study of human language in the investigation of a kind of communication found in another species at a different organizational level" (Tavolga 1968:272), and in his insistence that levels of integration in behavior are qualitatively different, requiring, as such, "distinctive instrumentation, experimental operations, and theoretical approaches" (p. 272). Nevertheless, his assertion that "communication does not exist as a single phenomenon" (p. 273) simply does not follow; on the contrary, highly insightful cross-phyletic comparisons have already been made (e.g., by Marler 1967), and will, we may confidently anticipate, continue to be made, provided that the analytical framework used is that of a well-developed theory of signs and not just of linguistic signs.

Parenthetically, it should be pointed out that the claim that a semiotic system, at any given time, functions independently of the processual forces that led to its formation (cf. the linguistic opposition of synchrony to diachrony) is not to say that a holistic analysis of, say, human gestures can afford to ignore their evolutionary antecedents. These can be traced in painstaking detail at least to the zoosemiotic behavior of primitive primates and insectivores, as R. J. Andrew (1963) has persuasively shown that many facial displays have evolved from such mechanisms as responses by which vulnerable areas are protected and those associated with respiration or grooming. On the other hand, there are two schools of thought about the origin of language: "there are those who, like Darwin, believe in a gradual evolution, but there have been others who have believed that speech is specifically a human attribute, a function *de novo*, different in kind from anything of which other animals are capable" (Pumphrey 1951). At any rate, there can be no facile generalizations overarching both language and the many well-identified zoosemiotic systems found in humans, such as the territorial, including temporal, spacing mechanism they share with the rest of the organic world (Hall 1968).

The question now arises whether a truly comparative science of signs is possible. We have argued that all natural languages are elaborations from a single template. If this is so, it would appear that the linguists' knowledge of "deep structure" suffers from the handicap of being restricted to a sample of one. The rules of language can, in some measure, be described; but, being unique, can they be explained, in the sense that these are logically deducible from a higher-level set of semiotic laws? The study and characterization of humans' other semiotic systems, and especially of the signaling behavior of the two million or so other extant species, are such immediately appealing tasks because they can perhaps point the way to an escape from the dilemma posed by the necessity for extrapolation from a sample of one and, in this way, enable us to discriminate what is necessary and what is contingent in systems of communication. This hope has fueled my own researches in these areas and motivated both the assembly of a volume on human communication (Sebeok et al. 1972) and a collection of papers on animal communication that includes exploratory inquiries concerning their implications for anthropology, psychology, linguistics, and the theory of communication (Sebeok 1968).

Ultimately, however, zoosemiotics as a whole must face the identical problem of extrapolation from a sample of one. This is because terrestrial organisms, from protozoans to humans, are so similar in their biochemical details as to make it virtually certain that all of them have evolved from a single instance of the origin of life. A variety of observations support the hypothesis that the entire organic world has descended lineally from primordial life, the most impressive fact being the ubiquity of the molecule DNA. The genetic material of all known organisms on earth is composed largely of the nucleic acids DNA and RNA, which contain in their structures information that is reproductively transmitted from generation to generation and which have, in addition, the capability for self-replication and mutation. In brief, the genetic code "is universal, or nearly so" (Crick 1966:3). Its decipherment was a stunning achievement, because it showed how "the two great polymer languages, the nucleic acid language and the protein language, are linked together" (Crick 1966:9; details in Clark and Marcker 1968). The Soviet mathematician A. A. Liapunov has further argued (1963) that all living systems transmit, through definitely prescribed channels, small quantities of energy or material containing a large volume of information that is responsible for the subsequent control of vast amounts of energy and materials. In this way, a host of biological as well as cultural phenomena can be comprehended as aspects of information handling: storage, feedback, message channeling, and the like. Reproduction is thus seen, in the end, to be in large measure information replication, or yet another sort of communication, a kind of control that seems to be a universal property of terrestrial life, independent of form or substance.

Five years ago, I called attention to a vision of new and startling dimensions: the convergence of the science of genetics with the science of linguistics, remarking that both are emerging "as autonomous yet sister disciplines in the larger field of communication sciences, to which, on the molar level, zoosemiotics also contributes" (Sebeok 1963a). The terminology of genetics is replete with expressions borrowed from linguistics and from the theory of communication, as was recently pointed out by Jakobson (1969–70), who also emphasized the salient similarities and equally important differences between the respective structures and functions of the genetic and verbal codes. These, of course, urgently need further elucidation and precision. Yet it is amply clear even now that the genetic code must be regarded as the most fundamental of all semiotic networks and therefore as the prototype for all other signaling systems used by animals, including humans. From this point of view, molecules that are quantum systems, acting as stable physical information carriers, zoosemiotic systems, and, finally, cultural systems, comprehending language, constitute a natural sequel of stages of ever more complex energy levels in a single universal evolution. It is possible, therefore, to describe language as well as living systems from a unified cybernetic standpoint. While this is perhaps no more than a useful analogy at present, hopefully providing insight if not yet new information, a mutual appreciation of genetics, animal communication studies, and linguistics may lead to a full understanding of the dynamics of semiosis, and this may, in the last analysis, turn out to be no less than the definition of life.

CHAPTER FIVE

"Animal" in Biological and Semiotic Perspective

Whatever else an animal may be, it is clear that each is a living system, or subsystem, a complex array of atoms organized and maintained according to certain principles, the most important among these being negative entropy. The classic statement emphasizing this fact is to be found in Schrödinger's famous book *What is life?* (1946:77), where he addresses an "organism's astonishing gift of concentrating a 'stream of order' on itself and thus escaping the decay into atomic chaos—of 'drinking orderliness' from a suitable environment."

The importance of Schrödinger's formulation, with its stress on the generation of order, seems to me to derive from two crucial implications. First, in invoking the notion of entropy, which in statistical mechanics is fundamental to the Second Law of Thermodynamics, it authenticates that life conforms to the basic laws of physics (Ling 1984). Secondly, since negative entropy is closely coupled with the notion (or, more accurately, *a* notion) of information—that which "embodies, expresses, and often specifies order" (Medawar and Medawar 1983:205)—it demonstrates the salience of semiotics to an understanding of life. Schrödinger himself (1946:79) hinted at the latter when he remarked on the power of a group of atoms—he called them a "tiny central office"—to produce "orderly events" in the isolated cell, and then went on to ask, "Do they not resemble stations of a local government dispersed through the body, communicating with each other with great ease, thanks to the code that is common to all of them?"

If the subject matter of semiotics "is the exchange of any messages whatever and of the systems of signs which underlie

Originally published in *What Is an Animal?*, ed. Tim Ingold, pp. 63–76 (London: Unwin Hyman, 1988).

them" (Sebeok 1985b:1), the amount of information is "a measure of the degree of order which is peculiarly associated with those patterns which are distributed as messages in time" (Wiener 1950:21). In short, life couples two transmutative processes, one energetic or physical, the other informational or semiosic. The former has to do with the conversion of low-entropy articles, integrating energy flowing from external sources, into high-entropy waste products disgorged into other open systems; the latter points to the transformation of signs into (as a rule) more-developed signs (an identification of organisms with signs that goes back at least to Peirce 1868).

There are two additional striking properties of life. One of these is hierarchical organization (cf. Bonner 1969; Salthe 1985). This is a universal characteristic which life shares with the rest of the cosmos and which defines, in the overall architecture of the universe, its position on a continuum of scale between the vanishingly small (leptons, photons, and quarks) and the indefinitely large (galactic superclusters).

The second conspicuous property lies in the contrast between, and fundamental invariance in, life's subjacent biochemistry (a virtually uniform pool of twenty animo acids) and the prodigal variety in the individual expressions thereof, the latter depending on shifts in the environmental context within the global biosphere.

Given that all animals are composed of matter in a "living state," it is equally clear that by no means all life-forms are animals. Competing definitions of life abound (e.g., Miller 1978), as well as miscellaneous paradigms to account for its origin (e.g., Schopf 1983), but these need not be discussed here. Indeed, such an exercise may not even serve any useful purpose, as N. W. Pirie (1937) has argued, especially considering the existence of borderline phenomena, comparable with the transition from, say, green to yellow or acid to alkaline. The supposedly ironclad distinction between life and nonlife becomes fuzzy not only if you look back far enough in time, but also in the light of recent developments in commingling and breeding life-forms (including humans) with manufactured objects, as is breathtakingly envisioned by Margulis and Sagan (1986b).

The place of animals among other living systems and their

distinctive features do, however, require consideration. Macrotaxonomy, the craft of classifying, is a vast (if not always fashionable) field of endeavor, masterfully explored in the realm of biology by Ernst Mayr (1982). However, the sole biologically valid classification of animals, since Charles Darwin's, is of subordinate classes whose members are united by common heritage or descent at one level of ancestry into superordinate classes whose members are united at the next ascending level. In Darwin's own words, "All true classification is genealogical" (1859:420; see also chap. 2).

There are many competing representations of evolutionary relations on all levels, and all of these are doubtless provisional. For example, the Linnaean plant versus animal dichotomy has been argued on quite different grounds by naturalists since the eighteenth century. Mayr (1965:418–420) lists eleven clusters of distinctive features among the more important differences which have been variously adduced. This notwithstanding, he concludes by noting that "it is important to emphasize that the species of animals and plants are nevertheless essentially similar. Plants and animals are virtually identical in their genetic and cytological mechanisms."

Thus, the choice of a classification scheme is ultimately (although, of course, within limits) a personal matter. I favor the one which seems to me to provide the maximum heuristic guidance. That is the codification proposed by R. H. Whittaker (1959), refined by him a decade later (1969).

Whittaker reviews the broad, conventional two-way classification of all organisms—into plants and animals—and enumerates its drawbacks, as well as those of an alternative quadripartite scheme proposed by H. F. Copeland (e.g., 1956). He then puts forward a pentad of his own, which, although having certain recognized deficiencies as well, seems to me the most comprehensive and cogent system worked out thus far. Whittaker's classification is based on a combination of two sets of distinctions, concerning, respectively, *levels* of organization and *types* of organization. The first is derived from the principle of hierarchy already mentioned. The second relates to three principal modes of nutrition, that is, to three different ways in which information (negentropy) is maintained by extracting order out of the environment.

This second set of distinctions sorts macroscopic entities into three complementary categories, called Superkingdoms, within the pervasive latticed configuration of the terrestrial biosphere. These are:

1. *Plants*, or producers, which derive their food from inorganic sources, by photosynthesis.

2. *Animals*, or ingestors, which derive their food—preformed organic compounds—from other organisms. They may be subdivided into three classes:

    a. If they eat plants, we call them herbivores;

    b. if they eat animals that eat plants, we call them carnivores (or predators);

    c. if they eat both, we call them omnivores.

Animals are designated "ingestors" because they incorporate food into their bodies, where the intake is then digested.

3. *Fungi*, or decomposers, in opposition to animals, do not incorporate food into their bodies, but they "secrete digestive enzymes into the environment to break down their food externally and they absorb the resulting small molecules from solution" (Margulis 1981:32).

On this macroscopic scale, animals can be cataloged as intermediate transforming agents midway between two polar opposite lifeforms: the composers, or organisms that "build up," and the decomposers, or organisms that "break down." Claude Bernard (1878:1, 37) once coined a pair of slogans, paradoxically entailing both production, *La vie, c'est la création*, and decay, *La vie, c'est la mort*. Of animals, it may well be added, *La vie, c'est l'entremise!*[1]

Most remaining life-forms can be negatively defined as non-plants, non-animals, and non-fungi. By application of the first principle of hierarchy, these fall into one of the following two groups.

4. *Protoctists*, comprising the remaining eukaryotes, all of them being microorganisms lacking embryogenesis but displaying alimentary heterogeneity, including the familiar triad of photosynthetic, ingesting as well as absorbing species (here belong algae, protozoa, slime molds and nets, etc.).

5. *Prokaryotes*, the Monera, where bacteria belong, are generally single-celled creatures which, although nutritionally diverse, are incapable of ingestion (see also Margulis and Sagan 1986a).[2]

Let me now consider further the classification of animals. In addition to Whittaker's double characterization: first by level of entitation—a term coined by the physiologist W. Ralph Gerard (1969:218–219) to mean "the identification of entity," and which he considered vastly more important than the concept of quantitation— and second, by nutritional mode, two further principles may be introduced; one embryological, the other biosemiosic. The former is stated by Margulis (1981:32) thus: "In all animals, the zygote formed by the fertilization of the female by the male gamete develops into a ball of cells called a blastula," which unambiguously separates animals from all other forms by virtue of their development.

All animates are bombarded by signs emanating from their environment, which includes a *milieu intérieur*, as well as, of course, other animates sharing their environment, some conspecific, some not (for further pertinent particulars, see Sebeok 1986d: chap. 3). Such inputs are eventually transmuted into outputs consisting of strings of further signs. This sign-process is called semiosis. The pioneer explorer of the decisive role of semiosis in the origin and operation of life processes was Jakob von Uexküll, who was also a preeminent founder of modern ethology. He advanced a highly original and integrated theory of semiosis in the framework of what came to be known as *Umweltforschung*, the study of phenomenal worlds, self-worlds, or the subjective universe.[3]

Although *Umwelt* research has focused almost wholly on animals including humans (e.g., Sebeok 1977a: chap. 38), plants are also discussed, contrastively if briefly, and there have been allusions even to plasmodial slime molds—now in a phylum of the Protoctista, although classified by Uexküll and others among the Fungi (J. von Uexküll 1982:35–36). As Uexküll maintained (1982:33–34), and as Martin Krampen (1981b) later greatly elaborated, plants differ from animals in that they lack a "functional cycle" (J. von Uexküll 1980: chap. 3) which would link receptor organs via a mesh of nerve fibers to effector organs. They are rather immersed directly in their habitat. The relationships of a plant with its habitat, or casing, "are altogether different from those of the animals with their Umwelts." However, Krampen (1981b:203) concludes that the "vegetative world is nevertheless structured according to a base semiotics which cuts across all living beings, plants, animals, and humans alike." He argues that while plants exhibit predominantly indexical signs, in animals both indexical and iconic signs appear, whereas human sign-processes encompass the entire gamut from indexicality via iconicity to symbolicity.[4] However this may be—and in my opinion the entire subject cries out for more empirical investigation—it is already obvious that, at least as a working assumption, one must suppose that there arc bound to be substantive differences among the several branches of biosemiotics (or biocommunication, as in Tembrock 1971): endosemiotics (J. von Uexküll 1980:291; T. von Uexküll 1986:204), zoosemiotics (Sebeok 1963a), phytosemiotics (Krampen 1981b) and, *in posse*, mycosemiotics.[5]

These and related subfields are very unevenly developed. The literature of zoosemiotics alone—even discounting human communication—is so prodigious that no summary can be attempted here, although one point pertinent to the topic of this chapter perhaps does need to be emphasized.

It seems to me beyond reasonable doubt that the symbiotic theory of the origin and evolution of cells is correct. This means that eukaryotic forms composed of nucleated cells—including such advanced forms as animals—evolved in consequence of certain symbioses between ancestral prokaryotes in the Proterozoic Aeon, by about 800 million years ago, and thereafter continued to diversify (see Margulis and Sagan 1986a: especially chaps. 8 and 9).

"Symbiosis," including commensalism, mutualism, and so forth, is plainly a form of semiosis: "Mutual cooperation is often facilitated by simple forms of *communication* between the participants," as *The Oxford Companion to Animal Behavior* puts it, with undue caution (MacFarland 1982:540). Biologists appear reluctant to describe it as such, yet the most obvious fact about symbionts is that they are types of communicants. They are organisms of different species living together, in ceaseless informative commerce, for most of the life-cycles of each, and to their mutual benefit. "Semiochemical effects occur between organisms of all types" (Albone 1984:2; for the sharing of semiochemicals in human bonding-related behavior, see Nicholson 1984). Their exchanges are accomplished by chemical messengers of precision and subtlety; the topics of their "conversations" have to do largely with territory or reproduction. The exosemiotic chemical signals yoking microorganisms together—hormonal and chemical neurotransmitters—evolved in life-forms such as animals into specialized and localized endosemiotic cells within the body tissue (Krieger 1983:977). Such cells facilitate exceedingly complex mutual communicative interactions between the immune and nervous systems, known as "neoroimmunomodulation." Research in this area has far-reaching clinical as well as philosophical implications, some of which I have reviewed elsewhere (Sebeok and Rosenthal 1981).

Ernst Mayr (1982:146) defines *taxonomy* as "the theory and practice of delimiting kinds of organisms and of classifying them." However, this kind of enterprise, fathered in its evolutionary perspective by Darwin, is but a segment of the far more venerable as well as unbounded science of *systematics*, which, as George G. Simpson (1961, cf. Mayr 1982:145) taught it, has diversity as its subject matter. Systems of classification may depend on a whole variety of alternative, presumably complementary, approaches. For example, given that multiple biochemical pathways emerged for the biosynthesis of chlorophyll, plants can be reclassified according to how they fabricate their photosynthetic pigments. As Jerold Lowenstein (1984:541) for one has cogently claimed, comparisons based on DNA or on proteins can be vastly fecund, especially when it comes to "the inclusion of extinct species in phylogenies, the identification of species in fossil studies and museum collections, and broad systematic analysis of living animals and plants."

In short, all organisms—especially plants, animals, and fungi— pertain at once to a plurality of codes, each of which is capable of being transmuted into every other. To paraphrase a striking passage from Lévi-Strauss (1985:228), "Like a text less intelligible in one language than in several, from many different versions, rendered simultaneously, there might flow a sense richer and more profound than each of the partial and distorted meanings that any single version, taken in isolation, might yield to us."[6] Although his observation was meant to apply to myths, viewed as formulaic networks, the same surely holds for groupings of animals into biologically relevant assemblages and into anthropologically as well as semiotically relevant folk arrangements, such as were discussed, for instance, for English animal categories by Edmund Leach (1964), or to adumbrate the "meaning of life" in assorted African societies, by Roy G. Willis (1974). Lévi-Strauss (1966b:42–43) has remarked on the "evidence of thought which is experienced in all the exercises of speculation and resembles that of the naturalists and alchemists of antiquity and the middle ages....Native classifications are not only methodical and based on carefully built up theoretical knowledge. They are also at times comparable, from a formal point of view, to those still in use in zoology and botany." Thus, it is hardly surprising that Aristotle classified whales as fish, and that, despite their replacement in 1693 by John Ray (refined by Carl von Linné in 1758) into that class of vertebrates biologists call the Mammalia, infraclass Eutheria, order Cetacea, many laypersons still believe that whales are, indeed, fish. Whales are, of course, both, and other entities— e.g., Moby Dick—to boot.

The transience from code to code can become critical. In certain societies a plant can substitute for an animal, as a cucumber for an ox in the well-known case of the Nuer (Evans-Pritchard 1956), and, as elsewhere in Africa, a token of a plentiful animal species can take the place of a religiously prescribed but rare one. A fortiori, a beast can stand in, symbolically, for a human in a sacrificial rite. Nor should one overlook liminoid creatures belonging to overlapping codes—Victor Turner (1974:253) singles out the centaur Cheiron as a classical prototype epitomizing such liminality—which render the would-be cataloger's chore so wearisome. Just how much they do so is beautifully explored in Vercors's penetrating novel centering on an imaginary creature named *Paranthropus erectus* (Bruller 1953).

Cecil H. Brown is concerned with folk zoological life-forms. Appendix B to his book *Language and Living Things* (1984) contains a rich source of lexical data on zoological life-form coding from more than 220 globally scattered languages, postulating six stages of terminological growth, ranging, for example, from no zoological forms to a mammal—"wug" (i.e., worm + bug)—dichotomy, on to a bird-fish-snake trichotomy, and so forth.

To appreciate what counts as an animal for humans, and in what ways, finally requires a concentrated semiotic enquiry, which can only be hinted at in the following paragraphs. An animal is upgraded to a cultural object, an object of value, as a by-product of structuring, ordering, and classifying: the animal, in short, becomes a *marker* in Dean MacCannell's (1976:110) sense, a chunk of concentrated information, a signifier segregated from a signified by virtue of "the superimposition of a system of social values" (MacCannell 1976:119).

From this point of view it seems promising to consider the many and varied circumstances under which humans may encounter animals. In what follows I shall identify and briefly comment on some of the most common situations. The following list is presented in no particular order, and is certainly not all-embracing. Moreover, the different situations are not necessarily exclusive, and may partially coincide.

1. *Homo sapiens as predator.* Humans prey upon, or even annihilate, animal species for different reasons. Some, like antelopes, may be hunted as game; certain carnivores, such as the East African crocodile, are condemned as "vermin" (a distancing label, discussed by Serpell [1986:159–162] under the heading of justificatory "misrepresentation"); primates are overused in medical research; marsupials are killed for their hides; and cetaceans are exploited for their oil. In effect, every time a population of animals is exterminated, the draining of the gene pool is concurrently and irreversibly accompanied by the elimination of a unique communicative code.

2. *Homo sapiens as prey.* Humans become the casualty of an animal's depredations: e.g., human malaria is caused by any of four sporozoites (parasitic protozoans). Each is transmitted from human to human by a female *Anopheles* mosquito, which injects saliva containing plasmodian sporozoites as it bites (even today, more people die every year of mosquito-borne disease than from any other single cause; cf. Stanier et al. 1985:646). Another forceful illustration is provided by V. Geist's speculations on the prehistoric bears of North America, and their possible role in delaying human colonization of that continent (Geist 1986).

3. *Homo sapiens as "partner."* Humans coexist with an animal in some sort of partnership (see Katcher and Beck 1983), as for example in a purely guest-host relationship (as aquarium fishes with their keeper) or in a nexus of mutual dependence (such as in beekeeping; seeing-eye dogs assisting blind people; dogs used for hauling, such as Arctic sled-dogs; dogs or cheetahs used for tracking; birds as fishing partners, such as a cormorant catching fish for a Japanese fisherman in exchange for a food reward matching the size of the catch; birds as hunting partners, such as the raptors described by Frederick II [1194–1250] in his classic and innovative account,

De arte venandi cum avibus; and pets as therapists [Beck and Katcher 1983: chap. 8; Serpell 1986: chap. 6]).

A special set of subproblems in this category can be identified when animals are used as sexual partners by either men or women, a phenomenon known as "cross-species attachment" (Money 1986:75–76). Bestiality, or the carnal exploitation of animals, has been known at least since Apuleius (ca. 125–175; cf. an "ancient pre-Columbian custom among Indians of the Caribbean coast of Columbia," cited by John Money (1986:75–76), "that associates the attainment of manhood with the exercise of copulating with donkeys"). Zoophilic acts, involving cattle, horses or donkeys, dogs, monkeys, or barnyard fowl, are a common theme of pornographic literature; there is also a variant called "formicophilia," "in which arousal and orgasm are dependent on the sensations produced by small creatures like snails, frogs, ants or other insects creeping, crawling, or nibbling the genitalia and perianal area, and the nipples" (Money 1986:75–76). In some urban environments animals are used as social facilitators, or catalysts; thus, dogs are used by European female, as well as male, streetwalkers to assist in striking up conversations with potential clients. The curious Western phenomenon of pet cemeteries could further be mentioned here.

4. *Sport and entertainment.* Animals have been long and variously used for human amusement: in Roman circuses (gladiators wrestling with big cats), bullfighting rings, alligator wrestling, cock fights, and frog-jumping contests. Here, too, belong horse and dog races and, perhaps marginally, birdwatching, (urban) pigeon feeding, and, more generally, safaris with photographic intent.

5. *Parasitism.* Parasitism may work in either direction:

a. The activities of humans in relation to reindeer, for instance, can be described as those of a social parasite; interspecific associations, in relation to parasitism and other concepts, are discussed by Tim Ingold (1980:30–31). He writes: "It is a matter of personal experience, since when I was first in the field in Lapland, an old reindeer named Enoch made a habit of coming round, at 11 o'clock every morning, to visit the place where I regularly urinated outside my cabin" (personal communication, 1986).

b. Each of us has about as many organisms on the surface of our skin as there are people on earth. The mite *Demodex*, crab lice, fleas, and bedbugs are a few samples of the teeming miniature parasitic population sharing the ecological niche constituted by human bodies (Andrews 1976).[7]

6. *Conspecificity*. An animal may accept a human as a conspecific; this is also known as "zoomorphism." As early as 1910, Otto Heinroth described the attachment of incubator-hatched greylag goslings to human beings. These goslings reject any goose or gander as parent objects, opting instead to look upon humans as their exclusive parents. Many other hand-reared birds were later found to have transferred their adult sexual behavior toward their human caretakers. Ramona Morris and Desmond Morris (1966:182–183) have recounted attempts by a "fully humanized" female panda, Chi-Chi, to mate with her keepers; and the sexual advances of a male dolphin, Peter, toward his female trainer, Margaret Howe, were recorded in her published protocol (Lilly 1967:282). The latter episode was represented as an accomplished, although fictional, aquatic congress in Ted Mooney's 1981 novel, *Easy Travel to Other Planets* (cf. also under item 3, above).

7. *Insentience*. An animal may define a human as part of its inanimate *Umwelt*, as when young birds will perch on the keeper's head or even on his or her outstretched arm, as though it were a branch. Fascinating behaviors of this sort were extensively analyzed by Heini Hediger (1969:81–83), who explains one of the tricks performed by snake charmers on the basis of this principle of misapprehending a human limb for an insensate substrate. According to Hediger, mammals such as the koala may also regard humans as a place for climbing, and make use of them accordingly. Especially intriguing is Hediger's discussion (1969:91–95) of the "centaur-like fusion" of human and motor vehicle, especially in the context of big-game reserves, and of how wild animals view such relatively novel combinations.

8. *Taming*. Taming, defined as the reduction or possibly total elimination of an animal's flight reaction from humans, may be deliberately induced. It is an indispensable precondition for both training and domestication. In the latter, not only the care and feeding but, most particularly, the breeding of an animal—or the communication of genetic information from one generation to the

next—have to some degree come under human control. When the biologically altered domesticated animal breeds out of control, it is referred to as "feral," as opposed to "wild."

9. *Training*. Humans' training of animals may take one of two counterpolar forms:

a. A rat forced to swim under water to escape drowning is taught to take the alley in a submerged Y-shaped maze when the correct decision is indicated by the brighter of two alleys; a porpoise is brought under behavioral control to locate and retrieve underwater objects. Such efforts are called *apprentissage*, loosely rendered as "scientific" or "laboratory training" (cf. Silverman 1978) or, in German, *wissenschaftliche Dressur*.

b. A horse is taught to perform a comedy act for the purposes of exhibition (cf. Bouissac 1985: chap. 4); a porpoise is taught to play basketball. Such efforts are called *dressage*, or circus (viz. oceanarium) training, or *höhere Dressur* (as with the Lippizaners of the Spanish Riding School).

Note that *apprentissage* and *dressage* are fundamentally distinct ways of shaping behaviors, although from a semiotic point of view they constitute complementary measures, in particular as regard their pragmatic import. This distinction was intuitively appreciated by Heini Hediger as early as 1935, in his dissertation, and was later materially advanced in several of his published writings (for example, Hediger 1979:286). For instance, Hediger insightfully emphasized that *apprentissage* entails a reduction of the animal-human nexus to as close to zero as feasible. *Dressage*, conversely, requires a maximum intensification of the ligature, with the richest possible emotional involvement. This is one dimension of semiotic variation.

Apropos *dressage*, Keller Breland and Marian Breland (1966:108) relate an arresting informal observation concerning the emotional component of a parrot's vocalization. In the exhibition in question the bird picks up a toy telephone, holds it up to his ear, and says "Hello!" Afterward he receives a peanut. It was noted that every time the bird said "Hello!," "the pupils of his eyes contracted and dilated remarkably." The sign is emitted solely in an emotionally charged situation, for the pupil-size cue may not occur if the bird is "talking" merely for peanuts (kindred observations have been made of domestic cats).

A second dimension of semiotic variation lies, in Hediger's words, between *Dressur ohne Affektaufwand* (or without affective display) and *Dressur mit bedeutendem Affektaufwand* (or with significant affective display).

There are many other juxtapositions of human and animal which could fruitfully be examined; concerning some of these there of course already exist more- or less-substantial studies (see Ingold 1988: chap. 4). These areas include the representation of animals in mythology, oral and written literature, cartoons, on the stage and in the performing arts generally (especially the cinema and television), or in the shape of dolls, puppets, toys, and robots. Animals are often featured, by design, in magazine and television advertising.

Moreover, there exist countless studies dealing with interactions between humans and particular sets of demarcated animals, individual anthropomorphic animals, and classes of exploited captives, such as primates (Erwin, Maple, and Mitchell 1979), or species in the aggregate (Clutton-Brock 1981; Craig 1981; Houpt and Wolski 1982: chap. 2), birds in general (Murton 1971), or horses in particular (Lawrence 1985). A synthesis of this vast literature, especially in its fascinating semiotic ramifications, is long overdue.

Saint Augustine was once asked, "What is time?" He answered: "If no-one asks me, I know; if I wish to explain it to one that asks, I know not."

To recapitulate, the central purpose of this chapter was to enquire what, broadly speaking, an animal is. That question ought to be preceded by another: What is life? Although there may not be an absolutely rigorous distinction between inanimate matter and matter in a living state, it is clear enough that animates undergo semiosis, i.e., they exchange, among other items, messages, which are strings of signs.

Paying heed, first, to biologically valid (meaning strictly genealogical) classificatory schemes, five major life-forms were distinguished, among which, on the macro level, the mediating position of animals between plants and fungi was accentuated. The critical relevance of *Umweltforschung* to an understanding of animals was mentioned, but was not further developed. The recalcitrant term *Umwelt* had best be rendered in English by the word *model* (as expounded in Sebeok 1986g). The biologist's notion of symbiosis, it was also suggested, is equivalent to the philosopher's notion of semiosis.

Turning back to systematics, of which taxonomy is but one component, animals were reassessed from the standpoint of folk classification. In this perspective it was argued that an animal always belongs at once to a multiple array of codes, some natural, or "scientific," others disparately cultural. Far from being irreconcilable, such codes complement one another. Therefore, it is perfectly in order, as one illustration, to regard a whale as being simultaneously a mammal and a fish, as well as, moreover, an enigmatic creature of the human imagination.

The anthropological, or semiotic, definitions of "animal" acquire concreteness and saliency within different types of human-animal confrontation, but their enumeration cannot be carried out exhaustively in the compass of a brief essay such as this. Nevertheless, even the very incomplete and preliminary listing attempted here may serve to elicit further investigation.

Notes

1. In semiosis, signs tend to function in a trinity of mutually exclusive classes as the intermediate transforming agents between "objects" and "interpretants." This is highly pertinent to Peirce's man-sign (more broadly, animal-sign) analogy. For a recent discussion by an anthropologist, see Milton Singer (1984: especially pp. 1-2, 55-56, 61).

2. It is at present unclear whether the thermophillic ("black smoker") bacteria of the East Pacific Rise, employing symbiotic chemosynthesis, thus surviving in utter independence of the sun (i.e., without photosynthesis) and seemingly constituting the only closed geothermal (terrestrial) ecosystem not integrated with the rest of life, can or cannot be grouped with "ordinary" bacteria (see Baross and Demming 1983; Jannasch and Mottl 1985). The giant worms subsisting, by absorption, upon these microbial symbionts thus also derive their energy from underwater volcanoes, not sunlight.

3. Among Uexküll's many writings, *The Theory of Meaning* (1982), creatively amplified by his elder son, Thure, is one of the most important and readily accessible in English; see also "Die Umweltlehre als Theorie der Zeichenprozesse" (J. von Uexküll 1980:291-388); Lorenz (1971:273-277); and Sebeok (1989b: chap. 10).

4. Peirce's trichotomous classification of signs into iconic, indexical, and

symbolic is fundamental in semiotics. It has been discussed by many commentators, notably Arthur Burks (1949), F. J. Ayer (1968:149-158), Thomas Sebeok (1975b) and, most recently, Christopher Hookway (1985: chap. 4); see also the entries under each of these three lemmata, and Joseph Ransdell's article on Peirce, in Sebeok (1986c).

5. See Bonner (1963) for semiosis in the Acrasieae—however classified, they must be reckoned aggregation organisms *par excellence*. See also Stanier et al. (1985:543-544).

6. "Comme un texte peu intelligible en une seule langue, s'il est rendu simultanément dans plusieurs, laissera peut-être émaner de ces versions differentes un sens plus riche et plus profond qu'aucun de ceux, partiels et mutilés, auquel chaque version prise à part eût permis d'accéder."

7. In the framework of Jakob von Uexküll, the ecological niche could best be described as "*Umwelt*-from-outside," from the standpoint of the observer of the subject concerned.

In What Sense Is Language a "Primary Modeling System?"

The expression "primary modeling system"—coupled, as a rule, with the contrasting concept "secondary modeling system," which emphasizes its derivational character in relation to natural language—has been central to Soviet semiotics of the Moscow-Tartu School since 1962, when it was proposed by A. A. Zaliznjak, V. V. Ivanov, and V. N. Toporov (in English in Lucid 1977:47–58; see also Rudy 1986 and Shukman, in Sebeok 1986c: vol. 1, pp. 166–168, 558–560).

In 1974, I interpreted the inferred concept—having checked my provisional understanding, when I gave a lecture at the University of Tartu in August 1970, with Professor Ivanov—as follows:

> The notion of a secondary modeling system, in the broad sense, refers to an ideological model of the world where the environment stands in reciprocal relationship with some other system, such as an individual organism, a collectivity, a computer, or the like, and where its reflection functions as a control of this system's total mode of communication. A model of the world thus constitutes a program for the behavior of the individual, the collectivity, the machine, etc., since it defines its choice of operations, as well as the rules and motivations underlying them. A model of the world can be actualized in the various forms of human behavior and its products, including linguistic texts—hence the emphasis on the verbal arts—social institutions, movements of civilization, and so forth. [Sebeok 1985b:23 n. 38]

This essay was originally published in *Proceedings of the Twenty-Fifth Symposium of the Tartu-Moscow School of Semiotics*, ed. Henri Broms and Rebecca Kaufmann, pp. 67–80 (Helsinki: Arator, 1988). In the same year the essay appeared elsewhere in English (*World Behind Words*, ed. F. Steurs [Leuven, The Netherlands: Leuven University Press, 1988]), and, in a French/Portuguese version (*Cruzeiro Semiotico* Jan. 1988:1,002–1,012).

Although Ivanov graciously acquiesced at the time to my *ad hoc* formulation, in retrospect, it seems to me to require further elucidation. Accordingly, the following remarks are intended to provide amplification and clarification.

The canonical definition of a modeling system was formed by Jurij M. Lotman in 1967 (rendered in English in Lucid 1977:7) as

> a structure of elements and of rules for combining them that is in a state of fixed analogy to the entire sphere of an object of knowledge, insight or regulation. Therefore a modeling system can be regarded as a language. Systems that have a natural language as their basis and that acquire supplementary superstructures, thus creating languages of a second level, can appropriately be called secondary modeling systems.

Natural language, in brief, is thus posited as the primary, or basic, infrastructure for all other (human) sign systems; and the latter—such as myth or religion—are held to be resultant superstructures constructed upon the former. In 1971, Jurij Lotman and B. A. Uspensky (in English, 1978) elaborated their view of the semiotic study of culture, noting that, in their scheme, language is viewed as carrying out a specific communicative function by providing the collective with a presumption of communicability.

An underlying question concerns, more generally, the concept of "model"—which is essentially a reductive analogy, and therefore ultimately a kind of icon—and its applications, if any, as a technical term in semiotics of the nonverbal and verbal in particular. Certainly, it is a fashionable appellation in the literature and philosophy of science, where it has, however, acquired many different connotations. Some of the more important of these—notably in logic, mathematics, and physics—are provocatively discussed by Mary Hesse (1967).

The only recorded discussion of linguistic models that I am aware of took place at the 1960 International Congress of Logic, Methodology and Philosophy of Science, with the participation (among others) of Yehashua Bar-Hillel and Noam Chomsky. The proceedings include a highly useful, although neglected, paper by Yuen Ren Chao, which correctly notes that, while "the term 'model' is relatively new in linguistics...the use of what may reasonably be regarded as models is as old as the study of language" (Chao 1962:558; for later references, see Welte 1974: vol. 1, p. 386–387 and Stewart 1976; also cf. Koch 1986). Chao claims that the earliest mention of models in (American?) linguistics was in 1944, by Z. S. Harris. The term was thereafter used with increasing frequency, yet in a bewildering variety of senses: Chao lists no less than thirty synonyms or more or less equivalent phrases of "model" for the fourteen years he surveyed. But none of these seem to conform to, or possess the scope of, the uses of "model" in the Soviet tradition.

Some twentieth-century pre-Chao and post-Chao models of semiosis are illustrated by the following graphic displays, a modest sample chosen almost at random out of a far larger number (cf. Fiske 1982: chap. 2, for models by George Gerbner, T. Newcomb, B. Westley, and M. MacLean, among others). It should also be noted that these models are all, more or less, linked intertextually among one another; namely, their framers were aware of earlier models and their interpretations of these models were repositioned in the lights of each later model.

A "convenient diagram of Symbol, Reference and Referent" (Fig. 6-1) was created in the 1920s by C. K. Ogden and I. A. Richards (1938:11).

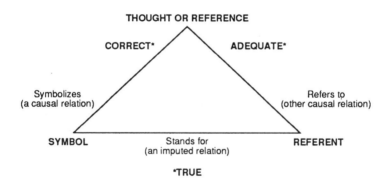

Fig. 6-1
Diagram of symbol, reference, and referent.
(Ogden and Richards 1938:11)

In Europe, the "organon model" of language (Fig. 6-2), created by Karl Bühler (1965:28), became widely influential after the mid-1930s.

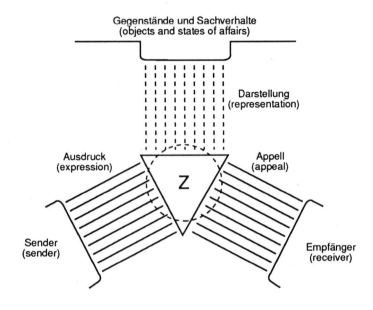

Fig. 6-2
Organon model of language. (Bühler 1965:28)

Claude E. Shannon and Warren Weaver's (1949:5) schematic flowchart (Fig. 6-3), representing a general communication system, has become a classic that is frequently copied with all sorts of variations, for it is heuristically valuable and suggests ways of expanding the theory embedded in it.

In the early 1960s, I (Sebeok 1972:14) tried to depict by way of a Morley Triangle the relationships between Bühler's model and Jakobson's (1960:253, 257) more comprehensive information-theoretical schema of six constitutive factors, each of which is posited to determine a different function of language; this diagram (Fig. 6-4) was, in turn, actuated by the Shannon and Weaver model.

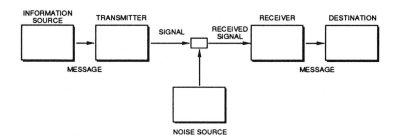

Fig. 6-3
Schematic flowchart representing
a general communication system.
(Shannon and Weaver 1949:5)

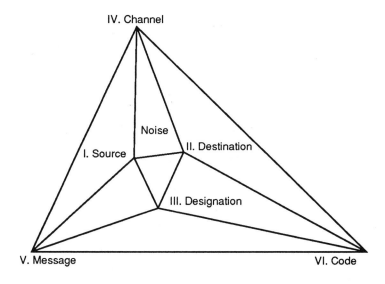

Fig. 6-4
Morley Triangle showing the relationships between Bühler's model and
Jakobson's more comprehensive information-theoretical schema of six
constitutive factors. (Sebeok 1972:14)

Chao does not press his own views, but it is clear that, had he
developed them, they would have mirrored common semiotic principles by changing their parity. What he does say is that, in his
model of models, "there are things and models of things, the latter
being also things but used in a special way" (1962:564). One would
nowadays rather say that there are objects and signs of objects, the
former also being signs but used in a special way (cf. Sebeok
1986b).

This statement can be rephrased in standard semiotic idiom in
this way: a cabbage (*aliquid*) stands for (*stat pro*) a king (*aliquo*). If
it is likely that much of what is true of one (i.e., of the sign "cabbage")
is also true of the other (i.e., of the object "king"), then perhaps one
might amplify, with Peirce (2.257), that the cabbage tends to be a
Decent Sinsign, involving both "an Iconic Sinsign to embody the
information and a Rhematic Indexical Sinsign to indicate the Object
to which the information refers." However, if very little is true of
one that is also true of the other (even though it is not entirely zero),
one might say, again with Peirce (2.261), that the cabbage tends to
be a Rhematic Symbol or a Symbolic Rheme, such as a common
noun. In Jakobson's much simplified version of semiosis (1980:11–
22), a model M, a cabbage, could be said to function as a *renvoi* to
the thing T, a king, and this referral could, by virtue of an effective
similarity, be iconic (after all, as Morris [1971:273] taught us,
"iconicity is...a matter of degree"). On the other hand, by virtue of
an imputed, conventional, habitual contiguity, the referral could be
symbolic, much as, for the experimental dog in the Pavlovian paradigm, the sound of a metronome became an arbitrarily paired symbol
(i.e., a conditioned reflex) for dry food.

Soviet conceptions of model and modeling systems clearly owe
much to Jakob von Uexküll's theory of meaning (1982; cf. Gipper
1963: chap. 6 and Sebeok 1989b: chap. 10), developed, in Hamburg
during the first four decades of this century, by this great biologist
in a series of sagacious if quirky contributions to semiotics. Ju. S.
Stepanov (1971:27–32), for instance, singles Uexküll out for extended mention in the course of his sketch of (then) current trends in
modern (bio)semiotics.

Uexküll's highly original *Umweltforschung*—which its creator
viewed as a scientific theory anchored in Kant's *a priori* intuitions—

is truly a fundamental theory as much of sign processes (or semiosis) as of vital functions. Moreover, his conception at once *utilizes* a pivotal model—the famous "functional cycle." This simple, albeit not linear, diagram by which, as Konrad Lorenz (1971:274) noted, "a vast programme of research is implied," in itself *constitutes* a cybernetic theory of modeling so fundamental that the evolution of language, as I have recently argued elsewhere (Sebeok 1986g; Sebeok 1987c), cannot be grasped without it. Uexküll's functional cycle is diagrammed in figure 6-5.

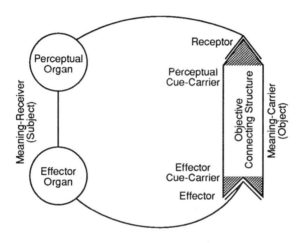

Fig. 6-5
Uexküll's functional cycle.

The term *Umwelt* has proved notoriously recalcitrant to translation, although "subjective universe," "phenomenal world," and "self-world" variously approximate Uexküll's intent. However, "model" renders it more incisively, especially in the view of his credo that "every subject is the constructor of its Umwelt" (J. von Uexküll 1982:87).

As François Jacob later explained with utmost clarity: "Every organism is so equipped as to obtain a certain perception of the outer world. Each species thus lives in its own unique sensory world, to which other species may be partially or totally blind...What an organism detects in its environment is always but a part of what is around. And this part differs according to the organism" (1982:55). The-world-as-perceived depends crucially on each organism's total sensorium and on the way its brain integrates sensory with motor events. But the inclusive behavioral resources of any organism must be reasonably aligned with its model of "reality" (*Natur*), that is, the system of signs its nervous system is capable of assembling—or it will surely be doomed, by natural selection, to extinction.

T. C. Schneirla's biphasic approach/withdrawal (A/W) theory (1965) furnishes a *minimal model* which must have been crucial for the survival of all animal types, from protozoans to primates (including humans). Such a miniature model—or "modelita," in Chao's (1962:565) sobriquet—evidently requires much the same organs, but is played out in two functionally opposed systems, one for the reaching of food and mates, the other for the evasion of noxious situations. A key postulate of this holistic, oppositive A/W theory, allowing, as it does, for plasticity through experience, is that it cyclically relates every organism's *Innenwelt* (or inner world, "comprising," as Lorenz explains [1971:275], "the whole of its bodily structures and/or functions") to its characteristic habitat (*Umgebung*, or observer's *Umwelt*; after J. von Uexküll 1909).

The *Innenwelt* of every animal comprises a model—whether of a minimal A/W type or of a more elaborate kind—that is made up of an elementary array of several types of nonverbal signs (variously elaborated by Jakob von Uexküll [1982:10–11] under such labels as *Ordnungszeichen*, *Inhaltszeichen*, *Lokalzeichen*, *Richtungszeichen*, *Wirkzeichen*, and the like, none of which will be discussed here). Solely in the genus *Homo* have verbal signs emerged. To put it in another way, only hominids possess two mutually sustaining repertoires of signs, the zoosemiotic nonverbal, plus, superimposed, the anthroposemiotic verbal. The latter is the modeling system which the Soviet scholars call primary, but which, in truth, is phylogenetically as well as ontogenetically secondary to the nonverbal; and, therefore, what they call "secondary" is actually a further, tertiary augmentation of the former. The congruity of this expanded paradigm with Karl Popper's famous Worlds 1-2-3 model (Eccles 1979: lecture 6; Sebeok 1989b:204–205) is unmistakable: his World 3 is the World of Culture; his World 2, "the other uniquely human world" (Eccles 1979:115–116), explicitly encompasses language and develops together with the former "in some kind of symbiotic interaction"; and his World 1 is the whole material world of the cosmos, both inorganic and organic, including machines and biology.

The earliest known species in the genus *Homo* is the form Louis Leakey named *habilis*, first described in 1964, and now usually regarded as a short-lived, transitional African form, of some two million years ago, ancestral to all later hominid species. With a brain capacity of 600–800 cubic centimeters, this ancestral creature must have had a mute verbal modeling device lodged in its brain (Sebeok 1986b; Sebeok 1986c), but it could not encode it in articulate, linear speech. Language is, in fact, among its quintessential taxonomic markers (in conjunction with chipped pebbles and clusters of animal bone that evince deliberate cutting and breaking).

The evolutionary success of *habilis* is corroborated by the very swift appearance, a mere half a million years later, of the succeeding species, *H. erectus*, with a brain volume of 800–1,200 cubic centimeters; this speedy attainment is undoubtedly due to the species' linguistic competence, also indirectly manifested by its possession of tool kits exhibiting standardized design, the use of fire, and its rapid global dispersion.

Starting around 300,000 years ago, an archaic form of *H. sapiens* evolved out of the *erectus* species, with a growth of skull capacity up to 1,400 cubic centimeters, and many concurrent novelties. It is reasonable to conclude that this pre-modern human already had the capacity to encode language into speech and the concomitant ability to decode it at the other end of the communication loop. *H. sapiens* appeared a mere 40,000 years ago, with brains averaging 1,500 cubic centimeters.

The cardinal points of this brief scenario are twofold: *that language evolved as an adaptation, whereas speech developed out of language as a derivative "exaptation"* over a succeeding period of approximately two million years. These twin propositions need to be made plain with reference to a suggestion by Stephen J. Gould and Elisabeth S. Vrba (1982). These authors emphasize the distinction between historical genesis and current utility, suggesting that characteristics which evolved for other uses (or none) may later come to be coopted for their current role. The former operation is customarily called *adaptation*; for the latter, they propose a new designation, "*exaptation*."

Accordingly, languages—consisting of a set of features that promotes fitness—can best be thought of as having been built by selection for the cognitive function of modeling and, as the philosopher Karl Popper and the linguist Noam Chomsky have likewise insisted (see Sebeok 1987c:356 n. 2) not at all for the message-swapping function of communication. The latter was routinely carried on by nonverbal means, as in all animals, and as it continues to be in the context of most human interactions today.

Several million years later, language, however, came to be "exapted" for communication, first in the form of speech (and later of script, and so forth). This relatively brief elapsed time was required for a plausible mutual adjustment of the encoding with the decoding capacity, but, since absolute mutual comprehension remains a distant goal, the system continues to be fine-tuned and tinkered with still. Gould and Vrba give many interesting examples of comparable biological processes, stressing that current utility carries no automatic implication about historical origin, and concluding with the empirical observation that "most of what the brain does now to enhance our survival lies in the domain of 'exaptation'" (1982:13). The common flaw in much evolutionary reasoning—"the inference of historical genesis from current utility"—egregiously contaminated virtually all research in the nineteenth century and even quite recently has confounded the problem of the origin of language, a problem which has therefore proved intractable to most probes based on such unbiological principles.

It is interesting that in the other universal domain of human modeling, where nonverbal—or, as Bullowa (1979:9–10) terms it, "extra-verbal"—communication clearly has exclusive primacy over language, to wit, in ontogenesis, the identical marring feature "has delayed the study of the earliest human communication," namely, "our habit of thinking of communication consisting mainly of language."

As Peirce taught us, "Every thought is a sign," (1.538) but as he also wrote, "Not only is thought in the organic world, but it develops there" (5.551). Every mental model is, of course, also a sign; and modeling is not only an indispensable characteristic of the human world but also a permeation of the entire organic world, where, indeed, it developed. The animals' *milieu exterieur* and *milieu interieur*, as well as the feedback links between them both, are created and sustained by such models. A model in this general sense is a semiotic production with carefully stated assumptions and rules for biological and logical operations.

This is as true of bees (Peirce 5.551) as it is, on a far vaster scale, of Isaac Newton's and Albert Einstein's grand models of the universe. Einstein constructed his model out of nonverbal signs, "of visual and some of muscular type," and labored long and hard "only in a secondary stage" to transmute this creation into "conventional worlds and other signs," so that he could communicate it to others. "The words of the language, as they are written or spoken," Einstein wrote in a letter to Jacques Hadamard, "do not seem to play any role in my mechanism of thought. The psychical entities which seem to serve as elements in thought are certain signs and more or less clear images which can be 'voluntarily' reproduced and combined" (in Hadamard 1945:142–143).

The relatively simple, nonverbal models that animals live by and that normal human infants likewise employ are more or less pliable representations which, as we saw, must fit "reality" sufficiently to tend to secure their survival in their ecological niche (an ethological expression which, in semiotic parlance, refers to the *Umwelt* as viewed by an observer of the subject under scrutiny). Such "top-down" modeling (to use current jargon borrowed from the cognitive sciences) can persist, and become very sophisticated indeed in the adult life of exceptionally gifted individuals, as borne out by Einstein's testimonial, or by what we know about Mozart's or Picasso's abilities to model intricate auditory or visual compositions in their heads in anticipation of transcribing them onto paper or canvas. This kind of nonverbal modeling is indeed primary, in both a phylogenetic and an ontogenetic sense.

Language itself is, properly speaking, a secondary modeling system, by virtue of the all-but-singular fact that it incorporates a syntactic component (for there are, as we know, no other in zoosemiotic systems, although this feature does abound in endosemiotic systems, such as the genetic code, the immune code, the metabolic code, and the neural code). Syntax makes it possible for hominids not only to represent immediate "reality" (in the sense discussed above) but also, among animals, uniquely to frame an indefinite number of possible worlds (in the sense of Leibniz).

Hence humans are able to fabricate tertiary modeling systems of the sort John Tyler Bonner (1980:186), for instance, calls "true culture," requiring "a system of representing all the subtleties of language," in contrast to "non-human culture," and thereby produce what the Moscow-Tartu group has traditionally been calling a "secondary modeling system." It is on this level, redefined now as tertiary, that nonverbal and verbal sign assemblages blend together in the most creative modeling that nature has thus far evolved.

CHAPTER SEVEN

Linguistics and Semiotics

The mutual relationship between semiotics and linguistics is to be conceived of as either coordinate or hierarchical. If the relationship is hierarchical, there are two possibilities: either linguistics is superordinate, i.e., it subsumes semiotics; or semiotics is superordinate, i.e., it subsumes linguistics. Each of these three conjunctions has been variously put forward, but only the third has enjoyed sustained support. The first two can thus be disposed of briefly.

The view that semiotics and linguistics are coequal is maintained on utilitarian rather than abstract grounds. As Christian Metz (1974:60), for instance, has expostulated:

> In theory, linguistics is only a branch of semiotics, but in fact semiotics was created from linguistics...For the most part semiotics remains to be done, whereas linguistics is already well advanced. Nevertheless there is a slight reversal. The post-Saussurians...have taken the semiotics he foresaw and are squarely making it into a translinguistic discipline. And this is very good, for the older brother must help the younger, and not the other way around.

Unfortunately, Metz's argument is riddled with fallacies, the most serious among them being the historical one: semiotics was not at all created from linguistics, but, most likely, out of medicine (Sebeok 1985b:181), and also has far deeper roots in the annals of humankind. Sometimes, however, the fraternal metaphor enjoys administrative sanction; thus Rice University, in 1982, created a Department of Linguistics and Semiotics (J. Copeland 1984:x).

Roland Barthes may have been unique in his advocacy of the radical stand that semiology (alias semiotics) is but

Originally published in *Developments in Linguistics and Semiotics, Language Teaching and Learning Communication Across Cultures*, ed. Simon P. X. Battestini, pp. 1–18 (Washington: Georgetown University Press, 1987), this essay has also appeared in German in *Gedankzeichen: Klaus Oehler zum sechzigsten Geburtstag*, ed. Regina Claussen and Roland Daube-Schackat, pp. 193–203 (Tübingen, Germany: Stauffenburg Verlag, 1988).

a part of linguistics: to be precise, it is that part covering the *great signifying unities* of discourse. By this inversion [of Saussure's celebrated dictum, more of which below], we may expect to bring to light the unity of the research at present being done in anthropology, sociology, psychoanalysis and stylistics round the concept of signification. [1967a:11]

Of this passage, one of Barthes' memorialists remarked:

Even if language were the only evidence semiologists had, this would not make semiology part of linguistics any more than the historians' reliance on written documents makes history a part of linguistics. But semiologists cannot rely on language alone; they cannot assume that everything named is significant and everything unnamed insignificant. [Culler 1983:73–74]

Luis J. Prieto's opinion (1975:133) that "malgré l'attrait que peut exercer ce point de vue [i.e., Barthes'], je considère qu'il est insoutenable," is shared by most semioticians and others.

The subject matter of semiotics is often said to be "the communication of any messages whatever" (Jakobson 1974:32) or "the exchange of messages whatever and of the system of signs which underlie them" (Sebeok 1985b:1). Its concerns include considerations of how messages are, successively, generated, encoded, transmitted, decoded, and interpreted, and how this entire transaction ("semiosis") is worked upon by the context. Further questions revolve around problems of coding, phylogenesis and history, ontogenesis, loss of semiosic capacity ("asemasia"; cf. Sebeok 1989b:71), and the like. A message is equivalent to a string of signs. Signs, defined by whatever rhetorical sleight of tongue—and, as Nietzsche observed, only what does not have a history can be defined, and surely semiotics has a very long history—are classifiable according to many (often partially overlapping) criteria. Common oppositions may comprehend subjective signs, or symptoms, vs. objective signs (Sebeok 1984a; T. von Uexküll 1987); "wanted" signs, or signals, vs. "unwanted" signs, or noise (Sebeok 1984a); signs vs. symbols (Maritain 1943; Cassirer 1944:31; Alston 1967b); icons vs. indexes, and both against symbols (involving one of many Peircean trichotomies; cf. 2.274–307); and so forth. The most immediately pertinent distinction here, however, is the one between nonverbal signs (the unmarked category) vs. verbal signs (the marked category). This differentiation—

which places semiotics in a superordinate position over both linguistics and the putative discipline, with, as yet, no universally agreed upon global designation, which studies nonverbal signs— enjoys a most respectable tradition among both philosophers and linguists.

The early development of the notion "verbal sign" out of its Stoic beginnings has been expertly tracked by Zsigmond Telegdi (1976:267–305), but for the continuation of the story since the seventeenth century we must begin anew with John Locke. In the two-page concluding chapter of his *Essay Concerning Human Understanding* (1975 [1690]:720–721), where he dealt with the division of the sciences, Locke abruptly introduced the term *semiotics* (with a minor variation in spelling), briefly defining it as "the Doctrine of Signs," and explaining that its business "is to consider the Nature of Signs, the Mind makes use of for the understanding of Things, or conveying its Knowledge to others." A bit further in the same paragraph, Locke goes on to observe:

> To communicate our Thoughts to one another, as well as record them for our own use, Signs of our *Ideas* are also necessary. Those which men have found most convenient, and therefore generally make use of, are articulate Sounds. The Consideration then of *Ideas* and *Words*, as the great Instruments of Knowledge, makes no despicable part of their Contemplation, who would take a view of humane Knowledge in the whole Extent of it.

Locke's epistemological classification here is based, as Robert Armstrong (1965:380) rightly points out, "upon the special theory of relations between *thing*, *idea*, and *word*." And as John Deely (1985:309–310) says, these key terms, "words and ideas," are here used by Locke synecdochically, i.e., by the former, Locke means verbal signs, in the ordinary sense of any and all units of language, whereas he equates the latter with objects (1975 [1690]). At any rate, in these short passages, Locke does establish two points: first, that "words," or the verbal, constitute but one class of signs, but that, second, for humans, this class is a privileged one.

The Alsatian philosopher Johann Heinrich Lambert, who was strongly influenced by Locke, published his workmanlike *Semiotik* some three-quarters of a century later, devoting the first of its ten chapters to types of signs other than verbal, while the rest of his

monograph dealt with language ("die Untersuchung der Nothwend-
igkeit der symbolischen Erkenntins überhaupt, und der Sprache
besonders," 1764:8). By this proportion, he implied his concurrence
with Locke.

The importance Peirce attached to his own doctrine of signs is
vividly illustrated by a famous quotation from a letter he wrote to
Lady Welby, on December 23, 1908:

> Know that from the day when at the age of 12 or 13 I took up, in my
> elder brother's room a copy of Whately's *Logic*, and asked him what
> Logic was, and getting some simple answer, flung myself on the floor
> and buried myself in it, it has never been in my power to study
> anything—mathematics, ethics, metaphysics, gravitation, thermody-
> namics, optics, chemistry, comparative anatomy, psychology, pho-
> netics, economic, the history of science, whist, men and women,
> wine, metrology, except as a study of semiotic...[in Hardwick
> 1977:85–86]

We can confidently take "phonetics" in this catalog as a *pars pro toto*
for what Peirce elsewhere (1.271) certified as "the vast and splen-
didly developed science of linguistics."

Among philosophers, Charles Morris (1946:220–23; 1964:60–
62) appears to have been the most circumspect about the links
between semiotics and linguistics. The suggestion he made in 1946,
and that I well remembered from seminars of his that I had attended
six years before that, was that semiotics was to provide "the metalanguage for linguistics," and thus that the terminology of linguistics would be defined in semiotic terms. "The carrying out of this
program consistently and in detail would mean the emergence of a
semiotically grounded science of linguistics" (Morris 1946:221).
Oddly enough, Morris's wish came true, in a way, four years after
his death, when Michael Shapiro made an earnest "attempt to found
a Peircean linguistics...along lines suggested by Peirce's semiotic
in the context of his entire philosophy" (1983:ix). This shot seems,
however, to have misfired, for it was either ignored by workers in
the mainstream of linguistics or condemned by other experts on
Peirce; for instance, one of these wrote:

> Die Gefahr besteht, dass dieses Buch [i.e., Shapiro's] als Vorwand
> dafür dienen könnte, dass andere Linguisten ihre Ausfuhrungen
> ebenfalls mit semiotischen Begriffen dekorieren und ihre Publikationen

dann als semiotische Analysen ausgeben. Eine Grundlagen-
wissenschaft wie die Semiotik darf nicht zum Dekor degradiert werden.
[Walther 1984:117]

And another, Newton Garver (1986:74), judged Shapiro's version
of semiotics "unsound, even from a Peircean point of view." (Actually, Shapiro's approach was anticipated by several other linguists, notably including Uriel Weinreich and Raimo Anttila, but
these treatments of linguistic data within a strongly semiotic framework, as Irmengard Rauch (1978:329) reminds us with characteristic understatement, "have not provoked a revolution in linguistic
method" either.)

Linguistics, Rudolf Carnap (1942:13) specified, "is the descriptive, empirical part of semiotic (of spoken or written languages...)." Morris expanded on Carnap's proposition by introducing the
very general notion of a *lansign-system*, applicable not only to spoken and written languages but also to mathematics and symbolic
logic, "and perhaps to the arts" (Morris 1964:60), noting that it is
commonly admitted (he mentions, however, only Louis Hjelmslev,
Leonard Bloomfield, and J. H. Greenberg) "that linguistics is part of
semiotic" (1964:62). His proposal to replace the word *language*
with *lansign-system* (Morris 1946:36), and associated terminological innovations, proved stillborn; but he was right in observing that
most linguists who have given the matter any thought at all did view
their discipline as a part of semiotics. Among linguists of this
persuasion, Ferdinand de Saussure is customarily discussed first.

Saussure, who used the word *semiology* rather than *semiotics*—
and sometimes the more apt, yet never espoused, French synonym
signologie—seems to have devoted very little time in his lectures to
thus situating linguistics. A compact, but revered and influential,
passage reads as follows:

> A language...is a social institution. But it is in various respects
> distinct from political, juridical and other institutions. Its special
> nature emerges when we bring into consideration a different order of
> facts...A language is a system of signs expressing ideas [cf. Locke!],
> and hence comparable to writing, the deaf-and-dumb alphabet,
> symbolic rites, forms of politeness, military signals, and so on. It is
> simply the most important of such systems...It is therefore possible
> to conceive of a science which studies *the role of signs as part of
> social life*. It would form part of social psychology, and hence of

general psychology. We shall call it *semiology* (from the Greek *semeion*, 'sign'). It would investigate the nature of signs and the laws governing them. Since it does not yet exist, one cannot say for certain that it will exist. But it has the right to exist, a place ready for it in advance. Linguistics is only one branch of this general science. The laws which semiology will discover will be the laws applicable in linguistics, and linguistics will thus be assigned to a clearly defined place in the field of human knowledge. [Saussure 1983:15–16]

Several essays were subsequently fashioned to carry out the implications of Saussure's program, the first among them being the thoughtful—and too long neglected—attempt of Eric Buyssens, who took it as given that "seul le point de vue sémiologique permet de déterminer scientifiquement l'objet de la linguistique" (1943:31). To the principle articulated here, according to which linguistic problems are "first and foremost semiological," and the "need will be felt to consider them as semiological phenomena and to explain them in terms of the laws of semiology" (Saussure 1983:16–17), another has to be juxtaposed, namely, that linguistics, in Saussure's view, was to serve as the model (*"le patron général"*) for semiology (or semiotics). (This formula, by the way, turned out to have been thoroughly mistaken, and fatally misleading for research endeavors, for instance, in such adjacent areas as "kinesics.")

Edward Sapir (1929:211) also viewed linguistic facts as "specialized forms of symbolic behavior" and he mentioned among

the primary communicative processes of society...language; gesture in its widest sense; the imitation of overt behavior; and a large and ill-defined group of implicit processes which grow out of overt behavior and which may be rather vaguely referred to as "social suggestion."

He then added that "language is the communicative process par excellence in every known society" (Sapir 1931:78–79). He did not, however, as far as I know, use any term of the "semiotics" family.

Alan Gardiner (1932:85) remarks about the "student of linguistic theory" that he

treats utterances solely as instruments of communication, as significant signs. His interest is, in fact, what has been variously called semasiology, significs, or semantics. It is a wide field, and when rightly understood, embraces the entire domain of both grammar and lexicography. [Cf. Sebeok 1985b:47–58 as to the terminological confusion inherent in the foregoing.]

Here should be mentioned, as well, Bloomfield's dictum (1939:55), that "linguistics is the chief contributor to semiotic"; and Uriel Weinreich's (1968:164), that "specialized research into natural human [*sic*] language—the semiotic phenomenon par excellence—constitutes linguistics." To round out such aphoristic dicta, one might finally cite A. J. Greimas and J. Courtés's (1982:177) interpretation of what linguistics is: this, they claim, "may be defined as a scientific study of language as semiotic system" (see further Mounin 1970).

The contributions of two major figures of twentieth century linguistics need to be singled out: Hjelmslev, who was thoroughly influenced by Saussure, and Jakobson, who was equally permeated by Saussure but far more persuaded by Peirce. Of Hjelmslev, Jürgen Trabant (1981:169 n. 10) observed:

> Zusammen mit Saussures vorbereitenden Bemerkungen zu einer allgemeinen Wissenschaft von den Zeichen stellt die Glossematik den eigentlich europäischen Beitrag zur allgemeinen Semiotik dar, der auch gleichzeitig der Betrag der Sprachwissenschaft zur Semiotik ist.

Greimas and Courtès (1982:288), ignoring history altogether, proclaimed that Hjelmslev "was the first to propose a coherent semiotic theory," a reckless exaggeration by which they seem to mean merely that he considers semiotics "to be a hierarchy...endowed with a double mode of existence, paradigmatic and syntagmatic...and provided with at least two articulation planes—expression and content." Natural semiotic systems then, in Hjelmslev's conception, comprehend natural languages. As Umberto Eco (1984:14) says, Hjelmslev's definition can indeed be taken "as a more rigorous development of the Saussurean concept," but it is also the case (as noted in chapter 2 of this book) that his program for semiotics "so confidently advertised has never been carried out successfully in any domain of science." Even Trabant (1981:149) concedes that "Hjelmslev hat selber die theoretisch radikale Konzeption seiner Theorie nicht konsequent durchgehalten," even while he tries to show Hjelmslev's originality in the development of modern linguistics in his only partially successful feat of having commingled it with general semiotics.

Jakobson's input into the doctrine of signs was every bit as pervasive as Hjelmslev's yet remains less readily identifiable (it is presented cogently and comprehensively in Eco 1977). Most pertinent here is that, while Jakobson (1974:32) concurred with other linguists that "of these two sciences of man," to wit, semiotics and linguistics, "the latter has a narrower scope," being confined to the communication of verbal messages, ":yet, on the other hand, any human communication of non-verbal messages presupposes a circuit of verbal messages, without a reverse implication," he unfurled an all-embracing multilayered hierarchy of the "communication disciplines" (actually refining a scheme originally put forward by Lévi-Strauss; cf. Lévi-Strauss 1958:95). According to this wider conception, in any (human) society, communication operates on three levels:

> exchange of messages, exchange of utilities (namely goods and services), and exchange of women (or, perhaps, in a more generalizing formulation, exchange of mates). Therefore, linguistics (jointly with the other semiotic disciplines), economics, and finally kinship and marriage studies "approach the same kinds of problems on different strategic levels and really pertain to the same field." All these levels of communication assign a fundamental role to language. [Jakobson 1974:33]

In my view, what vitiates this design is that it is not catholic enough by far; in particular, it fails to take into account the several fundamental divisions of biosemiotics or biocommunication (Tembrock 1971), such as endosemiotics (J. von Uexküll 1980:291), zoosemiotics (Sebeok 1963a), phytosemiotics (Krampen 1981b), and so forth, in none of which does language—an exclusively genus-specific propensity of *Homo*—play any role whatsoever. In short, while elegantly disposing of the chief departments in the "semiotics of culture," this scheme fails to account for those of the much broader domains in the "semiotics of nature," within which all of the foregoing are embedded. If semiotics is indeed to remain "the science of communicative sign systems," its immense responsibility for synthesizing linguistics with "research on animal behavior, particularly signaling systems, and much more" (Lekomcev 1977:39), is forfeited.

By and large, generative grammarians have paid no heed to

semiotics, although Noam Chomsky (1980:253) himself alludes to a "science of semiology" in the framework of which, he says, it "is tempting to draw an analogy...to rules of grammar, which relate various levels of linguistic representation." Such a science, he adds, "may not lie very far beyond the horizons of current inquiry," noting "some attempts at a general synthesis." The compatibility of Chomsky's theory with semiotic views of symbolic function remains to be explored but will probably find its explanation when both can be integrated into the fabric of a more comprehensive cognitive science.

At the end of the fourth paragraph of this chapter, I alluded to the fact that, while the study of verbal signs is everywhere called linguistics, the correlative province of nonverbal signs—the unmarked member of the pair—lacks a commonly accepted denomination. Since I have discussed the whys and wherefores of this state of affairs before (see Sebeok 1985b:158–162), let me merely cross-refer interested readers to that survey, with the assurance that none of the facts have changed.

In passing, allusion needs to be made to Jakob von Uexküll's consideration of the relationship between the sign-processes of nature and of language. The distinction between code and message, or, more narrowly, between *langue* and *parole*, corresponds to Uexküll's distinction between "active plan" and "concrete living existence." Of the plan, he wrote: "Our mind possesses an inner plan that reveals itself only in the moment when it starts to be active. Therefore we must observe the mind during the time in which it receives and works out impressions according to its activity";...or, "The form is never anything else but the product of a plan imprinted on the indifferent materia that could have taken another form as well" (J. von Uexküll 1982:5). (It should be kept in mind that this great innovator in theoretical biology had never heard of his elder contemporaries, Peirce and Saussure!)

A sweeping study of signs and systems of signs, whether verbal or nonverbal, demands both synchronic approaches (structural as well as functional) and an application of diachronic perspectives (developmental, or ontogenetic, and evolutionary, or phylogenetic) (cf. Sebeok 1989b:27–34, 57–60; and Sebeok 1985b:26–45). The following concluding remarks are intended to round out arguments previously introduced by reflecting on their historical dimensions.

As to the ontogeny of semiosis in our species, it is perfectly clear that manifold nonverbal sign systems are "wired into" the behavior of every normal neonate; this initial semiosic endowment enables children to survive and to both acquire and compose a working knowledge of their world (*Umwelt*) before they acquire verbal signs (in general, see, for example, Bullowa 1979 and Bruner 1983). The point to keep in mind is that nonverbal sign systems by no means atrophy (though they may, of course, become impaired; cf. Sebeok 1989b:69–73) in the course of reaching adulthood and old age. In other words, the two repertoires—the chronologically prior and the much, much younger—become and remain profoundly interwoven, to both complement and supplement one another throughout each human individual's life. This reliance on two independent but subtly intertwined semiotic modes—sometimes dubbed zoosemiotic and anthroposemiotic—is what is distinctively hominid, rather than the mere language propensity characteristic of our species.

When it comes to questions of phylogeny, I have previously contended (Sebeok 1985a and 1985c) that the emergence of life on earth, some 3.5 billions of years ago, was tantamount to the advent of semiosis. The life science and the sign science thus mutually imply one another. I have also argued that the derivation of language out of any animal communication system is an exercise in total futility, because language did not evolve to subserve human communicative exigencies. It evolved, to the contrary, as an exceedingly sophisticated modeling device (in the sense of J. von Uexküll's *Umweltlehre*, as discussed, for example, in chapter 6), surely present in *Homo habilis*. This ancestral member of our genus appeared, rather abruptly, only about 2 million years ago. Language, which was an evolutionary adaptation in the genus, became "exapted" (Gould and Vrba 1982) in the species *Homo sapiens* a mere 300,000 years ago in the form of speech. It took that long for the encoding abilities of *Homo sapiens* to become fine-tuned with our species' corresponding decoding abilities. Note that, as in human ontogeny, verbal semiosis has by no means replaced the far hoarier diversiform nonverbal manifestations, for reasons that were spelled out and elucidated by Gregory Bateson (1968:614):

> [The] decay of organs and skills under evolutionary replacement is a necessary and inevitable systemic phenomenon. If, therefore, verbal language were in any sense an evolutionary replacement of communication by [nonverbal] means...we would expect the old...systems to have undergone conspicuous decay. Clearly they have not. Rather, the [nonverbal sign uses] of men have become richer and more complex, and [nonverbal communication] has blossomed side by side with the evolution of verbal language.

In sum, a preponderance of expert opinion persuades that linguistics is a structurally rather than functionally autonomous branch of semiotics, the rest of which encompasses a wide variety of nonverbal systems of signification and communication which, in humans, flourish side by side with the former, related in reciprocity. In the longitudinal time section, whether in the life of organisms or the lives of men and women, nonverbal semiosis has substantial primacy. Studies of precisely how verbal and nonverbal signs intermingle with and modify each other in our multiform speech communities must be further considered conjointly by linguists and other semioticians.

All living beings interact by means of nonverbal message exchanges. Normal adult human beings interact by *both* nonverbal *and* verbal message exchanges. Although the latter, namely, language, is a semiautonomous structure, it does lie embedded in a labyrinthine matrix of other varieties of semiotic patterns used among us and variously inherited from our animal ancestry. "Since," as Jakobson (1974:39) emphasized, "verbal messages analyzed by linguists are linked with communication of nonverbal messages," and since, as Emile Benveniste (1971:14) insisted, "language is also human; it is the point of interaction between the mental and cultural life in man," efficacious language teaching should be regarded as an endeavor in what Morris (1946:353–354) has called "applied semiotic [which] utilizes knowledge about signs for the accomplishment of various purposes." The question that I would like to repeat here (from Sebeok 1985b:179, but first raised in 1975) is this:

> If, as is the case, we lavish incalculable amounts of energy, time, and money to instill in chidren and adults a range of foreign language competencies, why are the indissolubly parallel foreign gesticulatory skills all but universally neglected, especially considering that even linguists are fully aware that what has been called the total commu-

nication package, "best likened to a coaxial cable carrying many messages at the same time...," is hardly an exaggerated simile?

When I first asked this question, over a decade ago, very sparse materials existed for training in foreign gesticulatory skills; those that did were restricted to French and Spanish (Iberian, Colombian). Today, the situation has ameliorated, but not by much. The impact of nonverbal behavior on foreign language teaching was reviewed by Leo Ward and Walburga von Raffler-Engel (1980:287–304), but their paper described the results of a very modest experiment. Beginning in the late 1970s, our Research Center for Language and Semiotic Studies at Indiana University began to give this manifest lack of material some preliminary attention (the project was described in Johnson 1979 and in Wintsch 1979). Sahnny Johnson also completed a handbook on nonverbal communication for teachers of Japanese, which was accompanied by a widely used half-hour film in which Japanese people perform specific gestures and situational interactions. (In this connection, see also Tsuda 1984). Johnson likewise prepared a corresponding handbook for teachers of Gulf Arabic. Phyllis A. Harrison (1983) published a parallel handbook comparing Brazilian and North American social behavior, while Monica Rector and Aluizio Trinta (1985) produced an illustrated manual on nonverbal communication, i.e., gesturing, also in Brazil. All this, however, can be deemed only a mere beginning in what needs to be accomplished worldwide, and especially in the production of indispensable visual aids.

CHAPTER EIGHT

I Think I Am a Verb

I have heard—perhaps from my father, who enjoyed peppering me with historical anecdotes, especially tales from the Vienna Woods—that when the shrewd Austrian maneuverer of the Holy Alliance, Prince Metternich, died in 1859, diplomats everywhere kept asking, "What do you suppose he meant by it?"

This is the sort of question that people tend to raise about some of the recorded or, at least, reported "famous last words," or death-bed utterances, of celebrated humans. Julius Caesar's *"Et tu Brute?"* seems scarcely to require exegesis, nor does the testamentary injunction of King Charles II to his brother James, "Don't let poor Nellie [Gwyn] starve!" leave much room for ambiguity. On the other hand, to whom did Hegel refer when he closed, "Only one man ever understood me—and he didn't understand me"? Even Goethe's seemingly plain request for *"Mehr Licht!"* has been subjected to many interpretations, ranging from the literal to the jocular, and reaching for the oracular.

Ulysses S. Grant (1822–1885), eighteenth president of the United States, was supposed to have terminally whispered, plausibly enough, "Water!" thus foiling the efforts and expectations of the Reverend John P. Newman, the fashionable Methodist who ministered to him, that Grant would leave behind "some immortal saying of his relations to Christ." In the early summer of 1884, at dinner one day, Grant began to complain of suffering acutely from pain in his throat. By October he had difficulty in swallowing, and John H. Douglas, M.D., the leading throat specialist at the time in New York City, correctly diagnosed that Grant had cancer. Although his physician

First appearing as "Grant's Final Interpretant" (*MLN* 100 [1985]:922–934)—a version later translated into Spanish (*Semiosis* 19 [1988]:3–18)—this essay was published in its present form in Sebeok 1986d. It also appears in the Italian translation of that volume, *Penso de essere un verbo* (Palermo: Sellerio, 1989).

did not use the ominous word, Grant told a friend of his that the doctor "had told him that his throat was affected by a complaint with a cancerous tendency" (in Pitkin 1973:25). Henceforth, Grant continued to write his memoirs in a desperate race for time against an incurable malignancy. The poignant story is chronicled, in considerable detail, in Thomas M. Pitkin's workmanly book, *The Captain Departs: Ulysses S. Grant's Last Campaign* (1973), which has served as the principal source for the biographical information recounted in this and adjacent paragraphs.

By the following summer, Grant's voice had practically given out. He effectively ceased dictating and returned to writing. Dr. Douglas from the first treated his patient with a cocaine solution, and, increasingly, with morphine injections, and advised him to leave the city for Mount McGregor, New York. Grant was to die there, on July 23, at precisely eight o'clock in the morning.

A few days before the end, Grant, growing noticeably weaker, his voice now almost completely failed, and routinely communicating in the form of penciled notes, composed the following:

> I do not sleep though I sometimes doze a little. If up I am talked to and in my efforts to answer cause pain. The fact is I think I am a verb instead of a personal pronoun. A verb is anything that signifies to be; to do; or to suffer. I signify all three.

Preserved among the Ulysses S. Grant Papers at the Library of Congress, the chit is undated, but it is determined to have been among his last. The intended addressee was Dr. Douglas. Our arguably most enigmatic president's major biographer, William McFeely (1981:516), commented on the style with admirable sensitivity: "Grant's consciousness of his coming death had a magnificence not matched at any other time in his life. In a wonderfully heightened intensity, his notes to his doctor show flashes of intelligence that leaps past even the impressive power of the best prose of the *Memoirs*." Grant's words are, of course, touching; they are evocatively elegiac; and they are resplendently eloquent—but the quality which, magnetlike, drew me to this particular string of five sentences, constituting, in themselves, one complete utterance, inhered in their orphic semiotic understanding, compressed with stunning clarity and surety. What could Grant have meant by this note?

"It is hard for man to understand," Peirce (1984:241) knew, the identification of man and sign, man and word, man and part of speech. "It is sufficient to say," he thought,

> that there is no element whatever of man's consciousness which has not something corresponding to it in the word; and the reason is obvious. It is that the word or sign which man uses *is* the man himself. For, as the fact that every thought is a sign; taken in conjunction with the fact that life is a train of thought, proves that man is a sign; so, that every thought is an *external* sign, proves that man is an external sign. That is to say, the man and the external sign are identical, in the same sense in which the words *homo* and *man* are identical. Thus my language is the sum total of myself; for a man is the thought.

(The implications of this and related passages for a theory of culture, society, human nature, personality, and the self are explored in an important book by Milton Singer [1984]; they need not be pursued here.)

It is truly remarkable that these two great, roughly coeval, American figures—the soldier-politician and the scientist-philosopher—each finally a discerning victim of his incurable carcinoma at its most agonizing (on Peirce's use of cocaine and morphine, and cancer of bladder and rectum, see Will 1979), came to such consonant, if not commensurable, view of the nature of reality and the reality of the mind. Peirce's claim has been variously discussed, most specifically by Matthew Fairbanks (1976; cf. Sebeok 1989b:62). No one, however, has attempted to dilate upon Grant's seemingly cryptic minim of autobiography. I shall approach the puzzle, if that is what it is, by the modest means at a semiotician's disposal.

The organism is only an instrument of thought, Peirce (1984:241) insisted, or, following Richard Dawkins's (1982:263) controversial trope, the organism is a phenotypic manifestation of replicator molecules. Commonly called genes, these molecules function as mere sanctuaries to keep replicators surviving and reproducing. It is but a short vault to the inference that all survival-machines are only a sign's way of making another sign. Each survival-machine thus operates in the manner of a double agential transformer, as it were, of any "object" (more precisely: of the Heraclitean notion of *logos*, the formal structure that imparts any "object" its unity and stability) into a sign, by a process of "perceptual selection of sensed characteristics" (Gregory 1981:402), adhering to criteria we admittedly know all too little about. What are the teleonomic goals of such transformation? In other words, what is the function—the force—of semiosis, a criterial attribute of life, in general? I think the answers to these questions must be realized in terms of survival. In the short term, the process of sign-action guarantees to the subject a kind of lifelong cohesive solidarity. Sign-action maintains that identity of its semiotic self by a ceaseless rearrangement of its ego-quality (Jakob von Uexküll's *Ich-ton*; 1982 [1940]:84), propelled by the sort of ongoing dialogue so distinctly recognized by Peirce (6.338). In the long term, semiosis, by indefinitely spawning interpretants, permeates ("perfuses") the universe with likenesses (i.e., icons).

The position sketched here represents a compromise between what David Savan (1983) has called an extreme realist position— devoid of interest either to him or to me—and an extreme idealism, which he strives to refute. Semiotic idealism, according to Savan, comes in two flavors, one mild, the other strong, neither of which he finds palatable. He is inclined, as I am, to a middle way, as articulated about 1903 by Peirce himself: "Every sign stands for an object independent of itself; but it can only be a sign of that object in so far as that object is itself of the nature of a sign..." (1.538). I referred to this "object" as *logos* (Sebeok 1989b:34), after René Thom (1975:329 n. 5), following Heraclitus, in the sense of a formal go-between: "Richtig sagt Heraklit...ein Mittler ist der Logos, der beiden gemeinsam ist" (Kelber 1958:223). *Logos* has also been characterized as the manner in which all developmental laws inhere to the "primary essence," or *Grundwesen* (Heinze 1872:55; cf. Kerferd 1967, showing how Heraclitus's "*logos* doctrine" combined at least three ideas into one—our concept of the universe, the rational structure thereof, and its source). The constitutive characteristic of *logos* is therefore continuity of form, the persistence of structured pattern. It should also finally be pointed out that, in 1906, Peirce (see Hardwick 1977:196) wrote a fascinating paragraph to Lady Welby concerning sign as Form, and even specified that "the Form is the Object of the Sign."

Semiosis—all sensory experience, the causal flux of dancing beams of photons and shaped molecules impinging upon neurons— transpires within the boundaries of living entities, but organisms attribute those properties to "objects"; yet, over time, opinions change what are regarded as "objects." As Richard Gregory observes (1981:402), "Most objects are closed in form, and their parts move together. The common object characteristics become identifying principles—but they may structure random patterns to create object forms." We are deep into *Umweltforschung* here, for, in the program of Jakob von Uexküll (1982:85), every object belongs to some subject's, or organism's, *Umwelt*, and changes its meaning accordingly when perceived as one or the other, accompanied by modifications of the entirety of both its material and formal properties. Although Gregory may be right in emphasizing the *ignis fatuus* of object congruity, Uexküll was correct in regarding the constancy of subjects as far better substantiated (Sebeok 1989b: app. 1). Starkly stated, percepts are signs. Perceptual hypotheses are abductive acts, decisions, triggered by some impalpable logos "out there," selecting the most familiar out of an infinity of potentialities. As Percival Lowell conjured up an intricate network of Martian canals and cities that thrived at their intersections (Overbye 1984)—a romantic myth, based on a mistranslation of Giovanni Schiaparelli's *canali*, Italian for "channels," that swept the world, and Lo! multitudes beheld them—so we all tend to perceive what we believe. The Clever Hans effect (Sebeok and Rosenthal 1981; Fernald 1984) and the Barnum effect (Snyder, Shenkel, and Lowery 1977) illuminate the two facets of this maxim which have infused fair slices of my researches for about a decade, although neither phenomenon touches directly upon the question whether reality of the world of "objects" is or is not an arbitrary contrivance. It need not be altogether so, for a creative abductive leap, or preparatory speculative modeling, calls for induction, or the scrutiny of testing, a search for facts by "experiments which bring to light the very facts to which the hypothesis had pointed" (Peirce 7.218), each new fact linked to a long chain of connections which asymptotically increase confidence in today's version of reality. May I reiterate the ancient adage cited earlier (in chapter 2): *Nosce teipsum*? This insinuates that the locus of "objects" is situated within ourselves, and that therefore the cosmos is an internalized system of signs, a knowledge of which will yield the true key to an apprehension of the universe.

Without a doubt, each survival-machine is programmed to

transform "objects" into signs; but, according to the ironclad requirement of Peirce's indivisible triad, nothing can be a sign that is not interpretable as signifying some "object," in virtue of the latter's being a sign *in posse*. Since the process of sign-interpretation, or semiosis, inheres to the very nerve center of the semiotic emprise, much has been written about this teleological concept and its types, distinguished by Peirce with finespun—and some would say nubilous—delicacy: the immediate, the final, and the dynamic interpretant; the emotional, energetic, and logical interpretant; and the ultimate interpretant, which requires no further interpretation. The last is identified as a habit (5.538) which need not be final, and is best regarded as a hypothetical construct within an inchoate and incomplete theory of meaning. Since Peirce's notions about the interpretant in general, and its multifold intersecting classifications in particular, nowhere exist in a single canonical form—for he continued to revise his schemes until at least 1908—it suffices to focus here on his famous phrase (4.127) that specifies meaning (4.536) to be "the translation of a sign into another system of signs." In other words, an interpretant is likewise a transformation into a sign of a previous sign, such that the organism's total understanding of that is invariably enriched, until the entire semiosic cycle, if it ever does in practice, achieves its closure.

    An elementary example will do: consider some interpretants of the nominal vocable *dog*. These could be (partial) synonyms, like *canine, hound, bowwow*, or the like, or an extended dictionary definition, such as the *OED*'s, beginning: "A quadruped of the genus *Canis*. . ." They could be (roughly) equivalent foreign nouns, like *chien, Hund, kutya*, etc. They might be folkloristic or literary representations (of which I listed many in Sebeok 1981b: chap. 7), including entire novels, such as Jack London's *The Call of the Wild* or Olaf Stapledon's *Sirius*, or scientific treatises, such as Michael W. Fox's book, *The Dog*. These are just a few obvious instances of monolingual or multilingual verbal interpretants. The singing and drumming dog drawn by an Aztec artist in the Madrid Codex, the Pompeian artisan's *cave canem* monitory illustration, and Charles Schulz's Snoopy are each a nonverbal interpretant for *dog*, as is also any movie about Rin Tin Tin, Fellow, Lassie, or Benji. And, of course, any "actual" dog I choose to point to becomes, by virtue of that gesture, its interpretant as well.

It is useful at this juncture to recall again Peirce's most comprehensive definition of *sign*, which usefully enlarges upon the prototypal *aliquid stat pro aliquo*: "A sign...is something which stands to somebody for something in some respect or capacity" (2.228). The something that the sign stands for he calls "its *object*," but, as we have seen, any object, or "a sort of [Platonic] idea" of it (in 1.551 called the *ground* of the representamen), is itself a sign. The equivalent sign, "or perhaps a more developed sign," that the former sign creates in the mind Peirce calls "the *interpretant*," but that is also, by definition, a sign. Again: the object is a sign; the sign is, of course, a sign; and the interpretant is a sign.

The question remains: Is the "somebody" mentioned in the definition a sign as well? Peirce dealt with this issue, in a masterly manner, in his (editorially titled) lecture on "Consciousness and Language" (7.579–596), where he concluded that "the general answer to the question, What is man?, is that he is a symbol" (7.583); the crucial confirmation he offered was the fact that "man"—and, by augmentation, any organism—is conscious of "his" interpretant, which is to say, "his own thought in another mind" (7.591). Thus the fourth term of the above definition is a sign as well, or, to recompose the definition *à la* Gertrude Stein: "A sign is a sign is a sign is a sign." Little wonder, then, that Peirce, by 1905, was obliged to face up to this "strange thing, when one comes to ponder over it, that a sign should leave its interpreter to supply a part of its meaning; but the explanation of the phenomenon lies in the fact that the entire universe...the universe which we are all accustomed to refer to as 'the truth'—that all this universe is perfused with signs, if it is not composed exclusively of signs" (5.448 n.).

Reverting to Grant's meditative paragraph, it should first be noted that this brief piece of discourse is not so much referential as contextually appropriate (a dying patient communicating with his medical attendant), as well as internally consistent. In the latter respect, we can accredit Grant's matter-of-course equation of thought with expression (cf. Peirce 1.349), that "man is a language, a process of communication" (Fairbanks 1976:20), or, as semioticians nowadays prefer to term it, a text (Sebeok 1989b:62). It is no coincidence that patients suffering from malignant neoplasms in their vocal tracts, when administered Rorschach tests, tend to produce a statistically significant number of organ-specific interpretations, related to acts of consumption, anatomical images of speech-involved body parts, and, all the more, indulging in, or yielding to, language-fastened fantasies (cf. esp. the work of C. B. Bahnson and M. B. Bahnson, in Thure von Uexküll et al. 1979:695). The cascade of semblances evidently entered Grant's consciousness while he dozed a little—to wit, during "the play of musement" (Sebeok 1981b). (The Russian formalist device, *ostranenie*, sometimes rendered as "defamiliarization," promoted by Victor Shklovsky among others, may correspond in poetic art to alienative projective deformations enabling certain terminal patients to cope at specific stages with their malady.)

Given Grant's parity of his persona with his language, we must further probe: why a particular part of speech? Why shun a personal pronoun? Why opt for a verb? Curiously, eighty-five years later, another usually careful and original thinker, R. Buckminster Fuller (1970), with no reference to Grant, denominated a McLuhanesque collaborative pictorial paperback pastiche of a book *I Seem To Be a Verb*. Its title page depicts a vigorous Fuller apparently carrying a stroke to natural completion after hitting an (invisible) ball. This image, one supposes, is meant to exteriorize "the energy of the mind of the speaker," a phrase James Burnet used repeatedly when he enumerated the "essential" aspects signified by all verbs (e.g., Burnet 1774: vol. 2, p. 118), just as James Harris (1771:94, 173) had earlier affirmed that "all Verbs, that are strictly so called, denote…Energies." Harris regarded a verb as a generic intellection, including within it both motion and its privation—as co-present in the Fuller photo—both implying time as their concomitant. In the next century, Karl W. L. Heyse, in 1856, went so far as to depict human freedom of action as dependent on our ability to develop a linguistic expression for the activity of the subject, namely, the verb (cf. Stankiewicz 1974:175).

In his erudite essay, Edward Stankiewicz (1974) reopened the problem (at times a pseudoproblem) of how certain frequently twinned parts of speech—nouns and verbs—were ranked in the history of Western linguistics. He demonstrated that the noun, in genetic rather than logical perspective, was generally assigned priority up to the end of the eighteenth century, when the verb gained ascendancy as to both its development and functional priority. Stankiewicz insightfully aligned this shift with the historical swing from realism to idealism. He tells how, these debates notwithstanding even in our century, ideas about the verb's supremacy were eventually integrated into the mainstream of modern linguistic thought. Concerning the relative importance of the verb and the noun, the swirling controversies now seem as inane as a question would be, in cosmology, about the whyfor of the ratio of matter to antimatter. Although, in the beginning, there was a slight excess of the former over the latter—no one knows why one type should outnumber the other—such inelegant but natural asymmetry must have been the case, for numerical equality would have resulted in mutual annihilation, leaving only radiation. No astronomical or vital bodies would ever have appeared, and I would not then be writing these lines (cf. the discussion of the anthropic principle in chapter 2). In linguistics, we well know, it is the dichotomous opposition of categories, which Stankiewicz (1974:184) befittingly postulates as "a system of implicational terms," that is pivotal, not the special properties of the substance of any particular part of speech: "Entre eux il n'y a qu'*opposition*," in Saussure's (1972:167) pithy formulation of the fundamental issue, "opposition of sign, or diametrical oppositions," as Ogden (1967 [1932]:33) more generally confronted it. Thus, for instance, Jakobson devoted a great deal of fruitful work, especially in the 1930s, to studying "l'opposition contradictoire" played out in Russian between "le système verbal," as decomposed into series of binary oppositions (e.g., Jakobson 1971b:213).

Grant chose not to contrast the class of verbs, called by Edward Sapir (1944:94) "occurrents," with the traditional class of nouns (Sapir's "existents"), but with the class of personal pronouns. Peirce (2.330) labeled a token pertaining to this kind of word-type a "subindex," a "genuine index" (2.305), or an "indexical symbol." (An interesting observation of Jakobson's [1981:95] draws attention to occasional suggestive comparisons of the relation between pronouns and non-pronominal words, e.g., by A. Zareckji and others, with the relation between geometrical attributes and physical bodies, but this analogy cannot be addressed here.) For Peirce, moreover, the noun was that part of speech which is "put in place of a pronoun" (5.153)—an imperfect substitute at that. This view stands in sharp reversal of ancient doctrine, which, according to him, "was exploded early in the thirteenth century." A pronoun, he then presses, "ought to be defined as *a word which may indicate anything to which the first and second persons have suitable real connections, by calling the attention of the second person to it*" (2.287 n.). Grant opposed himself as a verb in lieu of a personal pronoun neither by grammatical nescience nor by mischance; the antithesis was amply justified within the fabric of a respectable linguistic convention, exemplified and propounded, albeit casually, by Peirce.

When Grant wrote that he thought he was *not* a personal pronoun, presumably "the person who is uttering the present instance of the discourse containing *I*" (Benveniste 1971:218), the interpretation of Paul Ricoeur, commenting on Benveniste's analysis, acquires the right ring. Ricoeur links not merely this single shifter with the subject that speaks—that much is standard procedure in pragmatic linguistics—but with the thinking, feeling subject as well, imparting to the verbalization, as it were, an additional "hermeneutics of the I am" burden, as in the following passage: "Outside the reference to a particular individual who designates himself in saying *I*, the personal pronoun is an empty sign that anyone can seize: the pronoun is waiting there, in my language, like an instrument available for converting the language into discourse through my appropriation of the empty sign" (Ricoeur 1974:255). In Milton Singer's opinion (1984:61), Ricoeur's suggestions offer a new basis "for a reconciliation between structuralism, psychoanalysis, and philosophy." Grant's pronominal personal awareness effectively diminishes his identity, by a flash of self-understanding, into a sort of vanishing artifact. His ego is then recreated in action, or interaction, through a dialectical resolution of a dramatized confrontation with *alter* (in this instance, Dr. Douglas), and is at the same time objectively mirrored in the sequence of the verbs he enumerates. The dissolution—and impending extinction—of the general's, and former president's, selfhood is transsubstantiated into a trio of "occurrents": two of the most common active verbs, that signify—to reiterate his *mots justes*—"to be," "to do," reinforced by a final, plangently passive, "to suffer." This very sequence, from the most universal to the progressively more specific, is far from unconsidered but, to the contrary, meaningful; it is a textlet that exhibits a highly productive, permutational open-ended intertextuality. The cornerstone of this miniature mosaic is the basic human existential "to be," that we have come to associate chiefly with Hamlet's questioning as well as with Descartes' cogitative certitude of "therefore I exist." Thereupon follows the general's—the man of public action's, the president's— "to do," that another Elizabethan playwright aphoristically juxtaposed with "...or die," a phrase perhaps better known from Tennyson's "The Charge of the Light Brigade." Finally, "to suffer" is a more private affection, which Shakespeare catechizes, in respect to "the slings and arrows of outrageous fortune," in immediate consecution to his "to be or not to be?"

In passing, it might further be noted that, underlying the train "to bé, to dó, to súffèr," there is a discernible pattern consisting of a metronomic alternation of minimal CV syllables (that is, a consonant followed by a vowel in the same syllable), one syllable containing an unaccented vowel, immediately followed by one containing an accented vowel (save for the last, which thus contains a surplus mora). The trimetric flow of iambic feet repeats, of course, the rhythm of "I think I am a verb." This mutual contrast is therefore realized as an opposition between more prominence or less: CV̆CV́, CV̆CV́, CV̆CV́CV̆. (For an ingenious paranomasiac analysis of "to be" and "to do," as permutated by Socrates, Sartre, and Sinatra, respectively, cf. Holenstein 1983:69–70, and see also Capelle 1982:51.) Furthermore, the vocalism of the three cardinal verbs exhibits the nearly universal scheme of acute versus grave on the horizontal axis (*be* vs. *do*, or /i/~/u/), with both opposed on the vertical axis to the optimally compact vowel (*suf-* , or /a/), followed by its diffuse unstressed counterpart (*-fer*, or /ə/).

Out of Grant's prismatic thesis one can fashion a unique model of an echo chamber imbued with unlimited semiosis, resonating into the unfathomable future. Because of this potential, and the inherent poignancy of this once mighty but enigmatic man's last silent cry embodied in his cardinal claim, his phraseology seemed apt for the title of the concluding volume (Sebeok 1986d) of my semiotic tetralogy.

References

Albone, Eric S. 1984. *Mammalian Semiochemistry: The Investigation of Chemical Signals Between Mammals.* Chicester, England: Wiley.

Alston, William P. 1967a. Language. In *The Encyclopedia of Philosophy* 4:384–386. New York: Macmillan.

———. 1967b. Sign and Symbol. In *The Encyclopedia of Philosophy* 7:437–441. New York: Macmillan.

Altmann, S. A., ed. 1967. *Social Communication Among Primates.* Chicago: University of Chicago Press.

Anderson, Myrdene, John Deely, Martin Krampen, Joseph Ransdell, Thomas A. Sebeok, and Thure von Uexküll. 1984. A Semiotic Perspective on the Sciences: Steps Toward a New Paradigm. *Semiotica* 52:7–47.

Andrew, R. J. 1963. Evolution of Facial Expression. *Science* 142:1,034–1,041.

Andrews, Michael. 1976. *The Life that Lives on Man.* New York: Taplinger.

Anschen, Ruth Nanda, ed. 1957. *Language: An Enquiry into Its Meaning and Function.* New York: Harper and Brothers.

Apel, Karl–Otto. 1959. Sprache und Wahrheit in der gegenwärtigen Situation der Philosophie. *Philosophische Rundschau* 7:161–184.

———. 1973. Charles Morris und das Problem einer pragmatisch integrierten Semiotik. Introduction to *Zeichen, Sprache und Verhalten,* by Charles Morris, 9–66. Düsseldorf: Schwann.

Armstrong, Daniel, and C. H. van Schooneveld, eds. 1977. *Roman Jakobson: Echoes of His Scholarship.* Lisse, The Netherlands: Peter de Ridder Press.

Armstrong, Robert L. 1965. John Locke's "Doctrine of Signs": A New Metaphysics. *Journal of the History of Ideas* 26:369–382.

Ayer, F. J. 1968. *The Origins of Pragmatism: Studies in the Philosophy of Charles Sanders Peirce and William James.* London: Macmillan.

Babcock, Barbara A., and John J. MacAloon. 1987. Victor W. Turner (1920–1983). *Semiotica* 65:1–27.

Baer, Eugen. 1975. *Semiotic Approaches to Psychotherapy.* Bloomington: Indiana University Press.

———. 1987. Thomas A. Sebeok's Doctrine of Signs. In *Classics of Semiotics,* ed. Martin Krampen et al., 181–210. New York and London: Plenum.

Bailey, Richard W., and Seymour Chatman. 1974. Literary Semiotics in

North America. *Versus* 8/9:227–244.

Barber, Janet M., and Peter A. Dillman. 1981. *Emergency Patient Care for the EMT–A.* Reston, Va.: Reston.

Baron, Naomi S. 1988. When Seeing's Not Believing: Language, Magic, and AI. *American Journal of Semiotics* 5:321–339.

Baross, John A., and Jody W. Demming. 1983. Growth of "Black Smoker" Bacteria at Temperatures of at Least 250°C. *Nature* 303:423–426.

Barthes, Roland. 1964. Eléments de sémiologie. *Communications* 4:91–135.

———. 1967a. *Elements of Semiology.* New York: Hill and Wang.

———. 1967b. *Systèmes de la mode.* Paris: Editions du Seuil.

———. 1988. *The Semiotic Challenge.* New York: Hill and Wang.

Bateson, Gregory. 1968. Redundancy and Coding. In *Animal Communication: Techniques of Study and Results of Research,* ed. Thomas A. Sebeok, 614–626. Bloomington: Indiana University Press.

Beck, Alan, and Aaron Katcher. 1983. *Between Pets and People: The Importance of Animal Companionship.* New York: G. P. Putnam's Sons.

Beckner, Morton. 1959. *The Biological Way of Thought.* New York: Columbia University Press.

Beniger, James R. 1986. *The Control Revolution: Technological and Economic Origins of the Information Society.* Cambridge: Harvard University Press.

Bense, Max. 1984. The So-Called "Anthropic Principle" as a Semiotic Principle in Empirical Theory Formation. *American Journal of Semiotics* 2(4):93–97.

Benveniste, Emile. 1971 [1966]. *Problems in General Linguistics.* Coral Gables, Fla.: University of Miami Press.

Bernard, Claude. 1878. *Leçons sur les phénomènes de la vie communs aux animaux et aux végétaux.* Paris: Baillière.

Birdwhistell, Ray L. 1963. The Kinesic Level of the Investigation of the Emotions. In *Expression of the Emotions in Man,* ed. P. H. Knapp, 123–139. New York: International Universities Press.

———. 1970. *Kinesics and Context: Essays on Body Motion Communication.* Philadelphia: University of Pennsylvania Press.

Blois, Marsden S. 1984. *Information and Medicine: The Nature of Medical Descriptions.* Berkeley: University of California Press.

Bloomfield, Leonard. 1939. Linguistic Aspects of Science. In *International Encyclopedia of Unified Science,* ed. Otto Neurath, 1:215–278. Chicago: University of Chicago Press.

Blumer, Herbert. 1969. *Symbolic Interaction: Perspective and Method.* Englewood Cliffs, N. J.: Prentice-Hall.

Bonner, John Tyler. 1963. How Slime Molds Communicate. *Scientific American* 209:284–293.

————. 1969. *The Scale of Nature*. New York: Harper and Row.

————. 1980. *The Evolution of Culture in Animals*. Princeton: Princeton University Press.

Bouissac, Paul. 1976. The "Golden Legend" of Semiotics. *Semiotica* 17:371–384.

————. 1985. *Circus and Culture: A Semiotic Approach*. Lanham, Md.: University Press of America.

Bouissac, Paul, Michael Herzfeld, and Roland Posner, eds. 1986. *Iconicity: Essays on the Nature of Culture (Festschrift for Thomas A. Sebeok on his 65th Birthday)*. Tübingen: Stauffenberg Verlag.

Breland, Keller, and Marian Breland. 1966. *Animal Behavior*. London: Collier–Macmillan.

Broughton, Panthea Reid, ed. 1979. *The Art of Walker Percy*. Baton Rouge: Louisiana State University Press.

Brown, Cecil H. 1984. *Language and Living Things: Uniformities in Folk Classification and Naming*. New Brunswick, N. J.: Rutgers University Press.

Bruller, John [Vercors]. 1953. *You Shall Know Them*. Boston: Little, Brown.

Bruner, Jerome. 1983. *Child's Talk: Learning to Use Language*. New York: W. W. Norton.

Bruner, Jerome S., J. J. Goodnow, and G. A. Austin. 1956. *A Study of Thinking*. New York: Wiley.

Bühler, Karl. 1965. *Sprachtheorie: Die Darstellungsfunktion der Sprache*. Stuttgart: Gustav Fischer Verlag.

Bullowa, Margaret. 1979. Prelinguistic Communication: A Field for Scientific Research. In *Before Speech: The Beginning of Interpersonal Communication*, ed. Margaret Bullowa, 1–62. Cambridge: Cambridge University Press.

Bunge, Mario. 1980. *The Mind–Body Problem: A Psychobiological Approach*. Oxford: Pergamon Press.

Burke, Kenneth. 1966. *Language as Symbolic Action*. Berkeley: University of California Press.

Burks, Arthur W. 1949. Icon, Index, and Symbol. *Philosophy and Phenomenological Research* 9:673–689.

Burnet, James [Lord Monboddo]. 1774. *Of the Origin and Progress of Language*, vol. 2. Edinburgh: J. Balfour.

Buyssens, Eric. 1943. *Les langages et le discours*. Brussels: Office de Publicité.

Cairns–Smith, A.G. 1985. *Seven Clues to the Origin of Life: A Scientific Detective Story*. Cambridge: Cambridge University Press.

Capelle, Thorsten. 1982. *Rettet dem Dativ!* Münster, Germany: Coppenrath Verlag.

Carlson, Marvin. 1988. Semiotics of Theater. In *The Semiotic Web 1987*, ed. Thomas A. Sebeok and Jean Umiker-Sebeok, 323–353. Berlin:

Mouton de Gruyter.

Carnap, Rudolf. 1942. *Introduction to Semantics*. Cambridge: Harvard University Press.

Casalis, Matthieu. 1983. The Semiotics of the Visible in Japanese Rock Gardens. *Semiotica* 44:349–362.

Cassirer, Ernst. 1944. An Essay on Man. *An Introduction to a Philosophy of Human Culture*. New Haven: Yale University Press.

———. 1945. Structuralism in Modern Linguistics. *Word* 1:99–120.

———. 1946. *Language and Myth*. New York: Harper and Brothers.

———. 1953–1957. *Philosophy of Symbolic Forms*, 3 vols. New Haven: Yale University Press.

———. 1964 [1923–1929]. *Philosophie der symbolischen Formen*. Darmstadt: Wissenschaftliche Buchgesellschaft.

Chao, Yuen Ren. 1962. Models in Linguistics and Models in General. In *Logic, Methodology and Philosophy of Science: Proceedings of the 1960 International Congress*, eds. Ernest Nagel, Patrick Suppes and Alfred Tarski, 558–566. Stanford: Stanford University Press.

———. 1968. *Language and Symbolic Systems*. Cambridge: Cambridge University Press.

Chomsky, Noam. 1965. *Aspects of the Theory of Syntax*. Cambridge: The MIT Press.

———. 1967. The General Properties of Language. In *Brain Mechanisms Underlying Speech and Language*, ed. Frederic L. Darley, 73–88. New York: Grune and Stratton.

———. 1979. Species of Intelligence. *The Sciences* 19(9):6–11, 23.

———. 1980. *Rules and Representations*. New York: Columbia University Press.

Clark, B. F. C., and K. A. Marcker. 1968. How Proteins Start. *Scientific American* 218:36–42.

Clutton–Brock, Juliet. 1981. *Domesticated Animals from Early Times*. London: British Museum (Natural History).

Coles, Robert. 1978. *Walker Percy: An American Search*. Boston: Little, Brown.

Copeland, H. F. 1956. *The Classification of Lower Organisms*. Palo Alto: Pacific Books.

Copeland, James E., ed. 1984. *New Directions in Linguistics and Semiotics*. Houston: Rice University Studies.

Coquet, J. C. 1982, *Sémiotique—L'Ecole de Paris*. Paris: Hachette.

Cowan, M., trans. 1963. *Humanist Without Portfolio: An Anthology of the Writings of Wilhelm von Humboldt*. Detroit: Wayne State University Press.

Craig, James V. 1981. *Domestic Animal Behavior: Causes and Implications for Animal Care and Management*. Englewood Cliffs, N.J.: Prentice-Hall.

Craik, K. J. W. 1967. *The Nature of Explanation*. Cambridge: Cambridge University Press.

Crick, F. H. C. 1966. The Genetic Code—Yesterday, Today and Tomorrow. In *The Genetic Code,* ed. Leonora Frisch. Cold Spring Harbor Symposia on Quantitative Biology 31:1, 3–9. Cold Spring Harbor, Long Island, N.Y.: Cold Spring Harbor Laboratory of Quantitative Biology.

Crumrine, Ross N. and Marjorie Halpin, eds. 1983. *The Power of the Symbol: Masks and Masquerade in the Americas.* Vancouver: University of British Columbia Press.

Crystal, David. 1974. Paralinguistics. In *Current Trends in Linguistics,* ed. Thomas A. Sebeok, 12:265–295. The Hague: Mouton.

———. 1980. *A First Dictionary of Linguistics and Phonetics.* London: André Deutsch.

Culler, Jonathan. 1983. *Roland Barthes.* New York: Oxford University Press.

———. 1986. *Ferdinand de Saussure.* Ithaca: Cornell University Press.

Daiches, David. 1971. *A Third World.* Sussex: Sussex University Press.

Darley, F. L., ed. 1967. *Brain Mechanisms Underlying Speech and Language.* New York: Grune and Stratton.

Darwin, Charles. 1859. *On the Origin of Species by Means of Natural Selection, or the Preservation of Favoured Races in the Struggle for Life.* London: John Murray.

———. 1872. *The Expression of the Emotions in Man and Animals.* London: John Murray.

Dauben, Joseph W. 1982. Peirce's Place in Mathematics. *Historia Mathematica* 9:311–325.

Davies, Paul. 1980. *Other Worlds.* New York: Simon & Schuster.

Davis, Martha. 1972. *Understanding Body Movement: An Annotated Bibliography.* Bloomington: Indiana University Press.

Dawkins, Richard. 1982. *The Extended Phenotype: The Gene as the Unit of Selection.* Oxford: W. H. Freeman.

Deely, John. 1982. *Introducing Semiotic: Its History and Doctrine.* Bloomington: Indiana University Press.

———. 1985. Semiotic and the Liberal Arts. *The New Scholasticism* 59:296–322.

———. 1986. Semiotic in the Thought of Jacques Maritain. *Recherches Sémiotiques/Semiotic Inquiry* 6:112–142.

———. 1988. The Semiotic of John Poinsot: Yesterday and Tomorrow. *Semiotica* 69:31–127.

———. 1989. A Global Enterprise. Preface to Sebeok 1989b:vii–xiv.

Deely, John, Brooke Williams, and Felicia E. Kruse, eds. 1986. *Frontiers in Semiotics.* Bloomington: Indiana University Press.

de Lauretis, Teresa. 1984. *Alice Doesn't: Feminism, Semiotic, Cinema.* Bloomington: Indiana University Press.

Deledalle, Gérard. 1979. *Théorie et pratique du signe.* Paris: Payot.

Demers, Richard A. 1988. Linguistics and Animal Communication. In *Linguistics: The Cambridge Survey*, ed. Frederick J. Newmeyer, 3:314–335.

Douglas, Mary. 1982. The Future of Semiotics. *Semiotica* 38:197–203.

Duncan, Hugh Dalziel. 1968. *Symbols in Society*. New York: Oxford University Press.

Eakins, Barbara. 1972. Charles Morris and the Study of Signification. Ph.D. diss., University of Iowa.

Eccles, John. 1979. *The Human Mystery*. New York: Springer International.

————., ed. 1982. *Mind and Brain: The Many–Faceted Problems*. Washington, D.C.: Paragon House.

Eco, Umberto. 1977. The Influence of Roman Jakobson on the Development of Semiotics. In *Roman Jakobson: Echoes of His Scholarship*, eds. Daniel Armstrong and C. H. van Schooneveld, 39–58. Lisse, The Netherlands: Peter de Ridder Press.

————. 1979. *The Role of the Reader: Explorations in the Semiotics of Texts*. Bloomington: Indiana University Press.

————. 1983. Proposals for a History of Semiotics. In *Semiotics Unfolding*, ed. Tasso Borbé, 1:75–89. Berlin: Mouton de Gruyter.

————. 1984. *Semiotics and the Philosophy of Language*. Bloomington: Indiana University Press.

————. 1987. The Influence of Roman Jakobson on the Development of Semiotics. In *Classics of Semiotics*, eds. Martin Krampen, Klaus Oehler, Roland Posner, Thomas A. Sebeok, and Thure von Uexküll, 109–127. New York and London: Plenum.

————. Forthcoming. History and Historiography of Semiotics. In *Semiotik: Ein Handbuch zu den zeichentheoretischen Grundlagen von Natur und Kultur*, eds. Roland Posner, Klaus Robering, and Thomas A. Sebeok. Berlin: Walter de Gruyter.

Eco, Umberto, and Thomas A. Sebeok, eds. 1983. *The Sign of Three: Dupin, Holmes, Peirce*. Bloomington: Indiana University Press.

Efron, David. 1972 [1941]. *Gesture, Race and Culture*. The Hague: Mouton.

————. 1979. Semiotics and Telepathy. In *A Semiotic Landscape*, eds. Seymour Chatman, Umberto Eco, and Jean-Marie Klinkenberg, 1,102–1,108. The Hague: Mouton.

Eibl–Eibesfeldt, I., and H. Hass. 1967. Film Studies in Human Ethology. *Current Anthropology* 8: 477–479.

Eisele, Carolyn, ed. 1976. *The New Elements of Mathematics by Charles S. Peirce*. 4 vols. The Hague: Mouton.

Eisenberg, J. F., and Wilton Dillon, eds. 1971. *Man and Beast: Comparative Social Behavior*. Washington, D.C.: Smithsonian Institution Press.

Ekman, Paul, and Wallace C. Friesen. 1969. The Repertoire of

Nonverbal Behavior: Categories, Origins, Usage, and Coding. *Semiotica* 1:49–98.

Elstein, Arthur S., Lee S. Shylman, and Sarah A. Sprafka. 1978. *Medical Problem Solving: An Analysis of Clinical Reasoning.* Cambridge: Harvard University Press.

Engler, Rudolf. 1968. *Lexique de la terminologie Saussurienne.* Utrecht: Spectrum.

Epstein, Robert, Robert P. Lanza, and B. F. Skinner. 1980. Symbolic Communication Between Two Pigeons (*Columbia livia domestica*). *Science* 207:543–545.

Erwin, Joseph, Terry L. Maple, and G. Mitchell. 1979. *Captivity and Behavior: Primates in Breeding Colonies, Laboratories, and Zoos.* New York: Van Nostrand.

Esposito, Joseph L. 1980. *Evolutionary Metaphysics: The Development of Peirce's Theory of Categories.* Athens: Ohio University Press.

Evans-Pritchard, E. E. 1956. *Nuer Religion.* Oxford: Oxford University Press.

Fabrega, Horatio, Jr. 1980 [1974]. *Disease and Social Behavior: An Interdisciplinary Approach.* Cambridge: The MIT Press.

Fairbanks, Matthew J. 1976. Peirce on Man as a Language: A Textual Interpretation. *Transactions of the Charles S. Peirce Society* 12(1):18–32.

Fann, K. T. 1970. *Peirce's Theory of Abduction.* The Hague: Martinus Nijoff.

Faye, J. P., J. Paris, and J. Roubaud. 1972. Entretien avec Roman Jakobson. In *Hypothèses: Trois entretiens et trois études sur la linguistique et la poétique,* 33–49. Paris: Seghers/Laffont.

Fernald, Dodge. 1984. *The Hans Legacy: A Story of Science.* Hillsdale, N.J.: Lawrence Erlbaum.

Fiordo, Richard. 1974. A System of Criticism Constructed from the Thought of Charles Morris and Its Applications. Ph.D. diss., University of Illinois.

Firth, John Rupert. 1949. Atlantic Linguistics. *Archivum Linguisticum* 1:95–116.

Firth, Raymond. 1957. *Man and Culture.* London: Routledge and Kegan Paul.

Fisch, Max H. 1986. *Peirce, Semeiotic, and Pragmatism: Essays by Max H. Fisch,* ed. Kenneth Laine Ketner and Christian J. W. Kloesel. Bloomington: Indiana University Press.

Fiske, John. 1982. *Introduction to Communication Studies.* London: Methuen.

Fitzroy, Dariel. 1943. *Showmanship for Magicians.* Oakland, Calif.: Magic Limited, Lloyd E. Jones.

———. 1944. *The Trick Brain.* Oakland, Calif.: Magic Limited, Lloyd E. Jones.

————. 1945. *Magic by Misdirection*. Oakland, Calif.: Magic Limited, Lloyd E. Jones.

Florence, P. Sargant, and J. R. L. Anderson. 1977. *C. K. Ogden: A Collective Memoir*. London: Elek Pemberton.

Flynn, Pierce Julius. 1990. *The Ethnomethodological Method: A Sociosemiotic Approach*. The Hague: Mouton.

Foote, Kenneth E. 1985. Space, Territory, and Landscape: The Border-lands of Geography and Semiotics. *Recherches Sémiotiques/Semiotic Inquiry* 5:158–175.

————. 1988. Object as Memory: The Material Foundations of Human Semiosis. *Semiotica* 69:243–268.

Fox, Sidney. 1988. *The Emergence of Life: Darwinian Evolution from the Inside*. New York: Basic Books.

Frank, L. K. 1957. Tactile Communication. *Genetic Psychology Monographs* 56:209–255.

French, A. P., and P. J. Kennedy, eds. 1985. *Niels Bohr: A Centenary Volume*. Cambridge: Harvard University Press.

Fuller, R. Buckminster et al. 1970. *I Seem to Be a Verb*. New York: Bantam Books.

Galan, F. W. 1985. *Historic Structures: The Prague School Project, 1928–1946*. Austin: University of Texas Press.

Gardin, Jean-Claude. 1988. Semiotics and Archaeology. In *The Semiotic Web*, ed. Thomas A. Sebeok and Jean Umiker-Sebeok, 377–387. Berlin: Mouton de Gruyter.

Gardin, Jean-Claude, Paul Bouissac, and Kenneth E. Foote. 1984. A Program for Semiotics. *Semiotica* 52:1–5.

Gardiner, Alan H. 1932. *The Theory of Speech and Language*. Oxford: Clarendon Press.

Gardner, Martin. 1983. *Order and Surprise*. Buffalo: Prometheus Books.

Garver, Newton. 1986. Review of *The Sense of Grammar: Language as Semeiotic*, by Michael Shapiro (1983). *Transactions of the Charles S. Peirce Society* 22:68–74.

Geist, V. 1986. Did Large Predators Keep Humans Out of North America? Paper presented at the World Archaeological Conference, Cultural Attitudes to Animals Including Birds, Fish and Invertebrates.

Gerard, W. Ralph. 1969. Hierarchy, Entitation, and Levels. In *Hierarchical Structures*, ed. L. L. Whyte, A. G. Wilson, and D. Wilson, 215–228. New York: American Elsevier.

Gipper, Helmut. 1963. *Bausteine zur Sprachinhaltforschung Neuere Sprachbetrachtung im Austausch mit Geistes- und Naturwissenschaft*. Düsseldorf: Pädigogischer Verlag Schwann.

Glass, D. C. 1967. Genetics and Social Behavior. Social Science Research Council *Items* 21:1–5.

Glassie, Henry. 1973. Structure and Function, Folklore and the Artifact. *Semiotica* 7:313–351.

Glynn, Prudence. 1982. *Skin to Skin: Eroticism in Dress.* New York: Oxford University Press.

Goffman, Erving. 1961. *Encounters.* Indianapolis: Bobbs-Merrill.

———. 1963. *Stigma: Notes on the Management of Spoiled Identity.* Englewood Cliffs, N.J.: Prentice-Hall.

———. 1979. Footing. *Semiotica* 25:1 –29.

Golliher, Jeffrey Mark. 1987. The Meaning of Bodily Artifacts: Variation in Domain Structure, Communicative Functions, and Social Context. *Semiotica* 65:107–127.

Gombrich, Ernst H. 1981. Image and Code: Scope and Limits of Conventionalism in Pictorial Representation. In *Image and Code,* ed. Wendy Steiner, 11–42. Ann Arbor: Michigan Studies in the Humanities.

Goodman, Nelson. 1968. *Languages of Art: An Approach to a Theory of Symbols.* Indianapolis: Bobbs-Merrill.

Gould, Stephen J., and Elisabeth S. Vrba. 1982. Exaptation—A Missing Term in the Science of Form. *Paleobiology* 8(1):4–15.

Grace, George W. 1987. *The Linguistic Construction of Reality.* London: Croom Helm.

Greenberg, J. H., ed. 1963. *Universals of Language.* Cambridge: The MIT Press.

———. 1966. Language Universals. In *Current Trends in Linguistics,* ed. Thomas A. Sebeok, 3:61–112. The Hague: Mouton.

Gregory, Richard L. 1981. *Mind in Science: A History of Explanations in Psychology and Physics.* Cambridge: Cambridge University Press.

Greimas, A. J., and J. Courtés. 1982 [1979]. *Semiotics and Language: An Analytical Dictionary.* Bloomington: Indiana University Press. [Trans. of *Sémiotique: dictionnaire raisonné de la théorie du langage.* Paris: Classiques Hachette, 1979.]

Gribble, Charles E., ed. 1968. *Studies Presented to Professor Roman Jakobson by His Students.* Cambridge, Mass.: Slavica.

Grinker, Roy Richard. 1956. *Toward a Unified Theory of Human Behavior.* New York: Basic Books.

Guiraud, Pierre. 1971. *La sémiologie.* Paris: Presses Universitaires de France.

Hadamard, Jacques. 1945. *An Essay on the Psychology of Invention in the Mathematical Field.* Princeton: Princeton University Press.

Hall, Edward T. 1968. Proxemics. *Current Anthropology* 9:83–108.

Hall, R. A., Jr. 1975. *Stormy Petrel in Linguistics.* Ithaca: Spoken Language Services.

Hanke, Michael. 1986. G. Weltrings 'Semeion in der Aristotelischen, Stoischen, Skeptischen und Epikureischen Philosophie.' *Kodias/Code* 9:7–118.

Hanna, Judith Lynne. 1986. Dance. In *Encyclopedic Dictionary of Semiotics,* ed. Thomas A. Sebeok, 1:170–172. Berlin: Mouton de

Gruyter.

Hardwick, Charles S., ed. 1977. *Semiotic and Significs: The Correspondence between Charles S. Peirce and Victoria Lady Welby.* Bloomington: Indiana University Press.

Harland, Richard. 1987. *Superstructuralism: The Philosophy of Structuralism and Post-Structuralism.* London: Methuen.

Harris, James. 1771 [1751]. *Hermes, or a Philosophical Inquiry Concerning Universal Grammar.* London: John Nourse.

Harrison, Phyllis A. 1983. *Behaving Brazilian: A Comparison of Brazilian and North American Social Behavior.* Rowley, Mass.: Newbury House.

Hasenmueller, Christine. 1984. Images and Codes: Implications of the Exegesis of Illusionism for Semiotics. *Semiotica* 50:335–357.

Hatten, Robert S. 1982. Toward a Semiotic Model of Style in Music: Epistemological and Methodological Eases. Ph.D. diss., Indiana University, Bloomington.

Heath, Robert L. 1986. *Realism and Relativism: A Perspective on Kenneth Burke.* Macon, Ga.: Mercer University Press.

Hediger, Heini. 1969. *Man and Animal in the Zoo: Zoo Biology.* New York: Delacorte.

———. 1979. *Beobachtungen zur Tierpsychologie im Zoo und im Zirkus.* Berlin: Henschelverlag.

Heinze, Max. 1872. *Die Lehrer vom Logos in der Griechischer Philosophie.* Oldenberg, Germany: F. Schmidt.

Heisenberg, Werner. 1955. *The Physicist's Conception of Nature.* New York: Harcourt Brace Jovanovich.

Henle, Paul, ed. 1958. *Language, Thought, and Culture.* Ann Arbor: The University of Michigan Press.

Herzfeld, Michael. 1983. Signs in the Field: Prospects and Issues for Semiotic Ethnography. *Semiotica* 46:99–106.

———. 1987. *Anthropology Through the Looking Glass.* Cambridge: Cambridge University Press.

Hesse, Mary. 1967. Models and Analogy in Science. In *The Encyclopedia of Philosophy*, 5:354–359. New York: Macmillan.

Hinde, R. A. 1966. *Animal Behavior: A Synthesis of Ethology and Comparative Psychology.* New York: McGraw-Hill.

Hjelmslev, Louis. 1953. *Prolegomena to a Theory of Language.* International Journal of American Linguistics Memoir 7. Baltimore: Waverly.

Holenstein, Elmar. 1976. *Roman Jakobson's Approach to Language: Phenomenological Structuralism.* Bloomington: Indiana University Press.

———. 1983. Natural and Artificial Intelligence: Computer Science and Phenomenology. *Philosophy of Science* (Tokyo) 16:63–84.

Hookway, Christopher. 1985. *Peirce.* London: Routledge and Kegan

Paul.

Houpt, Katherine A., and Thomas R. Wolski. 1982. *Domestic Animal Behavior for Veterinarians and Animal Scientists*. Ames: Iowa State University Press.

Hudson, Deal W., and Matthew J. Mancini, eds. 1987. *Understanding Maritain: Philosopher and Friend*. Macon, Ga.: Mercer University Press.

Hume, David. 1739–1740. *A Treatise of Human Nature*. London: John Noon.

————. 1748. *Enquiry Concerning Human Understanding*. London: Millar.

Husserl, Edmund. 1913. *Ideen zu einer reinen Phänomenologie und phänomenologischen Philosophie*, vol. 1. Halle: Martin Niemeyer.

Hymes, Dell. 1968. Essays on Life, Literature, and Method. *Language* 44:664–669.

Ingold, Tim. 1980. *Hunters, Pastoralists and Ranchers: Reindeer Economies and Their Transformations*. Cambridge: Cambridge University Press.

————., ed. 1988. *What Is an Animal?* London: Unwin Hyman.

Innis, Robert E. 1985. *Semiotics: An Introductory Anthology*. Bloomington: Indiana University Press.

Jacob, François. 1965. *Leçon inaugurale*. Paris: Collège de France.

————. 1982. *The Possible and the Actual*. Seattle: University of Washington Press.

Jakobson, Roman. 1960. Linguistics and Poetics. In *Style in Language*, ed. Thomas A. Sebeok, 350–377. New York: Wiley.

————. 1964. On Visual and Auditory Signs. *Phonetica* 11:216–220.

————. 1965. Quest for the Essence of Language [Interview]. *Diogenes* 51:21–37.

————. 1966. *Selected Writings 4: Slavic Epic Studies*. The Hague: Mouton.

————. 1967. About the Relation Between Visual and Auditory Signs. In *Models for the Perception of Speech and Visual Form*, ed. W. Wathen-Dunn, 1–7. Cambridge: The MIT Press.

————. 1968. The Beginnings of National Self-Determination in Europe. In *Readings in the Sociology of Language*, ed. Joshua Fishman, 585–597. The Hague: Mouton.

————. 1969–70. Linguistics and Adjacent Sciences. In: *Actes du Xe congrès international des linguistes*, ed. A. Graur. Bucharest: Editions de l'Academie de la République Socialiste de Roumanie.

————. 1971a. Concluding Note. *International Journal of Slavic Linguistics and Poetics* 14:209.

————. 1971b. *Selected Writings 2: Word and Language*. The Hague: Mouton.

————. 1972. The Editor Interviews Roman Jakobson. *Modern Occa-*

sions Winter:14–20.

————. 1973. *Questions de poétique*. Paris: Seuil.

————. 1974 [1973]. *Main Trends in the Science of Language*. New York: Harper and Row.

————. 1980. *The Framework of Language*. Ann Arbor: Michigan Studies in the Humanities.

————. 1981. *Selected Writings 3: Poetry of Grammar and Grammar of Poetry*. The Hague: Mouton.

Jakobson, Roman, and Krystyna Pomorska. 1983. *Dialogues*. Cambridge: The MIT Press.

Jannasch, Holger W., and Michael J. Mottl. 1985. Geomicrobiology of Deep-Sea Hydrothermal Vents. *Science* 229:717–725.

Jastrow, Joseph. 1900. *Fact and Fable in Psychology*. Boston: Houghton Mifflin.

————. 1916. Charles S. Peirce as a Teacher. *Journal of Philosophy* 13:723–726.

————. 1935. *Wish and Wisdom: Episodes in the Vagaries of Belief*. New York: D. Appleton-Century.

Jerne, Niels K. 1985. The Generative Grammar of the Immune System. *Science* 229:1,057–1,059.

Jervis, Robert. 1970. *The Logic of Images in International Relations*. Princeton: Princeton University Press.

————. 1987. *The Symbolic Nature of Nuclear Politics*. Urbana: University of Illinois Department of Political Science.

Johnson, Alexander Bryan. 1947 [1836]. *A Treatise on Language*, ed. David Rynin. Berkeley: University of California Press.

Johnson, Mark. 1987. *The Body in Mind: The Bodily Basis of Meaning, Imagination, and Reason*. Chicago: The University of Chicago Press.

Johnson, Sahnny. 1979. Nonverbal Communication in the Teaching of Foreign Languages. Ph.D. diss., Indiana University, Bloomington.

Jowitt, D. Humanity on the Move. *Village Voice* 32 (10 November 1987):97–98.

Kantor, J. R. 1936. *An Objective Psychology of Grammar*. Bloomington: Indiana University Press.

Karp, Ivan. 1986. Anthropology. In *Encyclopedic Dictionary of Semiotics*, ed. Thomas A. Sebeok, 1:30–35. Berlin: Mouton de Gruyter.

Katcher, Aaron H., and Alan M. Beck, eds. 1983. *New Perspectives on Our Lives with Companion Animals*. Philadelphia: University of Pennsylvania Press.

Katz, J. J., and P. Postal. 1964. *An Integrated Theory of Linguistic Descriptions*. Cambridge: The MIT Press.

Kelber, Wilhelm. 1958. *Die Logoslehre: von Heraklit bis Origenes*. Stuttgart: Verlag Urachhaus.

Kendon, Adam. 1986. Nonverbal Communication. In *Encyclopedic*

Dictionary of Semiotics, ed. Thomas A. Sebeok, 2:609–622. Berlin: Mouton de Gruyter.

Kerferd, G. B. 1967. Logos. In *The Encyclopedia of Philosophy*, ed. Paul Edwards, 5:83–84. New York: Macmillan.

Kevelson, Roberta. 1986. Semiotics in the United States. In *The Semiotic Sphere*, eds. Thomas A. Sebeok and Jean Umiker-Sebeok, 519–554. New York and London: Plenum.

———. 1988. *The Law as a System of Signs*. New York and London: Plenum.

Klaus, Georg. 1962. *Semiotik und Erkenntnistheorie*. Munich: Wilhelm Fink Verlag.

Kluckhohn, C. 1953. Universal Categories of Culture. In *Anthropology Today: An Encyclopedic Inventory*, ed. A. L. Kroeber, 507–523. Chicago: University of Chicago Press.

Koch, Walter. 1986. *Philosophie der Philologie und Semiotik*. Bochum: Studienverlag Dr. Norbert Brockmeyer.

Krampen, Martin. 1981a. The Developmental Semiotics of Jean Piaget (1896–1980). *Semiotica* 34:193–218.

———. 1981b. Phytosemiotics. *Semiotica* 36:187–209.

Krampen, Martin, Klaus Oehler, Roland Posner, Thomas A. Sebeok, and Thure von Uexküll. 1987. *Classics of Semiotics*. New York and London: Plenum.

Krieger, Dorothy T. 1983. Brain Peptides: What, Where, and Why? *Science* 222:975–985.

Kristeva, Julia. 1967. L'Expansion de la sémiotique. *Social Science Information* 6:169–181.

Krois, John Michael. 1987. *Cassirer: Symbolic Forms and History*. New Haven: Yale University Press.

Lacan, Jacques. 1966. *Ecrits*. Paris: Seuil.

Lakoff, George. 1987. *Women, Fire, and Dangerous Things: What Categories Reveal about the Mind*. Chicago: University of Chicago Press.

Lakoff, George, and Mark Johnson. 1980. *Metaphors We Live By*. Chicago: University of Chicago Press.

Lamb, Sydney M. 1981. On the Gains of Linguistics. In *The Seventh LACUS Forum 1980*, ed. James E. Copeland and Philip W. Davis, 17–27. Columbia, S.C.: Hornbeam Press.

———. 1984. On the Aims of Linguistics. In *New Directions in Linguistics and Semiotics*, ed. James E. Copeland, 1–11. Houston: Rice University Studies.

Lambert, Johann Heinrich. 1764. *Semiotik oder Lehre von der Bezeichnung der Gedanken und Dinge*. Leipzig: Johann Wendler.

Landowski, Eric. 1988. Towards a Semiotic and Narrative Approach to Law. *International Journal for the Semiotics of Law* 1:79–105.

Langacker, Ronald W. 1987. *Foundations of Cognitive Grammar*. Vol.

1, *Theoretical Prerequisites*. Stanford: Stanford University Press.

Langer, Susanne K. 1942. *Philosophy in a New Key: A Study in the Symbolism of Reason, Rite, and Art*. New York: Penguin.

―――. 1962. *Philosophical Sketches*. Baltimore: The John Hopkins University Press.

Lavers, Annette. 1982. *Roland Barthes: Structuralism and After*. London: Methuen.

Lawrence, Elisabeth Atwood. 1985. *Hoofbeats and Society—Studies in Human–Horse Interaction*. Bloomington: Indiana University Press.

Leach, Edmund. 1964. Anthropological Aspects of Language: Animal Categories and Verbal Abuse. In *New Directions in the Study of Language*, ed. E. H. Lenneberg, 23–63. Cambridge: The MIT Press.

―――. 1984. *Semiotics, Ethology, and the Limits of Human Understanding*. Patten Foundation Lecture, Indiana University, Bloomington.

Lee, Benjamin, and Greg Urban, eds. 1989. *Sign, Self, and Society*. Berlin: Mouton de Gruyter.

Lekomcev, Ju. K. 1977. Foundations of General Semiotics. In *Soviet Semiotics*, ed. Daniel P. Lucid, 39–44. Baltimore: The Johns Hopkins University Press.

Lenneberg, E. H. 1967. *Biological Foundations of Language*. New York: Wiley.

Leroi–Gourhan, André, Pierre Champion, and Monique de Fontanes, eds. 1964. *Sixième Congrès International des Sciences Anthropologiques et Ethnologiques*, vol. 2. Paris: Musée de l'homme.

Lévi–Strauss, Claude. 1945. L'Analyse structurale en linguistique et en anthropologie. *Word* 1:33–53.

―――. 1956. Structure et dialectique. In *For Roman Jakobson*, ed. Morris Halle, Horace G. Lunt, Hugh McLean, and Cornelius H. van Schooneveld, 289–294. The Hague: Mouton.

―――. 1958. *Anthropologie structurale*. Paris: Librairie Plon.

―――. 1962a. Les limites de la notion de structure en ethnologie. In *Sens et usages du terme structure dans les sciences humaines et sociales*, ed. R. Bastide, 40–45. The Hague: Mouton.

―――. 1962b. *La pensée sauvage*. Paris: Plon.

―――. 1963. *Structural Anthropology* New York: Basic Books. [English edition of 1958.]

―――. 1966a. The Culinary Triangle. *Partisan Review* 33:586–595.

―――. 1966b. *The Savage Mind*. Chicago: University of Chicago Press. [English edition of 1962b.]

―――. 1973. *Anthropologie structurale deux*. Paris: Plon.

―――. 1985. *La potière jalouse*. Paris: Plon.

―――. 1986. L'avant–propos. In *Iconicity: Essays on the Nature of Culture*, eds. Paul Bouissac, Michael Herzfeld, and Roland Posner, 1–3. Tübingen: Stauffenberg Verlag.

Lévi–Strauss, Claude, Roman Jakobson, C. F. Voegelin, and Thomas A. Sebeok. 1953. *Results of the Conference of Anthropologists and Linguists.* International Journal of American Linguistics, Memoir 8. Baltimore: Waverly Press.

Liapunov, A. A., ed. 1963. *Prolemy Kibernetiki.* Moscow: State Publishing House.

Lieberman, Philip. 1988. Voice in the Wilderness: How Humans Acquired the Power of Speech. *The Sciences* 28(4):23–29.

Lilly, John. 1967. *The Mind of the Dolphin: A Nonhuman Intelligence.* Garden City, N.Y.: Doubleday.

Ling, Gilbert N. 1984. *In Search of the Physical Basis of Life.* New York and London: Plenum.

Lipset, David. 1980. *Gregory Bateson: The Legacy of a Scientist.* Englewood Cliffs, N.J.: Prentice–Hall.

Locke, John. 1975 [1690]. *An Essay Concerning Human Understanding,* ed. P. H. Nidditch. Oxford: Clarendon Press.

Lorenz, Konrad. 1965. *Evolution and Modification of Behavior.* Chicago: University of Chicago Press.

———. 1971. *Studies in Animal and Human Behaviour,* vol. 2. Cambridge: Harvard University Press.

Lotman, Jurij, ed. 1965. *Trudy po znakovym sistemam, II.* Transactions of the Tartu State University, vol. 181. Tartu, Soviet Union: Tartu State University.

———. ed. 1967. *Trudy po znakovym sistemam, III.* Transactions of the Tartu State University, vol. 198. Tartu, Soviet Union: Tartu State University.

Lotman, Jurij, and B. A. Uspensky. 1978. On the Semiotic Mechanism of Culture. *New Literary History* 9:211–232.

Loveday, Leo, and Satomi Chiba. 1985. Partaking with the Divine and Symbolizing the Societal: The Semiotics of Japanese Food and Drink. *Semiotica* 56:115–131.

Lovelock, J. E. 1979. *Gaia: A New Look at Life on Earth.* Oxford: Oxford University Press.

Lowenstein, Jerold M. 1984. Molecular Approaches to the Identification of Species. *American Scientist* 73:541–547.

Lowie, R. H. 1937. *The History of Ethnological Theory.* New York: Farrar & Rinehart.

Lucid, Daniel P., ed. 1977. *Soviet Semiotics: An Anthology.* Baltimore: The Johns Hopkins University Press.

Lurie, Alison. 1981. *The Language of Clothes.* New York: Random House.

MacCannell, Dean. 1976. *The Tourist: A New Theory of the Leisure Class.* New York: Schocken Books.

———. 1983. Erving Goffman. *Semiotica* 45:1–33.

———. 1986. Semiotics and Sociology. *Semiotica* 61:193–200.

MacCannell, Dean, and Juliet Flower MacCannell. 1982. *The Time of the Sign: A Semiotic Interpretation of Modern Culture.* Bloomington: Indiana University Press.

McCulloch, Warren S. 1965. *Embodiments of Mind.* Cambridge: The MIT Press.

McDowell, John H. 1986. Folkloristics. In *Encyclopedic Dictionary of Semiotics,* ed. Thomas A. Sebeok, 1:261–267. Berlin: Mouton de Gruyter.

MacFarland, D., ed. 1982. *The Oxford Companion to Animal Behavior.* Oxford: Oxford University Press.

McFeely, William S. 1981. *Grant: A Biography.* New York: W. W. Norton.

McNeill, David. 1979. *The Conceptual Basis of Language.* Hillsdale: Lawrence Erlbaum Associates.

Magli, Patrizia. 1986. De Iorio, Andrea (1769–1851). In *Encyclopedic Dictionary of Semiotics,* ed. Thomas A. Sebeok, 1:177–179. Berlin: Mouton de Gruyter.

Malinowski, Bronislaw. 1965 [1935]. *The Language of Magic and Gardening.* Vol. 2 of *Coral Gardens and Their Magic.* Bloomington: Indiana University Press.

Mallery, Garrick. 1880. *Introduction to the Study of Sign Language Among the North American Indians as Illustrating the Gesture Speech of Mankind.* Washington, D.C.: U.S. Bureau of American Ethnology.

———. 1972 [1881]. *Sign Language Among North American Indians Compared with that Among Other Peoples and Deaf-Mutes.* The Hague: Mouton.

Margulis, Lynn. 1981. *Symbiosis in Cell Evolution: Life and Its Environment on the Early Earth.* San Francisco: Freeman.

Margulis, Lynn and Dorion Sagan. 1986a. *Microcosmos: Four Billion Years of Evolution from Our Microbial Ancestors.* New York: Summit Books.

——— and ———. 1986b. Strange Fruit on the Tree of Life. *The Sciences* 26(3):38–45.

Maritain, Jacques. 1943. Sign and Symbol. In *Redeeming the Time,* 151–224, 268–276. London: Geoffrey Bles.

———. 1957. Language and the Theory of Sign. In *Language: An Enquiry into Its Meaning and Function,* ed. Ruth Nanda Anshen, 86–101. New York: Harper and Brothers.

Marler, P. 1961. The Logical Analysis of Animal Communication. *Journal of Theoretical Biology* 1:295–317.

———. 1967. Animal Communication Signals. *Science* 157:769–774.

Marrone, Gianfranco, ed. 1986. *Dove va la semiotica?* Notebooks of the Circolo Semiologico Siciliano, No. 24. Palermo.

Mayenowa, M. R. 1967. Semiotics Today: Reflections On the Second International Conference on Semiotics. *Social Science Information*

6:59–64.

Mayr, Ernst. 1965. *Animal Species and Evolution*. Cambridge: Harvard University Press.

———. 1982. *The Growth of Biological Thought: Diversity, Evolution, and Inheritance*. Cambridge: Harvard University Press.

Mead, George H. 1934. *Mind, Self, & Society: From the Standpoint of a Social Behaviorist*, ed. Charles W. Morris. Chicago: University of Chicago Press.

Mechling, Jay. 1987. Dress Right, Dress: The Boy Scout Uniform as a Folk Costume. *Semiotica* 64:319–333.

Medwar, P. B., and J. S. Medawar. 1983. *Aristotle to Zoo: A Philosophical Dictionary of Biology*. Cambridge: Harvard University Press.

Mehta, V. 1971. *John is Easy to Please: Encounters with the Written and the Spoken Word*. New York: Farrar, Straus & Giroux.

Merleau–Ponty, Maurice. 1964 [1960]. *Signs*. Evanston, Ill.: Northwestern University Press.

Merrell, Floyd. 1982. *Semiotic Foundations: Steps Toward an Epistemology of Written Texts*. Bloomington: Indiana University Press.

Mertz, Elizabeth, and Richard J. Parmentier. 1985. *Semiotic Mediation: Sociocultural and Psychological Perspectives*. Orlando: Academic Press.

Metz, Christian. 1974. *Film Language: A Semiotics of the Cinema*. New York: Oxford University Press.

Meyer, Leonard B. 1967. *Music, the Arts, and Ideas: Patterns and Predictions in Twentieth–Century Culture*. Chicago: University of Chicago Press.

Mick, David G. 1986. Consumer Research and Semiotics: Exploring the Morphology of Signs, Symbols, and Significance. *Journal of Consumer Research* 13:196–213.

———. 1988. Schema-theoretics and Semiotics: Toward More Holistic, Programmatic Research on Marketing Communication. *Semiotica* 70:1–26.

Miller, Benjamin F. 1978. *The Complete Medical Guide*. New York: Simon & Schuster.

Miller, Eugene F. 1979. Hume's Reduction Cause to Sign. *The New Scholasticism* 53:42–75.

———. 1986. David Hume. In *Encyclopedic Dictionary of Semiotics*, ed. Thomas A. Sebeok, 1:323–324. Berlin: Mouton de Gruyter.

Miller, James Grier. 1978. *Living Systems*. New York: McGraw–Hill.

Moles, Abraham. 1964. Les voies cutanées: compléments informationnels de la sensibilité de l'organisme. *Studium generale* 17:589–595.

———. 1986. Information Theory. In *Encyclopedic Dictionary of Semiotics*, ed. Thomas A. Sebeok, 1:349–351. Berlin: Mouton de Gruyter.

Money, John. 1986. *Lovemaps: Clinical Concepts of Sexual/Erotic Health and Pathology, Paraphilia, and Gender Transposition in Childhood, Adolescence, and Maturity.* New York: Irvington.

Mooney, Ted. 1981. *Easy Travel to Other Planets.* New York: Farrar, Straus & Giroux.

Morris, Charles. 1938. *Foundations of the Theory of Signs.* Chicago: University of Chicago Press.

———. 1946. *Signs, Language and Behavior.* New York: Prentice-Hall.

———. 1964. *Signification and Significance: A Study of the Relations of Signs and Values.* Cambridge: The M.I.T. Press.

———. 1970. *The Pragmatic Movement in American Philosophy.* New York: George Braziller.

———. 1971. *Writings on the General Theory of Signs.* The Hague: Mouton.

Morris, Desmond. 1977. *Manwatching: A Field Guide to Human Behaviour.* London: Jonathan Cape and New York. Harry N. Abrams.

———. 1981. *The Soccer Tribe.* London: Jonathan Cape.

Morris, Ramona, and Desmond Morris. 1966. *Men and Pandas.* New York: New American Library.

Mounin, Georges. 1970. *Introduction à la sémiologie.* Paris: Les Editions de Minuit.

———. 1985. *Semiotic Praxis: Studies in Pertinence and in the Means of Expression and Communication.* New York and London: Plenum.

Murdock, G. P. 1945. The Common Denominator of Cultures. In *The Science of Man in the World Crisis*, ed. Ralph Linton, 123–142. New York: Columbia University Press.

Murton, R. K. 1971. *Man and Birds.* London: Collins.

Nagel, Ernest. 1982. Charles Peirce's Place in Philosophy. *Historia Mathematica* 9: 302–310.

Nicholson, B. 1984. Does Kissing Aid Human Bonding by Semiochemical Addiction? *British Journal of Dermatology* 111:623–627.

Nida, Eugene A. 1975. *Componential Analysis of Meaning: An Introduction to Semantic Structures.* The Hague: Mouton.

Nöth, Winfried. 1972. *Strukturen des Happenings.* Hildesheim: Olms.

Ogden, C. K. 1967 [1932]. *Opposition: A Linguistic and Psychological Analysis.* Bloomington: Indiana University Press.

Ogden, C. K., and I. A. Richards. 1938 [1923]. *The Meaning of Meaning: A Study of the Influence of Language upon Thought and of the Science of Symbolism.* 5th ed. New York: Harcourt, Brace.

Ogilvie, John, ed. 1883. *The Imperial Dictionary of the English Language*, vol. 4. New York: The Century Co.

Osgood, Charles E., and Thomas A. Sebeok, eds. 1965 [1934]. *Psycholinguistics: A Survey of Theory and Research Problems.* Bloomington: Indiana University Press.

Overbye, Dennis. 1984. The Mystique of Mars. *Discover* 5(9):24–25.

Parry, Albert. 1933. *Tattoo: Secrets of a Strange Art.* New York: Simon and Schuster.

Paulson, William R. 1988. *The Noise of Culture: Literary Texts in a World of Information.* Ithaca: Cornell University Press.

Pederson, H. 1962. *The Discovery of Language: Linguistic Science in the Nineteenth Century.* Bloomington: Indiana University Press.

Peirce, Charles S. 1868. Some Consequences of Four Incapacities. *Journal of Speculative Philosophy* 2:140–151.

Peirce, Charles S., ed. 1883. *Studies in Logic, By Members of the Johns Hopkins University.* Boston: Little, Brown.

————. 1931–1966. *Collected Papers of Charles Sanders Peirce*, ed. Charles Hartshorne, Paul Weiss, and Arthur Burks. 8 vols. Cambridge: Harvard University Press. Citations to the *Collected Papers* are to volume and paragraph numbers. Unpublished manuscripts from the Peirce Edition Project, located at Indiana University–Purdue University at Indianapolis, are indicated as such within the text.

————. 1982. *Writings of Charles S. Peirce. A Chronological Edition.* vol. 1, 1857–1866. Bloomington: Indiana University Press.

————. 1984. *Writings of Charles S. Peirce. A Chronological Edition.* vol. 2. Bloomington: Indiana University Press.

Pelc, Jerzy. 1981. Theoretical Foundation of Semiotics. *American Journal of Semiotics* 1:15–45.

Percy, Walker. 1981. *The Message in the Bottle: How Queer Man Is, How Queer Language Is, and What One Has to Do with the Other.* New York: Farrar, Straus & Giroux.

Petitot–Cocorda, Jean. 1985. *Les catastrophes de la parole: de Roman Jakobson à René Thom.* Paris: Maloine.

Petrilli, Susan. 1987. Da Peirce (via Morris e Jakobson) a Sebeok: I segni di un percorso [Interview with Thomas A. Sebeok]. *Idee: Rivista di Filiosofia* 2 (5/6, December):123–132.

Pharies, David A. 1985. *Charles S. Peirce and the Linguistic Sign.* Amsterdam: John Benjamins.

Philodemus. 1978. *On Methods of Inference*, eds. Phillip Howard De Lacy and Estelle Allen De Lacy. Naples: Bibliopolis.

Pike, Kenneth L. 1945. *The Intonation of American English.* Ann Arbor: University of Michigan Press.

————. 1967 [1960]. *Language in Relation to a Unified Theory of the Structure of Human Behavior.* The Hague: Mouton.

Pirie, N. W. 1937. The Meaninglessness of the Terms Life and Living. In *Perspectives in Biochemistry*, eds. J. Needham and D. E. Green, 11–22. Cambridge: Cambridge University Press.

Pitkin, Thomas M. 1973. *The Captain Departs: Ulysses S. Grant's Last Campaign.* Carbondale: Southern Illinois University Press.

Poinsot, John. 1985. *Tractatus de Signis: The Semiotic of John Poinsot,* ed. John N. Deely. Berkeley: University of California Press.

Polanyi, Livia. 1985. *Telling the American Story: A Structural and Cultural Analysis of Conversational Storytelling.* Norwood, N.J.: Ablex.

Polanyi, Michael. 1958. *Personal Knowledge: Towards a Post-Critical Philosophy.* Chicago: University of Chicago Press.

Ponzio, Augusto. 1984. Notes on Semiotics and Marxism. *Recherches Sémiotiqes/Semiotic Inquiry* 4:293–302.

Posner, Roland, Tasso Borbé, Annemarie Lange-Seidl, Martin Krampen, and Klaus Oehler, eds. 1984. Und in alle Ewigkeit: Kommunikation über 10 000 Jahre. *Zeitschrift für Semiotik* 6:195–330.

Poteat, Patricia Lewis. 1985. *Walker Percy and the Old Modern Age: Reflections on Language and the Telling of Stories.* Baton Rouge: Louisiana State University Press.

Preziosi, Donald. 1986. Architecture. In *Encyclopedic Dictionary of Semiotics*, ed. Thomas A. Sebeok, 1:44–50. Berlin: Mouton de Gruyter.

Prieto, Luis J. 1975. *Etudes de linguistique et de sémiologie générales.* Geneva: Librairie Droz.

Pumphrey, R. J. 1951. *The Origin of Language.* Liverpool: The University Press.

Ransdell, Joseph. 1980. Semiotic and Linguistics. In *The Signifying Animal: The Grammar of Language and Experience*, ed. Irmengard Rauch and Gerald F. Carr, 135–185. Bloomington: Indiana University Press.

———. 1986. Peirce. In *Encyclopedic Dictionary of Semiotics*, ed. Thomas A. Sebeok, 2:673–695. Berlin: Mouton de Gruyter.

Rauch, Irmengard. 1978. The State of the Semiotics Curriculum. *Semiotic Scene* 2:151–155.

———. 1987. Peirce: "With No Pretension of Being a Linguist." *Semiotica* 65:25–43.

Read, Allen Walker. 1973. Approaches to Lexicography and Semantics. In *Current Trends in Linguistics*, ed. Thomas A. Sebeok, 10:145–205. The Hague: Mouton.

Rector, Monica, and Aluizio R. Trinta. 1985. Comuniccão não verbal: A gestualidade Brazileira. Petropolis: Editor Vozes.

Rey, Alain. 1984. What Does Semiotics Come From? *Semiotica* 52:79–93.

Rhétoré, Joëlle. 1988. La linguistique sémiotique de Charles S. Peirce: Propositions pour un grammaire phanéroscopique. Ph.D. diss., University of Perpignan.

Ricoeur, Paul. 1974. The Question of the Subject: The Challenge of Semiology. In *The Conflict of Interpretations: Essays in Hermeneutics*, ed. Don Ihde, 236–66. Evanston, Ill.: Northwestern University Press.

————. 1978. *The Rule of Metaphor: Multidisciplinary Studies of the Creation of Meaning in Language*. Toronto: University of Toronto Press, 1978.

Rjeznikov, L. O. 1964. *Gnosealogiceskie Voprosy Semiotiki*. Leningrad: Leningrad University.

Rossi–Landi, Ferruccio. 1953. *Charles Morris*. Rome: Fratelli Bocca.

————. 1974. Linguistics and Economics. In *Current Trends in Linguistics*, ed. Thomas A. Sebeok, 12:1,787–2,017. The Hague: Mouton.

Roth, Jesse, and Derek LeRoith. 1987. Chemical Cross Talk. *The Sciences* 27(3):51–54.

Rotman, Brian. 1987. *Signifying Nothing: The Semiotics of Zero*. New York: St. Martin's Press.

————. 1988. Towards a Semiotics of Mathematics. *Semiotica* 72:1–35.

Royce, Anya Peterson. 1987. Limits of Innovation in Dance and Mime. *Semiotica* 65:269–284.

Rudy, Stephen. 1986. Semiotics in the U.S.S.R. In *The Semiotic Sphere*, eds. Thomas A. Sebeok and Jean Umiker–Sebeok, 555–582. New York and London: Plenum.

Ruesch, Jurgen. 1961. *Therapeutic Communication*. New York: W. W. Norton.

————. 1972. *Semiotic Approaches to Human Relations*. The Hague: Mouton.

Ruesch, Jurgen, and Gregory Bateson. 1951. *Communication: The Social Matrix of Psychiatry*. New York: W. W. Norton.

Ruesch, Jurgen, and Weldon Kees. 1956. *Nonverbal Communication: Notes on the Visual Perception of Human Relations*. Berkeley: University of California Press.

Ruwet, N. 1967. Musicology and Linguistics. *International Social Science Journal* 12:79–87.

Rynin, David. 1967. Johnson, Alexander Bryan. In *The Encyclopedia of Philosophy*, ed. Paul Edwards, 4:286–290. New York: Macmillan.

Sagan, Dorion, and Lynn Margulis. 1987. Gaia and the Evolution of Machines. *Whole Earth Review* 55 (Summer):15–21.

Salthe, Stanley N. 1985. *Evolving Hierarchical Systems: Their Structure and Representation*. New York: Columbia University Press.

Sapir, Edward. 1927. Speech as a Personality Trait. *American Journal of Sociology* 32:892–905.

————. 1929. The Status of Linguistics as a Science. *Language* 5:207–214.

————. 1931. Communication. In *Encyclopaedia of the Social Sciences*, ed. Edwin R. A. Seligman, 4:78–81. New York: Macmillan.

————. 1944. Grading: A Study in Semantics. *Philosophy of Science* 11:93–116.

Saussure, Ferdinand de. 1967. *Cours de linguistique générale*, ed. R.

Engler. Wiesbaden: Otto Harrassowitz.

———. 1972. *Cours de linguistique générale*, ed. Tullio de Mauro. Paris: Payot.

———. 1983. *Course in General Linguistics*, ed. Roy Harris. London: Duckworth.

Savan, David. 1976. *An Introduction to C. S. Peirce's Semiotics.* Monographs, Working Papers, and Pre-publications of the Toronto Semiotic Circle, No. 1. Toronto: Victoria University.

———. 1983. Toward a Refutation of Semiotic Idealism. *Recherches Sémiotiques/Semiotic Inquiry* 3:1–8.

Schapiro, Meyer. 1970. On Some Problems in the Semiotics of Visual Art: Field and Vehicle in Image-Signs. In *Sign, Language, Culture*, 487–502. The Hague: Mouton.

Schelling, Thomas C. 1984. *Choice and Consequence: Perspectives of an Errant Economist.* Cambridge: Harvard University Press.

Schneirla, Theodore C. 1965. Aspects of Stimulation and Organization in Approach/Withdrawal Processes Underlying Vertabrate Behavioral Development. In *Advances in the Study of Behavior*, vol. 1, eds. Daniel S. Lehrman, Robert A. Hinde, and Evelyn Shaw. New York: Academic Press.

Scholes, Robert. 1982. *Semiotics and Interpretation.* New Haven: Yale University Press.

Schopf, J. William, ed. 1983. *Earth's Earliest Biosphere: Its Origins and Evolution.* Princeton: Princeton University Press.

Schrödinger, Erwin. 1946. *What Is Life?* Cambridge: Cambridge University Press.

Schuchardt, Hugo. 1912. Geschichtlich verwandt oder elementar verwandt? *Magyar Nyelvör* 44:3–13.

Sebeok, Thomas A., ed. 1960. *Style in Language.* New York: Wiley.

———. 1963a. Communication Among Social Bees; Porpoises and Sonar; Man and Dolphin. *Language* 39:448–466.

———. 1965a. Animal Communication. *Science* 147:1,006–1,014.

———. 1965b. Review of *Selected Writings I: Phonological Studies*, by Roman Jakobson. *Language* 41:77–88.

———. 1966. Introduction. In *Portraits of Linguists: A Biographical Source Book for the History of Western Linguistics 1746–1963*, ed. Thomas A. Sebeok. Bloomington: Indiana University Press.

———. 1967a. Animal Communication. *International Social Science Journal* 19:88–95.

———. 1967b. Discussion of Communication Processes. In *Social Communication Among Primates*, ed. Stuart A. Altmann, 363–369. Chicago: University of Chicago Press.

———. 1967c. On Chemical Signs. In *To Honor Roman Jakobson: Essays on the Occasion of his Seventieth Birthday*, 1,775–1,782. The Hague: Mouton.

————., ed. 1968. *Animal Communication: Techniques of Study and Results of Research*. Bloomington: Indiana University Press.

————. 1970. The Word "Zoosemiotics." *Language Sciences* No. 10:36–37.

————. 1972. *Perspectives in Zoosemiotics*. The Hague: Mouton.

————. 1974a. Semiotics: A Survey of the State of the Art. In *Current Trends in Linguistics*, ed. Thomas A. Sebeok, 12 (nos. 1–2):211–264. The Hague: Mouton.

————. 1974b. *Structure and Texture*. The Hague: Mouton.

————. 1975a. The Pertinence of Peirce to Linguistics. Address delivered to the Linguistic Society of America, San Francisco, December 30.

————. 1975b. Six Species of Signs: Some Propositions and Strictures. *Semiotica* 13:233–260.

————., ed. 1977a. *How Animals Communicate*. Bloomington: Indiana University Press.

————., ed. 1977b. *A Perfusion of Signs*. Bloomington: Indiana University Press.

————. 1978a. "Clever Hans" in a Semiotic Frame. *Diogenes* 28:112–137.

————. 1978b. Looking in the Destination for What Should Have Been Sought in the Source. *Diogenes* 104:112–137.

————. 1978c. Note on Martin Gardner and Charles Morris. *Semiotica* 23:1–4.

————. 1981a. The Image of Charles Morris. In *Zeichen über Zeichen über Zeichen*, ed. Achim Eschbach, 267–284. Tübingen: Gunter Narr Verlag.

————. 1981b. *The Play of Musement*. Bloomington: Indiana University Press.

————. 1984a. *Communication Measures to Bridge Ten Millennia*. Technical report prepared for the Office of Nuclear Waste Isolation. Columbus: Battelle Memorial Institute.

————. 1984b. Symptom. In *New Directions in Linguistics and Semiotics*, ed. James E. Copeland, 211–230. Houston: Rice University Studies.

————. 1985a. Communication, Language and Speech. *Recherches sémiotiques/Semiotic Inquiry* 5:361–367.

————. 1985b [1976]. *Contributions to the Doctrine of Signs*. Lanham, Md.: University Press of America.

————. 1985c. Modern Man, Communication, and Language. In *The Phylogeny and Ontogeny of Communication Systems*, ed. Clive Thomson, 163–169. Kingston, Ont.: Queen's University.

————. 1986a. Clever Hans Redivivus. *The Skeptical Inquirer* 10:314–318.

————. 1986b. The Doctrine of Signs. *Journal of Social and Biological*

Structures 9(4):345–352.

———, ed. 1986c. *Encyclopedic Dictionary of Semiotics*. 3 vols. Berlin: Mouton de Gruyter. [Referred to as *EDS*]

———. 1986d. *I Think I Am a Verb: More Contributions to the Doctrine of Signs*. New York and London: Plenum.

———, comp. 1986e. On the Goals of Semiotics. *Semiotica* 61:369–388.

———. 1986f. The Origin of Language. In *Pragmatics and Linguistics: Festschrift for Jacob L. Mey*, ed. Jørgen Dines Johansen and Harly Sonne, 187–195. Odense: Odense University Press.

———. 1986g. The Problem of the Origin of Language in an Evolutionary Frame. *Language Sciences* 8:169–176.

———. 1986h. A Signifying Man. *The New York Times Book Review*, March 30, pp. 14–15.

———. 1987a. In hoc signo vinces: Sign Design. In *Language Topics: Essays in Honour of Michael Halliday*, ed. Ross Steele and Terry Threadgold, 231. Amsterdam: John Benjamins.

———. 1987b. Linguistics and Semiotics. In *Developments in Linguistics and Semiotics, Language Teaching, and Learning Communication Across Cultures*, ed. Simon P. X. Battestini, 1–18. Washington: Georgetown University Press.

———. 1987c. Toward a Natural History of Language. *Semiotica* 65:141–145.

———. 1988a. "Animal" in Biological and Semiotic Perspective. In *What Is an Animal?*, ed. Tim Ingold, 63–76. London: Unwin Hyman.

———. 1988b. In What Sense Is Language a "Primary Modeling System"? In *Proceedings of the Twenty-Fifth Symposium of the Tartu–Moscow School of Semiotics*, ed. Henri Broms and Rebecca Kaufmann. Helsinki: Arator.

———. 1988c. Semiosis and Semiotics: What Lies in Their Future? *International Semiotic Spectrum* 10:2.

———. 1989a. The Semiotic Self Revisited. In *Sign, Self, and Society*, ed. Benjamin Lee and Greg Urban. Berlin: Mouton de Gruyter.

———. 1989b [1979]. *The Sign and Its Masters*. 2d ed. Lanham, Md.: University Press of America.

———. Forthcoming. The Evolution of Semiosis. In *Semiotik: Ein Handbuch zu den zeichentheoretischen Grundlagen von Natur und Kultur*, ed. Roland Posner, Klaus Robering, and Thomas A. Sebeok. Berlin: Walter de Gruyter.

Sebeok, Thomas A., and Alexandra Ramsay, eds. 1969. *Approaches to Animal Communication*. The Hague: Mouton.

Sebeok, Thomas A., Alfred S. Hayes, and Mary Catherine Bateson, ed. 1972 [1964]. *Approaches to Semiotics: Transactions of the Indiana University Conference on Paralinguistics and Kinesics*. The Hague: Mouton.

Sebeok, Thomas A., and Jean Umiker–Sebeok, eds. 1980a. *Speaking of Apes: A Critical Anthology of Two–Way Communication with Man.* New York and London: Plenum.

———. and ———. 1980b. *"You Know My Method"*: A Juxtaposition of Charles S. Peirce and Sherlock Holmes. Bloomington: Gaslight Publications.

———. and ———. 1981. Clever Hans and Smart Simians: The Self–Fulfilling Prophecy and Kindred Methodological Pitfalls. *Anthropos* 76:89–165.

———. and ———., eds. 1986. *The Semiotic Sphere*, New York and London: Plenum.

———. and ———., eds. 1987–1989. *The Semiotic Web.* Berlin: Mouton de Gruyter.

Sebeok, Thomas A., and R. Rosenthal, eds. 1981. *The Clever Hans Phenomenon: Communication with Horses, Whales, Apes, and People.* Annals of the New York Academy of Sciences, vol. 364. New York: New York Academy of Sciences.

Sebeok, Thomas A., S. M. Lamb, and J. O. Regan. 1988. *Semiotics in Education: A Dialogue. Issues in Communication,* vol. 10. Claremont, Calif.: The Claremont Graduate School.

Seeley, Thomas D. and Royce A. Levien. 1987. A Colony of Mind. *The Sciences* 27(4):39–42.

Seielstad, George A. 1983. *Cosmic Ecology: The View from the Outside In.* Berkeley: University of California Press.

Serpell, James. 1986. *In the Company of Animals: A Study of Human–Animal Relationships.* Oxford: Blackwell.

Shands, Harley C. 1960. *Thinking and Psychotherapy: An Inquiry into the Processes of Communication.* Cambridge: Harvard University Press.

Shannon, Claude E., and Warren Weaver. 1949. *The Mathematical Theory of Communication.* Urbana: University of Illinois Press.

Shapiro, Marianne. 1981. Preliminaries to a Semiotics of Ballet. In *The Sign in Music and Literatures,* ed. Wendy Steiner, 216–227. Austin: University of Texas Press.

Shapiro, Michael. 1983. *The Sense of Grammar: Language as Semeiotic.* Bloomington: Indiana University Press.

Shaumyan, Sebastian. 1987. *A Semiotic Theory of Language.* Bloomington: Indiana University Press.

Sherzer, Dina, and Joel Sherzer. 1987. *Humor and Comedy in Puppetry: Celebration in Popular Culture.* Bowling Green: Bowling Green State University Popular Press.

Sherzer, Joel. 1971. Conference on Interaction Ethology. *Language Sciences* 14:19–21.

Short, T. L. 1982. Life Among the Legisigns. *Transactions of the Charles S. Peirce Society* 18:285–310.

———. 1988. The Growth of Symbols. *Cruzeiro Semiotico* January:81–87.

Silverman, Paul. 1978. *Animal Behavior in the Laboratory*. New York: Pica Press.

Simpson, George Gaylord. 1961. *Principles of Animal Taxonomy*. New York: Columbia University Press.

———. 1966. The Biological Nature of Man. *Science* 152:472–478.

Singer, Milton. 1984. *Man's Glassy Essence: Explorations in Semiotic Anthropology*. Bloomington: Indiana University Press.

Skinner, B. F. 1979. *The Shaping of a Behaviorist*. New York: Knopf.

Snow, C. P. 1959. *The Two Cultures and the Scientific Revolution*. New York: Cambridge University Press.

Snyder, C. R., Randee Jae Shenkel, and Carol R. Lowery. 1977. Acceptance of Personality Interpretations: The "Barnum Effect" and Beyond. *Journal of Consulting and Clinical Psychology* 45:104–114.

Sonea, Sorin. 1988. The Global Organism. *The Sciences* 28(4):38–45.

Staal, J. F. 1971. What Was Left of Pragmatics in Jerusalem. *Language Sciences* 14:29–32.

Stanier, Roger Y., John L. Ingraham, Mark L. Wheelis, and Page R. Painter. 1985. *The Microbial World*. Englewood Cliffs, N.J.: Prentice–Hall.

Stanislavsky, K. 1959. *My Life in Art*. Moscow: Foreign Languages Publishing House.

Stankiewicz, Edward. 1974. The Dithyramb to the Verb in the Eighteenth- and Nineteenth-Century Linguistics. In *Studies in the History of Linguistics: Traditions and Paradigms*, ed. Dell Hymes, 157–190. Bloomington: Indiana University Press.

Stanosz, Barbara. 1986. Communication. In *Encyclopedic Dictionary of Semiotics*, ed. Thomas A. Sebeok, 1:137–141. Berlin: Mouton de Gruyter.

Steiner, Wendy. 1978. Modern American Semiotics (1930–1978). In *The Sign: Semiotics Around the World*, ed. R. W. Bailey, L. Matejka, and P. Steiner, 99–118. Ann Arbor: Michigan Slavic Publications.

Stender–Petersen, Ad. 1949. Esquisse d'une théorie structurale de la littérature. *Travaux du cercle linguistique de Copenhague* 5:277–278.

Stepanov, Ju. S. 1971. *Semiotika*. Moscow: Nauka.

Stewart, Ann Harleman. 1976. *Graphic Representation of Models in Linguistic Theory*. Bloomington: Indiana University Press.

Structure of Language and Its Mathematical Aspects. 1961. *Proceedings of Symposia in Applied Mathematics* XII. Providence: American Mathematical Society.

Tannen, Deborah. 1984. *Conversational Style: Analyzing Talk Among Friends*. Norwood, N.J.: Ablex.

Tavolga, William N. 1968. Fishes. In *Animal Communication: Techniques of Study and Results of Research*, ed. Thomas A. Sebeok, 271–

288. Bloomington: Indiana University Press.

Telegdi, Zsigmond. 1976. Zur Herausbildung des Begriffs "sprachliches Zeichen" und zur stoischen Sprachlehre. *Acta Linguistica Scientiarum Hungaricae* 26:267–305.

Tembrock, Gunter. 1971. *Biokommunikation: Informationsvertragung im biologischen Bereich.* Berlin: Akademie-Verlag.

Thom, René. 1975. *Structural Stability and Morphogenesis: An Outline of a General Theory of Models,* trans. D. H. Fowler. Reading, Mass.: Benjamin/Cummings.

———. 1980. L'éspace et les signes. *Semiotica* 29:193–208.

———. 1983. *Mathematical Models of Morphogenesis.* Chichester, England: Ellis Horwood.

Thomas, Donald W. 1976. Semiotics: A Macroscope for Education. In *Proceedings of the Semiotic Society of America* 1:185–191. Atlanta: Georgia Institute of Technology.

Thomas, L. L. 1957. *The Linguistic Theories of N. Ja. Marr.* Berkeley and Los Angeles: University of California Press.

Tiefenbrun, Susan W. 1986. Legal Semiotics. *Cardozo Arts and Entertainment Law Journal* 5:91–156.

Tiger, L., and R. Fox. 1966. The Zoological Perspective in Social Science. *Man* 1:75–81.

Todd, Charles L., and Russell T. Blackwood, eds. 1969. *Language and Value. Centennial Conference on the Life and Works of Alexander Bryan Johnson.* New York: Greenwood.

Todorov, Tzvetan. 1984. *The Conquest of America: The Question of the Other.* New York: Harper and Row.

Tomas, David. 1982. The Ritual of Photography. *Semiotica* 40:1–25.

———. 1983. A Mechanism for Meaning: A Ritual and the Photographic Process. *Semiotica.* 46:1–39.

———. 1988. Toward an Anthropology of Sight: Ritual Performance and the Photographic Process. *Semiotica* 68:245–270.

Tomkins, Gordon M. 1975. The Metabolic Code. *Science* 189:760–763.

Trabant, Jürgen. 1981. Die Welt als Zeichen. In *Klassiker der modernen Semiotik,* ed. Martin Krampen, Klaus Oehler, Roland Posner, and Thure von Uexküll, 145–171. Berlin: Severin and Siedler.

Trevarthen, Colwyn. 1987. The Structure of Motives. *International Semiotic Spectrum* 8:1–2.

Tsuda, Aoi. 1984. *Sales Talk in Japan and the United States: An Ethnographic Analysis of Contrastive Speech Events.* Washington, D.C.: Georgetown University Press.

Turner, Victor. 1974. *Dramas, Fields, and Metaphors: Symbolic Action in Human Society.* Ithaca: Cornell University Press.

Uexküll, Jakob von. 1909. *Umwelt und Innenwelt der Tiere.* Berlin: Springer-Verlag.

———. 1926. *Theoretical Biology.* Trans. by D. L. Mackinnon.

International Library of Psychology, Philosophy, and Scientific
Method, C. K. Ogden, general ed. London: Kegan Paul, Trench,
Trubner.
─────. 1940 [1928]. *Bedeutungslehre.* Bios, No. 10. Leipzig: Johann
Ambrosius Barth.
─────. 1973 [1928] [1920]. *Theoretische Biologie.* Frankfurt:
Suhrkamp.
─────. 1980. *Kompositionslehre der Natur: Biologie als
undogmatische Naturwissenschaft,* ed. Thure von Uexküll. Frankfurt:
Verlag Ullstein (Propylaen).
─────. 1982 [1940]. The Theory of Meaning, ed. Thure von Uexküll.
Trans. by B. Stone and H. Weiner from *Bedeutungslehre. Semiotica*
42:1–87.
Uexküll, Thure von. 1986. Medicine and Semiotics. *Semiotica* 61:201–
217.
─────.1987. Semiotics and the Problem of the Observer. In *Semiotics
1982,* ed. John Deely and Jonathan Evans, 1–25. Lanham, Md.:
University Press of America.
─────., ed. 1979. *Lehrbuch der Psychosomatischen Medizin.* Munich:
Urban and Schwarzenberg.
Ullman, I. M. 1975. *Psycholinguistik und Psychosemiotik.* Göttingen:
Vandenhoeck und Ruprecht.
Umiker–Sebeok, Jean. 1977. Semiotics of Culture: Great Britain and
North America. *Annual Review of Anthropology* 6:121–135.
─────. 1978. You're Only as Old as You Look: Age Displays in
American Culture. Ms. Bloomington, Ind.
─────., ed. 1987. *Marketing and Semiotics: New Directions in the
Study of Signs for Sale.* Berlin: Mouton de Gruyter.
Umiker-Sebeok, Jean, and Thomas A. Sebeok., eds. 1976. *Speech
Surrogates: Drum and Whistle Systems.* 2 vols. The Hague: Mouton.
───── and ─────., eds. 1978. *Aboriginal Sign Languages of the
Americas and Australia.* 2 vols. New York and London: Plenum.
───── and ─────., eds. 1987. *Monastic Sign Languages.* Berlin:
Mouton de Gruyter.
Urban, Wilbur Marshall. 1939. *Language and Reality: The Philosophy
of Language and the Principles of Symbolism.* New York: Macmillan.
Vachek, J. 1966. *The Linguistic School of Prague: An Introduction to Its
Theory and Practice.* Bloomington: Indiana University Press.
Verene, Donald Phillip. 1986. Cassirer, Ernst (1874–1945). *Encyclope-
dic Dictionary of Semiotics,* ed. Thomas A. Sebeok. 1:103–105.
Berlin: Mouton de Gruyter.
Walther, Elisabeth. 1984. Die Beziehung zwischen Semiotik und
Linguistik. *Semiotica* 52:111–117.
Ward, Leo, and Walburga von Raffler-Engle. 1980. The Impact of
Nonverbal Behavior on Foreign Language Teaching. In *Aspects of*

Nonverbal Communication, ed. Walburga von Raffler-Engel, 287–304. Lisse, The Netherlands: Swets and Zeitlinger.

Weinreich, Uriel. 1968. Semantics and Semiotics. In *International Encyclopedia of the Social Sciences,* ed. David L. Sills, 14:164–169. New York: Macmillan.

———. 1980. *On Semantics.* Philadelphia: University of Pennsylvania Press.

Wellbery, David E. 1984. *Lessing's Laocoon: Semiotics and Aesthetics in the Age of Reason.* Cambridge: Cambridge University Press.

Wellek, René. 1986. *A History of Modern Criticism: 1750–1950.* Vol. 6, *The First Half of the Twentieth Century: English and American.* New Haven: Yale University Press.

Welte, Werner. 1974. *Moderne Linguistik: Terminologie/Bibliographie: Ein Handbuch und Nachschlagewerk auf der Basis der generativ-transformationellen Sprachtheorie.* Munich: Max Hüber Verlag.

West, Candace. 1984. *Routine Complications: Troubles with Talk Between Doctors and Patients.* Bloomington: Indiana University Press.

Wheeler, John Archibald. 1984. Bits, Quanta, Meaning. In *Problems in Theoretical Physics,* ed. A. Giovanni, F. Mancini, and M. Marinaro, 121–141. Salerno: University of Salerno Press.

———. 1987. How Come the Quantum. In *New Techniques and Ideas on Quantum Measurement Theory,* ed. D. M. Greenberger, 304–316. Annals of the New York Academy of Sciences 480.

Whitehead, Alfred North. 1919. *An Enquiry Concerning the Principles of Natural Knowledge.* Cambridge: Cambridge University Press.

———. 1927. *Symbolism: Its Meaning and Effect.* New York: Capricorn Books.

Whitney, William D., ed. 1891. *The Century Dictionary and Cyclopedia,* s.v. "Semiotics" (entry presumed to be written by Charles S. Peirce). pt. 19:5, 496. New York: The Century Co.

Whittaker, R. H. 1959. On the Broad Classification of Organisms. *Quarterly Review of Biology* 34:210–266.

———. 1969. New Concepts of Kingdoms of Organisms. *Science* 163:150–160.

Wiener, Norbert. 1948. *Cybernetics or Control and Communication in the Animal and the Machine.* Cambridge: The M.I.T. Press.

———. 1950. *The Human Use of Human Beings: Cybernetics and Society.* Boston: Houghton Mifflin.

Will, Marilyn Major. 1979. The Health of Charles S. Peirce: A Semiotic Perspective. Ms. Bloomington, Ind.

Williams, Allan, Gunter Bentele, Herbert Eagle, and Aage Hansen-Love. 1986. Cinema. In *Encyclopedic Dictionary of Semiotics,* ed. Thomas A. Sebeok, 1:110–121. Berlin: Mouton de Gruyter.

Williams, Brooke. 1985. What Has History to Do with Semiotic?

Semiotica 54:267–333.

Willis, Roy G. 1974. *Man and Beast*. London: Hart–Davis, MacGibbon.

Wintsch, Susan. 1979. The Vocabulary of Gestures: Nonverbal Communication in Foreign Languages. *Research and Creative Activity* 3:6–11.

Wollheim, Richard. 1987. *Painting as an Art*. Princeton: Princeton University Press.

Wright, Robert. 1987. Virtual Reality. *The Sciences* 67(6):8–10.

———. 1988. *Three Scientists and Their Gods: Looking for Meaning in an Age of Information*. New York: Times Books.

———. 1989. Charles S. Peirce Meets Douglas Hofstadter: Pragmatism and the Language of Modern Science. *Semiotica* 73:191–198.

Yates, F. Eugene. 1985. Semiotics as Bridge Between Information (Biology) and Dynamics (Physics). *Recherches Sémiotiques/Semiotic Inquiry* 5:347–360.

———, and Peter N. Kugler. 1984. Signs, Singularities and Significance: A Physical Model for Semiotics. *Semiotica* 52:49–77.

Zvegintsev, V. 1967. Structural Linguistics and Linguistics of Universals. *Acta Linguistica Hafniensia* 10:129–144.

Index

Carroll, John B.: 113
Carter, Brandon: 128
Cartoons: semiotics and, 71; animals in, 171
Casalis, Matthieu: 72
Cassirer, Ernst: 27, 35, 41, 42, 44–46, 50, 54, 66, 188; Langer and, 48
Catastrophe theory: 18, 87, 100
Cats: 171; gladiators and, 168; *see also* cheetahs
Cells, evolution of: 164–65
Cetaceans, 167; *see also* whales
Chalk, semiotic aspects of tailors': 154
Chao, Yuen Ren: 34, 118, 176–77, 180, 182
Charles II, King of England: 199
Charles S. Peirce Society: 76
Chatman, Seymour: 40
Cheetahs: 167
Cheiron: 166
Chemosynthesis: 172 n.2
Cherry, Colin: 70
Chiba, Satomi: 72
Chomsky, Noam: 34, 39, 42, 50, 70, 97, 103, 113, 150, 155, 176, 184, 195
Chrysippus: 30
Cinema: semiotics of, 6–7, 70; animals in, 171
Circuses, Roman: 168
Circus training: 170
Clark, B. F. C.: 157
Claussen, Regina: 187
Clever Hans effect: 203
Clothing, communicative function of: 72, 154
Clutton-Brock, Juliet: 171
Cock fights: 168
Codes(s): 188; animals and, 172; message and, 195; *see also* genetic code; immune code; metabolic code; neural code
Cognitive science, semiotics and: 22–23
Coles, Robert: 42
Collingwood, Robin G.: 74
Columbus, Christopher: 11, 12, 142
Commensalism: 164
Committee for the Scientific Investigation of Claims of the Paranormal: 88
Communication(s): Sebeok on, 16; language and, 17; nonverbal, 31, 184;

animal, 33, 152, 155, 157 (*see also* zoosemiotics); body motion as, 38 (*see also* gestures); mathematical theory of, 69; *Umwelten* and, 79–80; inter-body, 83; intercellular, 83; social systems and, 86; Jakobson on, 115, 194; cutaneous, 154; reproduction and, 157; signification and, 197; by plants (*see* phytosemiotics); science of human (*see* anthroposemiotics); theory of (*see* semiotics); verbal (*see* language(s)); *see also* conversation, semiotic analysis of; language(s); messages; neurocommunications; sign(s); speech
Communication engineering: 69
Computers: 22, 23, 85; semiotics and, 87; Sebeok on, 101
Conimbricenses: 74
Conspecificity: 169
Conversation, semiotic analysis of: 41
Copeland, H. F.: 161, 187
Coquet, J. C.: 120
Coral Gardens and Their Magic (Malinowski): 112
Cormorants: 167
Corpus Hippocraticum: 51
Cortes, Hernando: 11, 12
Courtés, J.: 120, 193
Cowan, M.: 150
Cows: 168; plants as signs for, 16
Crab lice: 169
Craig, James V.: 171
Craik, K. J. W.: 80, 93 n.16
Crick, F. H. C.: 157
Crocodiles: 167
Crumrine, Ross N.: 72
Cryptosemiotics: 25, 34
Crystal, David: 38
Culler, Jonathan: 91 n.5, 92 n.9
Culture, semiotics of: 194
Cuviers, George: 149
Cybernetics: 18, 93 n.15; Jakobson and, 69
Cybersemiosis: 14, 87
Cybersymbiosis: 87
Cyborgs: 101

Daiches, David: 111
Dalgarno, George: 29